The
NYSTROM
ATLAS
of
World
History

NYSTROM
DIVISION OF HERFF JONES, INC.

Table of Contents

UNIT 1

EARLY SETTLEMENTS AND CIVILIZATIONS *pages 6–15*
100,000 B.C. to 500 B.C.

People Migrate Across the Earth ➤ Agriculture and Early Settlements ➤ Civilization in Ancient Mesopotamia ➤ Babylonia and Assyria ➤ Hebrew Kingdoms ➤ Phoenician Trade

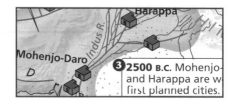

UNIT 2

ANCIENT EGYPT, CHINA, AND INDIA *pages 16–27*
6000 B.C. to 552 A.D.

Civilization in Ancient Egypt ➤ Ancient Egypt Under Foreign Rule ➤ Civilization in Ancient China ➤ Dynasties of Ancient China ➤ Ancient India and the Spread of Hinduism ➤ Ancient India and the Spread of Buddhism

UNIT 3

ANCIENT GREECE AND ROME *pages 28–41*
3000 B.C. to 500 A.D.

Civilizations of Ancient Greece ➤ Growth of Greek City-States ➤ The Conquests of Alexander the Great ➤ From Roman Republic to Roman Empire ➤ Height of the Roman Empire ➤ Judaism and Christianity in the Roman Empire ➤ Decline of the Roman Empire

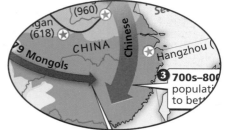

UNIT 4

EMPIRES AND CULTURES OF ASIA *pages 42–55*
395 to 1818

Cultures and Trade In and Around Asia ➤ The Spread of Islam ➤ Growth and Decline of the Byzantine Empire ➤ Tang and Sung Dynasties of China ➤ The Mongol Empire Spans Eurasia ➤ Ming Dynasty of China ➤ Kingdoms of Southeast Asia ➤ From Imperial to Feudal Japan ➤ India and the Mughal Empire

UNIT 5

EUROPE IN THE MIDDLE AGES *pages 56–69*
418 to 1580

Early Kingdoms of Medieval Europe ➤ Viking Impact on Europe ➤ Feudalism and the Holy Roman Empire ➤ Crusades to the Holy Land ➤ Trade Routes and Plague ➤ Moorish Spain ➤ The Hundred Years' War ➤ Age of European Exploration

10 9 8 7 6 5 4 3 2 1   10 09 08 07 06 05 04 03

ISBN 0-7825-0940-1 Product Code Number 9AWH
For information about ordering this atlas, call toll-free 800-621-8086.

Printed in U.S.A.

EDUCATIONAL CONSULTANTS

Michael Bruner, History Teacher, Chanute High School, Chanute, Kansas

Melissa Green, 6th Grade Teacher, Haven Middle School, Evanston School District #65, Evanston, Illinois

Lawrence W. McBride, Professor, Department of History, Illinois State University, Normal, Illinois

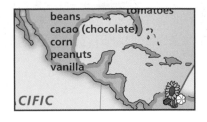

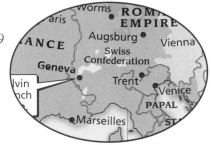
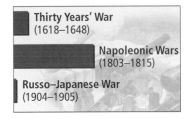

PHOTO CREDITS
Credit abbreviations: **AI/C** Archivo Iconographico, S.A./Corbis **ART** Art Resources **B/C** Bettmann/CORBIS
BAL Bridgeman Art Library **C** CORBIS **GDO/C** Gianni Dagli Orti/Corbis **GI** Getty Images **MF** Masterfile **PQ** PictureQuest
Position on page: **b** bottom; **l** left; **r** right; **t** top

front cover, t, © Louvre, Paris, France/BAL; **front cover**, b, © 2003 C; **7** t, © B/C; **7** b, © Vaka Taumako Project, 2002; **9** © Santokh Kochar/GI; **10** © GDO/C; **12** © Francoise de Mulder/C; **16** © 2003 C; **17** © C; **18** © The British Museum; **19** image provided by Gines Quinero Santiago; **20** © Daryl Benson/MF; **21** © Corbis Asian Arts & Archaeology/C; **22** © Dallas and John Heaton/C; **26** © Greg Stott/MF; **29** © Charlie Waite/GI; **31** © B/C; **32** © Royal Asiatic Society, London, UK/BAL; **35** © Charles & Josette Lenars/C; **36** © Richard T. Nowitz/C; **37** © Louvre, Paris, France/BAL; **39** © Christie's Images/C; **40** Scala/ART; **41** © Brian Redding/MF; **42** © GI; **44** © Bojan Brecelj/C; **45** © Michael Tropea/C; **47** © Reunion des Musees Nationaux/ART; **48** © Werner Forman/ART **49** © James L. Stanfield/National Geographic Image Collection; **50** © Victoria & Albert Museum/ART; **51** © Paul Chesley/National Geographic Image Collection; **53** © Natori Shunsen/BAL; **54** © Victoria & Albert Museum/ART; **55** © Scala/ART; **57** © AI/C; **58** painting by Michael P. Fräse, Swartz City, Michigan; **59** © AI/C; **60** © BAL/GI; **62** © AI/C; **63** © BAL/GI; **65** © BAL/GI; **67** Cliché musée des Beaux-Arts d'Orléans; **69** l, © GI; **69** r © B/C; **70** © AI/C; **71** © M.L. Sinibaldi/C; **72** © Michael Hampshire/Cahokia Mounds State Historic Site; **73** © Tom Bean/C; **74** © Schalkwijk/ART; **75** © Alison Wright/C; **77** © Historical Pictures Archives/C; **78** © The Granger Collection; **80** © GDO/C; **81** © Paul Almasy/C; **82** © AI/C; **84** © Wolfgang Kaehler/C; **85** © MIT Collection/C; **90** © Reunion des Musées Nationaux/ART; **91** © Scala/ART; **92** © The Corcoran Gallery of Art/C; **93** © Scala/ART; **94** © Scala/ART; **95** © Chris Hellier/C; **96** © John Farmar, Cordaiy Photo Library Ltd/C; **101** © B/C; **102** © Giraudon/ART; **103** © B/C; **104** © Leonard de Selva/C; **106** © B/C; **108** © AI/C; **111** © B/C; **112** © PQ; **115** © Hulton-Deutsch Collection/C; **116** l, © Christopher Morris/PQ; **116** r, © C; **118** © B.Press/PQ; **120** © AFP/C; **121** © Albert Normandin/MF.

How does this atlas work?

1 First read the **unit title**, which tells what the unit is about and what time period it covers.

2 Then read the **topic title** which tells what these two pages are about.

3 Next read the **introduction**, for more about the topic.

4 Now follow the **A B C D** markers for the clearest path through the pages.

The **A B C D captions** help you understand each map, graph, and picture.

Maps show places, movement, people, and events.

The **legend** gives the title of the map and explains what its colors and other symbols mean. Read the legend before studying the map.

Charts and graphs organize information visually.

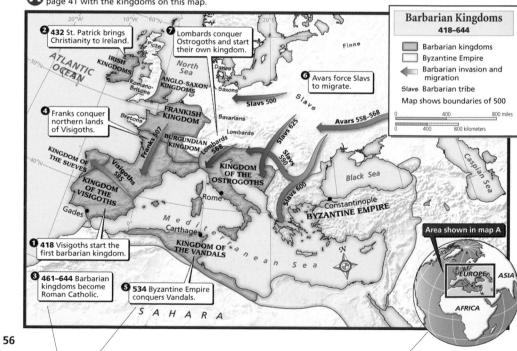

UNIT 5 — Europe in the Middle Ages
418 to 1580

711–1492 Moors rule Spain.

400 — **600** — **800**

418 Visigoths start a kingdom in Spain.

432 St. Patrick introduces Christianity to Ireland.

789 Vikings' first raid strikes Portland, England.

800 Charlemagne is crowned "Emperor of the West."

Early Kingdoms of Medieval Europe

During the **Middle Ages** or **medieval era**, many Europeans were poor, uneducated, and violent.

- Early in the Middle Ages, barbarian tribes settled in Western Europe and established their own kingdoms.
- Barbarian kings, wanting to be as civilized as the Romans, became Roman Catholic.
- One Frankish king, Charlemagne, conquered much of Western Europe.

Barbarians in Our Language

barbarian—*a brutal or uncultured person*	From **bar bar**, an imitation of how barbarians talked.
frank—*straightforward*	From the **Franks**, who thought violence was more direct than laws or diplomacy.
slave—*person held as property of another*	From the **Slavs**, a tribe that lost many people to slavery in the Roman Empire.
vandalism—*deliberate destruction of property*	From the **Vandals**, the tribe that looted Rome in 455.

B The table above shows some modern-day words, definitions, and histories.

A Compare the barbarian invasions on page 41 with the kingdoms on this map.

2 **432** St. Patrick brings Christianity to Ireland.

7 Lombards conquer Ostrogoths and start their own kingdom.

6 Avars force Slavs to migrate.

4 Franks conquer northern lands of Visigoths.

1 **418** Visigoths start the first barbarian kingdom.

3 **461–644** Barbarian kingdoms become Roman Catholic.

5 **534** Byzantine Empire conquers Vandals.

Barbarian Kingdoms 418–644

- Barbarian kingdoms
- Byzantine Empire
- Barbarian invasion and migration
- *Slavs* Barbarian tribe

Map shows boundaries of 500

0   400   800 miles
0   400   800 kilometers

Area shown in map A

Call-outs are mini-captions right on the map.

Locator maps explain what part of the world is shown.

56

4

The **unit timeline** shows key events from this time period. Use it to preview the unit.

At the end of the unit, use the timeline to review the sequence of key events.

What else can you find in this atlas?

1066 Normans take control of England.

1095 First Crusade is called by Pope Urban II.

1347 Plague-infected rats arrive in Sicily.

1498 Vasco da Gama reaches the Indies.

1519–1522 Magellan's crew circles the earth.

1000 | **1200** | **1400** | **1600**

936 Otto I creates what will be the Holy Roman Empire.

1215 Magna Carta gives rights to free men in England.

1337–1453 Hundred Years' War fought between England and France.

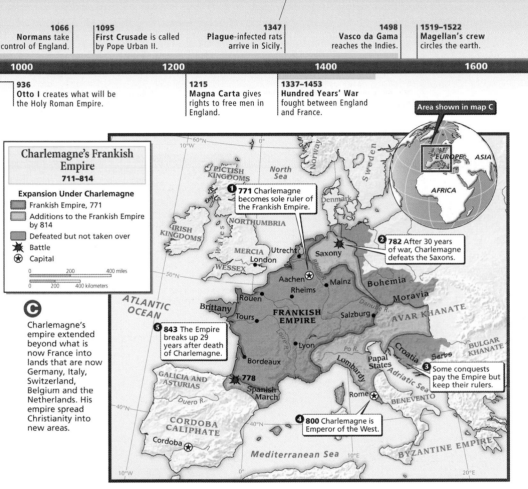

Area shown in map C

Charlemagne's Frankish Empire
711–814

Expansion Under Charlemagne

▢ Frankish Empire, 771

▢ Additions to the Frankish Empire by 814

▢ Defeated but not taken over

✸ Battle

★ Capital

0   200   400 miles
0   200   400 kilometers

771 Charlemagne becomes sole ruler of the Frankish Empire.

782 After 30 years of war, Charlemagne defeats the Saxons.

843 The Empire breaks up 29 years after death of Charlemagne.

Some conquests pay the Empire but keep their rulers.

800 Charlemagne is Emperor of the West.

C
Charlemagne's empire extended beyond what is now France into lands that are now Germany, Italy, Switzerland, Belgium and the Netherlands. His empire spread Christianity into new areas.

Milestones of World History on the inside front cover are a short list of key events.

Reference Maps on pages 122–131 can be compared to see how countries have changed over time.

Timetables of World History on 132–135 show what was happening in different places at the same time.

Glossary on 136–137 defines special words and names used in the atlas.

Index on 138–144 lists all the pages where people, places, or events are mentioned.

Thematic Index on the inside back cover lists all the pages related to certain big topics.

Abbreviations are explained on the inside back cover too.

D
The pope (center) crowned Charlemagne "Emperor of the West." Western Europeans hoped Charlemagne's rule would end centuries of chaos.

Who is the pope?
The pope is the Roman Catholic bishop of Rome and is the leader of the entire church. In the Middle Ages, the Catholic Church was very powerful in Western Europe. Today the pope leads over a billion Catholics worldwide.

57

Pictures show how people and places looked in the past.

History Questions help you understand key words or ideas.

5

8000 B.C.
Jericho is one of the first cities.

7000 B.C.
Symbols, earliest ancestors of writing, are first used.

100,000 B.C.	10,000 B.C.	8000 B.C.	6000 B.C.

100,000 B.C.
People migrate beyond East Africa.

9000 B.C.
Farming and herding begin in Fertile Crescent.

By 6000 B.C.
Farming begins in Egypt, India, and China.

People Migrate Across the Earth

About 100,000 B.C. early people began migrating from their African homeland.

- For thousands of years, people moved into new areas in search of food. They hunted animals and gathered wild plants.

- Ice ages killed much of their food, forcing people to move. They migrated on foot or in small boats.

- By 9000 B.C. people had migrated to most regions of the world.

A People first migrated to regions that had plenty of food and comfortable climates. Which continents had been reached by 30,000 B.C.?

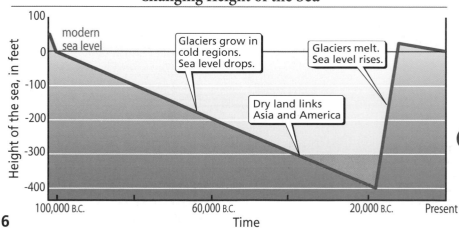

ARCTIC OCEAN

3 Route free of ice after 10,000 B.C.

30,000 B.C.

NORTH AMERICA

10,000 B.C.

4 As ice sheets melt, people migrate further south.

12,000 B.C.

PACIFIC OCEAN

ATLANTIC

5 Some Pacific islands are not reached until 1000 B.C.

SOUTH AMERICA

9000 B.C.

Routes by ice and sea are possible but not certain.

30°N

0°

30°S

60°S

Early Human Migration
100,000–9000 B.C.

Spread of Humans

→ 100,000–90,000 B.C.
→ 90,000–75,000 B.C.
→ 75,000–30,000 B.C.
→ 30,000–9000 B.C.

12,000 B.C. Approximate date of arrival in region

Ice Age

☐ Sea ice, 16,000 B.C.
☐ Glacier or ice sheet
Ice Age coastline
Coastline today

Equatorial Scale

0   2000   4000 miles
0   2000   4000 kilometers

Changing Height of the Sea

Height of the sea, in feet

100
0 — modern sea level
-100
-200
-300
-400

Glaciers grow in cold regions. Sea level drops.

Glaciers melt. Sea level rises.

Dry land links Asia and America

100,000 B.C.   60,000 B.C.   20,000 B.C.   Present

Time

B The earth's temperature began to fall around 100,000 B.C. Rivers froze, so water could not flow back to the sea and sea level dropped. Areas that had been underwater were exposed as dry land.

4000 B.C. Sahara gets drier, soon becomes desert.	3500 B.C. First civilization rises in Sumer. Bronze tools are made.	2350 B.C. First empire rises in Akkad.	By 1200 B.C. Hebrews live in Canaan.	539 B.C. Cyrus of Persia conquers Babylon.

4000 B.C.   **2000 B.C.**   B.C. ◄|► A.D.

5000 B.C. Irrigation is used in farming.	1800–1600 B.C. Assyria and Babylonia create empires in Mesopotamia.	900 B.C. Phoenicians sail to the Atlantic Ocean.

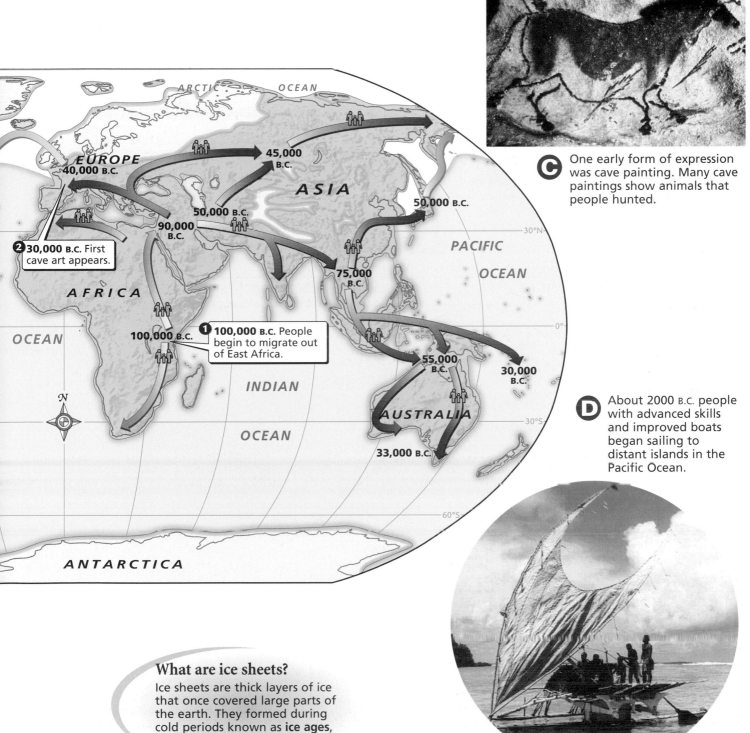

C One early form of expression was cave painting. Many cave paintings show animals that people hunted.

2 30,000 B.C. First cave art appears.

1 100,000 B.C. People begin to migrate out of East Africa.

D About 2000 B.C. people with advanced skills and improved boats began sailing to distant islands in the Pacific Ocean.

What are ice sheets?

Ice sheets are thick layers of ice that once covered large parts of the earth. They formed during cold periods known as **ice ages**, which lasted thousands of years.

Agriculture and Early Settlements

Agriculture, or growing plants and raising animals for food, changed human society forever. Agriculture was more reliable than hunting and gathering.

- People began to herd or keep wild animals in pens. They also planted seeds from wild grasses, using hoes and digging sticks. They had become farmers.

- Farmers could get their food in one place, so their settlements became permanent. Farming communities became villages.

- As farmers grew more food than they needed, some people became free to **specialize**. They worked at other jobs, such as making pots or tools.

Isn't that wild?

Wild dogs probably followed people to get food scraps. Early people trained these dogs to guard their camps and to help them hunt or herd other animals. The dog is the earliest known **domestic** animal, living with people or under their care.

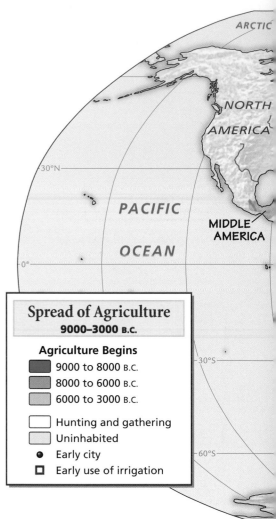

A Agriculture developed in several different regions of the world at about the same time. In areas unsuitable for farming, people continued to hunt and gather.

Spread of Agriculture
9000–3000 B.C.

Agriculture Begins
- 9000 to 8000 B.C.
- 8000 to 6000 B.C.
- 6000 to 3000 B.C.

- Hunting and gathering
- Uninhabited
- Early city
- Early use of irrigation

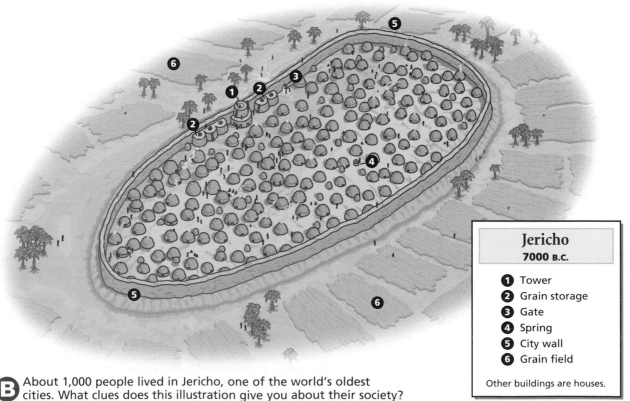

Jericho
7000 B.C.

1. Tower
2. Grain storage
3. Gate
4. Spring
5. City wall
6. Grain field

Other buildings are houses.

B About 1,000 people lived in Jericho, one of the world's oldest cities. What clues does this illustration give you about their society?

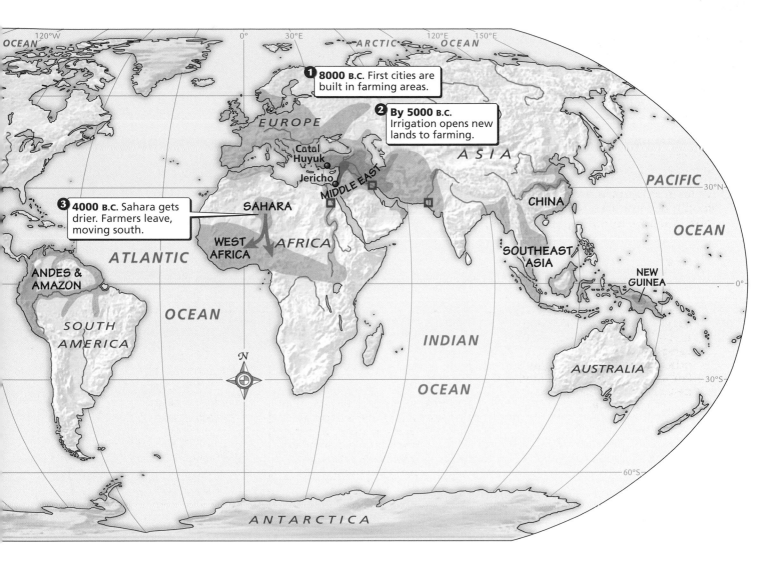

1 8000 B.C. First cities are built in farming areas.

2 By 5000 B.C. Irrigation opens new lands to farming.

3 4000 B.C. Sahara gets drier. Farmers leave, moving south.

C Hunters often returned empty-handed from a day of hunting. Herding animals, however, guaranteed a supply of meat, skins, and milk.

Earliest Domestic Plants and Animals

	PLANTS	ANIMALS
Middle East	barley, lentils, peas, wheat	cattle, goats, pigs, sheep
China	millet, rice	chickens, pigs, water buffalo
South and Southeast Asia	cotton, millet, rice, soybeans, sweet potatoes, taro	cattle, chickens, pigs, water buffalo
Africa	barley, millet, sorghum, wheat, yams	cattle, sheep
Europe	barley, rye, wheat	cattle, dogs, pigs
Americas	beans, peppers, potatoes, squash	dogs, turkeys

D Agriculture started with resources found in the environment. What were the most common domestic plants and animals?

Civilization in Ancient Mesopotamia

The earliest known civilization, Sumer, and the world's first empire, the Akkadian Empire, both developed in Mesopotamia.

■ The Sumerians developed the first written language and the first laws. They also traded with places as far away as Egypt and India.

■ Each Sumerian city-state was independent. Each had its own ruler, own special god, and own army.

■ People from the neighboring region of Akkad later conquered Sumer and the rest of the area around the Tigris and Euphrates Rivers. Once conquered, city-states were simply cities.

A Sargon was the first ruler of the Akkadian Empire. He conquered all of Mesopotamia and beyond.

Sumerians Develop Writing
7000–3000 B.C.

Word	Token 7000 B.C.	Pictograph 3500 B.C.	Cuneiform 3000 B.C.
Sheep	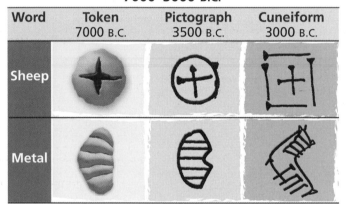		
Metal			

B People in Mesopotamia first used objects, or tokens, to record trades. Sumerians then drew the same shapes on clay tablets. Later they used triangular reeds to draw these shapes. These wedge shapes, or cuneiform, became the basis of written languages in Mesopotamia.

Is it a city or is it a state?

Early civilizations weren't part of a large country. Instead, people were governed by their own **city-state**. A city-state included a city and the surrounding countryside. There are a few city-states today, such as Monaco in Europe and Singapore in Asia.

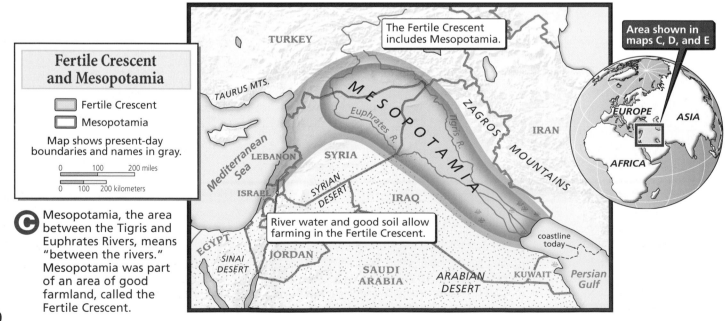

Fertile Crescent and Mesopotamia

- Fertile Crescent
- Mesopotamia

Map shows present-day boundaries and names in gray.

0   100   200 miles
0   100   200 kilometers

The Fertile Crescent includes Mesopotamia.

Area shown in maps C, D, and E

River water and good soil allow farming in the Fertile Crescent.

TURKEY
TAURUS MTS.
MESOPOTAMIA
Euphrates R.
ZAGROS MOUNTAINS
IRAN
Mediterranean Sea
LEBANON
SYRIA
ISRAEL
SYRIAN DESERT
Tigris R.
IRAQ
EGYPT
SINAI DESERT
JORDAN
SAUDI ARABIA
ARABIAN DESERT
KUWAIT
Persian Gulf
coastline today

EUROPE
ASIA
AFRICA

C Mesopotamia, the area between the Tigris and Euphrates Rivers, means "between the rivers." Mesopotamia was part of an area of good farmland, called the Fertile Crescent.

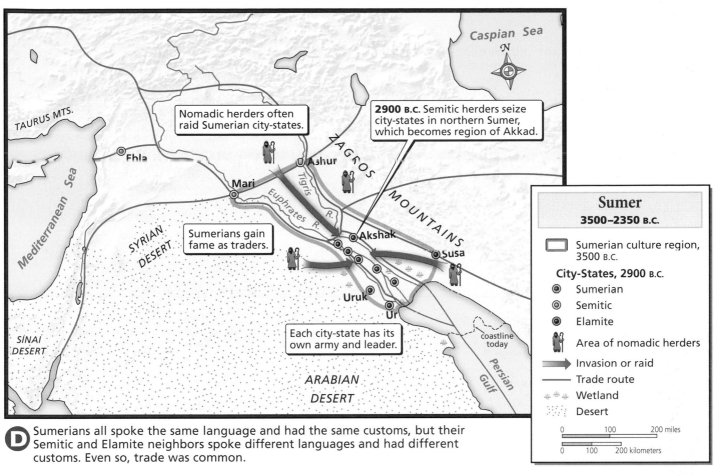

2900 B.C. Semitic herders seize city-states in northern Sumer, which becomes region of Akkad.

Nomadic herders often raid Sumerian city-states.

Sumerians gain fame as traders.

Each city-state has its own army and leader.

TAURUS MTS.

Ebla

Mediterranean Sea

SYRIAN DESERT

SINAI DESERT

ARABIAN DESERT

Mari

Ashur

Akshak

Uruk

Ur

Susa

ZAGROS MOUNTAINS

Tigris R.

Euphrates R.

Caspian Sea

N

Persian Gulf

coastline today

Sumer
3500–2350 B.C.

- ☐ Sumerian culture region, 3500 B.C.

City-States, 2900 B.C.
- ◉ Sumerian
- ◉ Semitic
- ◉ Elamite
- 🚶 Area of nomadic herders
- ➡ Invasion or raid
- — Trade route
- ⸻ Wetland
- ⸱⸱ Desert

0   100   200 miles
0   100   200 kilometers

D Sumerians all spoke the same language and had the same customs, but their Semitic and Elamite neighbors spoke different languages and had different customs. Even so, trade was common.

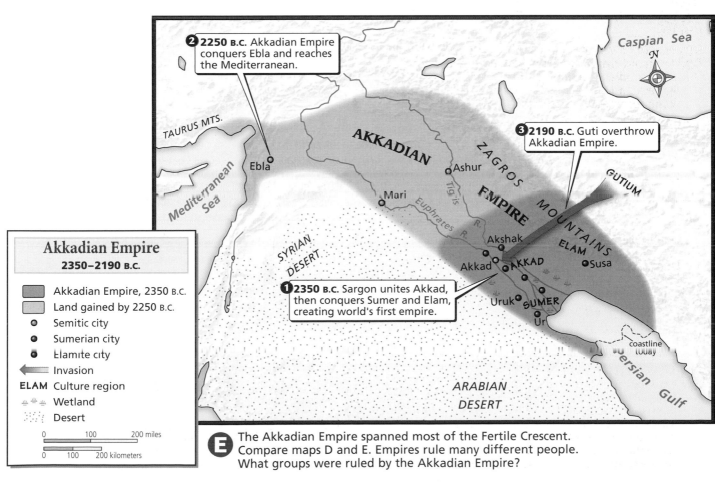

2 **2250 B.C.** Akkadian Empire conquers Ebla and reaches the Mediterranean.

3 **2190 B.C.** Guti overthrow Akkadian Empire.

1 **2350 B.C.** Sargon unites Akkad, then conquers Sumer and Elam, creating world's first empire.

TAURUS MTS.

AKKADIAN

EMPIRE

ZAGROS MOUNTAINS

GUTIUM

ELAM

Ebla

Mediterranean Sea

SYRIAN DESERT

ARABIAN DESERT

Mari

Ashur

Akshak

Akkad

AKKAD

Uruk

SUMER

Ur

Susa

Tigris R.

Euphrates R.

Caspian Sea

N

Persian Gulf

coastline today

Akkadian Empire
2350–2190 B.C.

- ▨ Akkadian Empire, 2350 B.C.
- ▨ Land gained by 2250 B.C.
- ◉ Semitic city
- ◉ Sumerian city
- ◉ Elamite city
- ← Invasion
- **ELAM** Culture region
- ⸻ Wetland
- ⸱⸱ Desert

0   100   200 miles
0   100   200 kilometers

E The Akkadian Empire spanned most of the Fertile Crescent. Compare maps D and E. Empires rule many different people. What groups were ruled by the Akkadian Empire?

Babylonia and Assyria

After the Akkadian Empire fell, two groups struggled for control of the Fertile Crescent. Babylonians from Babylon and Assyrians from Ashur became the major powers in the region.

- Babylon was long known as a center of learning. Babylonian science and literature were admired and imitated throughout the Fertile Crescent.

- In contrast, Assyria was known for its fierce army.

- Babylonia and Assyria fought each other often over the course of a thousand years. Each conquered the other more than once.

B The Babylonians and Assyrians built monuments to show their wealth and power. Above is a replica of Babylon's Ishtar Gate. The wealth came from conquests and taxes.

Area shown in maps A, C, and D

EUROPE ASIA
AFRICA

A The Babylonian Empire expanded under Hammurabi, one of Babylonia's most important kings. He is also remembered for his extensive law code.

HITTITE EMPIRE
Kanesh

1 **1813–1781 B.C.** Assyria controls upper Mesopotamia by force.

Caspian Sea

Tigris

ASSYRIA

Nineveh

Copper and tin are used for bronze weapons.

Ashur

Mediterranean Sea

Z A G R O S

KASSITE KINGDOM

SYRIAN DESERT

Akkad
Babylon ★ **BABYLONIA**

M T S.
ELAM

CANAAN

2 **1792–1750 B.C.** Under Hammurabi, Babylonia conquers most of Assyria.

Uruk
Ur

EGYPT

Persian Gulf

coastline today

3 After Hammurabi dies, Babylonia slowly fades away.

ARABIAN DESERT

Nile R.

Red Sea

Why do empires fail?

Akkad, Babylon, and Ashur all produced **empires**, ruling distant lands with languages and customs unlike their own. Such differences, along with the common preference for familiar rulers, make empires hard to govern.

Assyria and Babylonia
1800–1600 B.C.

☐	Assyria, 1800 B.C.
■	Babylonia, 1800 B.C.
▦	Babylonian gains by 1750 B.C.
←	Babylonian conquest
—	Trade route
▰	Copper
▱	Tin
★	Capital
EGYPT	Independent empire or state
ELAM	Culture region
⋰⋰	Desert

0	200	400 miles
0	200	400 kilometers

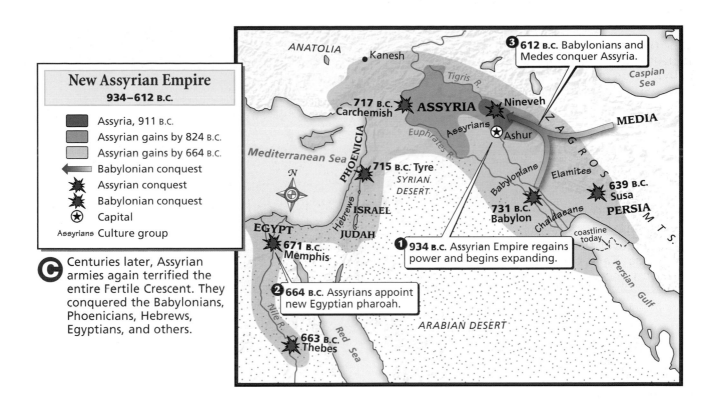

New Assyrian Empire
934–612 B.C.

- Assyria, 911 B.C.
- Assyrian gains by 824 B.C.
- Assyrian gains by 664 B.C.
- → Babylonian conquest
- ✶ Assyrian conquest
- ✶ Babylonian conquest
- ⊛ Capital
- Assyrians Culture group

C Centuries later, Assyrian armies again terrified the entire Fertile Crescent. They conquered the Babylonians, Phoenicians, Hebrews, Egyptians, and others.

❸ **612 B.C.** Babylonians and Medes conquer Assyria.

717 B.C. Carchemish

ASSYRIA Nineveh

715 B.C. Tyre

731 B.C. Babylon

639 B.C. Susa

❶ **934 B.C.** Assyrian Empire regains power and begins expanding.

671 B.C. Memphis

❷ **664 B.C.** Assyrians appoint new Egyptian pharoah.

663 B.C. Thebes

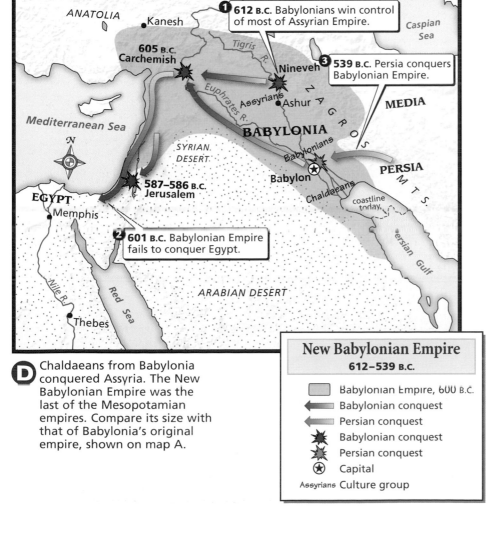

❶ **612 B.C.** Babylonians win control of most of Assyrian Empire.

605 B.C. Carchemish

Nineveh

❸ **539 B.C.** Persia conquers Babylonian Empire.

BABYLONIA

Babylon

587–586 B.C. Jerusalem

❷ **601 B.C.** Babylonian Empire fails to conquer Egypt.

D Chaldaeans from Babylonia conquered Assyria. The New Babylonian Empire was the last of the Mesopotamian empires. Compare its size with that of Babylonia's original empire, shown on map A.

New Babylonian Empire
612–539 B.C.

- Babylonian Empire, 600 B.C.
- → Babylonian conquest
- → Persian conquest
- ✶ Babylonian conquest
- ✶ Persian conquest
- ⊛ Capital
- Assyrians Culture group

Babylonian Contributions to Science

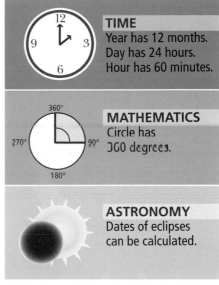

TIME
Year has 12 months. Day has 24 hours. Hour has 60 minutes.

MATHEMATICS
Circle has 360 degrees.

ASTRONOMY
Dates of eclipses can be calculated.

E Babylonians liked numbers that could be evenly divided by many other numbers. Notice how such numbers are used in Babylonian contributions to time and mathematics.

Hebrew Kingdoms

According to the Hebrew Bible, Hebrews came from southeastern Mesopotamia near the Persian Gulf. Around 1800 B.C., they migrated west to the Mediterranean coast.

- They are said to have settled in the area called "Canaan," which they felt their god had given them.

- History confirms that a Hebrew kingdom existed by 1200 B.C. Later the kingdom split into Israel and Judah.

- Wars and famine often forced Hebrews to leave their "Promised Land."

- The Hebrews came to be called **Jews** and their religion **Judaism**.

Area shown in maps A and B

1 1800 B.C. Abraham and relatives move from Ur to Canaan.

2 1700 B.C. Famine forces Hebrews to move to Egypt. They become slaves.

5 Hebrews reach Canaan and form a kingdom.

4 Moses gets divine Ten Commandments. Hebrews accept one god.

3 1200 B.C. Moses leads freed Hebrews from Egypt back to Canaan.

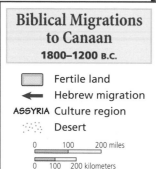

Biblical Migrations to Canaan
1800–1200 B.C.

- Fertile land
- ← Hebrew migration
- ASSYRIA Culture region
- Desert

0   100   200 miles
0 100   200 kilometers

A In the biblical accounts, leaders such as Abraham and Moses led the Hebrews to Canaan. Archeologists have not been able to confirm these accounts.

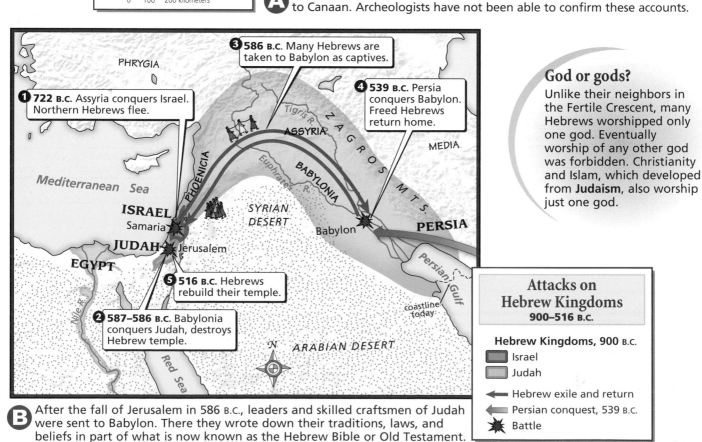

3 586 B.C. Many Hebrews are taken to Babylon as captives.

1 722 B.C. Assyria conquers Israel. Northern Hebrews flee.

4 539 B.C. Persia conquers Babylon. Freed Hebrews return home.

5 516 B.C. Hebrews rebuild their temple.

2 587–586 B.C. Babylonia conquers Judah, destroys Hebrew temple.

God or gods?

Unlike their neighbors in the Fertile Crescent, many Hebrews worshipped only one god. Eventually worship of any other god was forbidden. Christianity and Islam, which developed from **Judaism**, also worship just one god.

Attacks on Hebrew Kingdoms
900–516 B.C.

Hebrew Kingdoms, 900 B.C.
- Israel
- Judah
- ← Hebrew exile and return
- ← Persian conquest, 539 B.C.
- ✹ Battle

B After the fall of Jerusalem in 586 B.C., leaders and skilled craftsmen of Judah were sent to Babylon. There they wrote down their traditions, laws, and beliefs in part of what is now known as the Hebrew Bible or Old Testament.

Phoenician Trade

The Phoenician civilization, like that of the Hebrews, developed along the eastern edge of the Mediterranean Sea.

- By 2900 B.C. the Phoenicians had become the first major sea-going civilization. Their ships could travel long distances using either sails or oars.

- The Phoenicians established a large trade network. They also established colonies in North Africa, southern Spain, and on islands in the Mediterranean Sea.

- To make trade easier, the Phoenicians developed a simple writing system that used symbols for sounds instead of symbols for words or ideas.

Development of OurAlphabet

Phoenician 1000 B.C.	Greek 600 B.C.	Roman 300 A.D.
K	A	A
◁	B	B
△	△	D
ʒ	E	E

C Sumerians used over 500 symbols in their writing; Phoenicians used only 22. Other cultures adopted the Phoenician symbols, on which our modern alphabet is based.

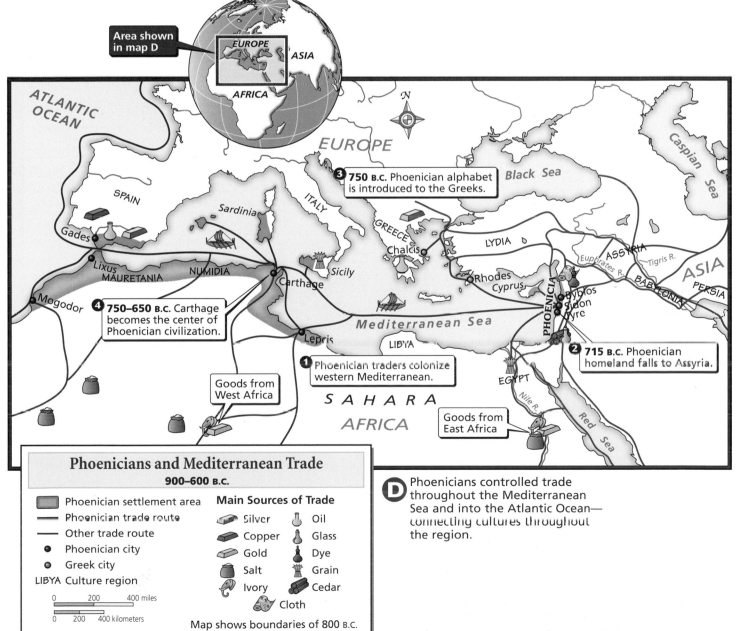

3 750 B.C. Phoenician alphabet is introduced to the Greeks.

4 750–650 B.C. Carthage becomes the center of Phoenician civilization.

1 Phoenician traders colonize western Mediterranean.

2 715 B.C. Phoenician homeland falls to Assyria.

Goods from West Africa

Goods from East Africa

Area shown in map D

Phoenicians and Mediterranean Trade
900–600 B.C.

- Phoenician settlement area
- Phoenician trade route
- Other trade route
- ● Phoenician city
- ● Greek city
- LIBYA Culture region

0   200   400 miles
0   200   400 kilometers

Main Sources of Trade
- Silver
- Copper
- Gold
- Salt
- Ivory
- Oil
- Glass
- Dye
- Grain
- Cedar
- Cloth

Map shows boundaries of 800 B.C.

D Phoenicians controlled trade throughout the Mediterranean Sea and into the Atlantic Ocean— connecting cultures throughout the region.

2500 B.C.
Planned cities are built in India.

6000 B.C.	5000 B.C.	4000 B.C.	3000 B.C.

6000 B.C.
Farming begins in western India.

5000 B.C.
Yangshao culture begins in China.

3100 B.C.
Upper and Lower Egypt unite.

Civilization in Ancient Egypt

Ancient Egypt is one of the oldest and longest lasting civilizations in the world. This civilization began in a river valley more than 5,000 years ago.

▬ Ancient Egypt arose along the Nile River in northeastern Africa.

▬ The first 2,000 years of Egyptian history are divided into three periods: the Old, Middle, and New Kingdoms.

▬ The ancient Egyptians developed an advanced civilization. They built cities, invented hieroglyphics (a form of writing), and created large monuments.

A During the Old Kingdom, a strong central government was established and the building of pyramids began. During the Middle Kingdom, Egypt expanded south along the Nile and conquered Lower Nubia.

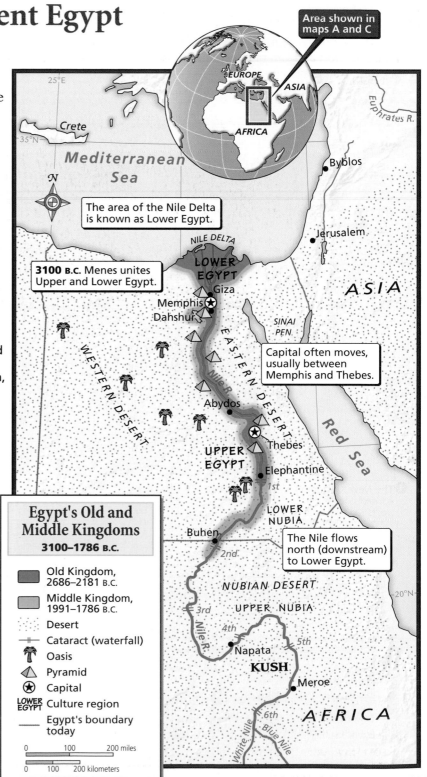

Area shown in maps A and C

The area of the Nile Delta is known as Lower Egypt.

3100 B.C. Menes unites Upper and Lower Egypt.

Capital often moves, usually between Memphis and Thebes.

The Nile flows north (downstream) to Lower Egypt.

Egypt's Old and Middle Kingdoms
3100–1786 B.C.

- ▮ Old Kingdom, 2686–2181 B.C.
- ▮ Middle Kingdom, 1991–1786 B.C.
- ⋯ Desert
- ⊢⊢ Cataract (waterfall)
- 🌴 Oasis
- △ Pyramid
- ✪ Capital
- LOWER EGYPT Culture region
- — Egypt's boundary today

0   100   200 miles
0   100   200 kilometers

B Thousands of workers built huge pyramids as tombs for Egyptian rulers. Farmers helped while the Nile was flooded.

16

1766 B.C. Shang dynasty, China's first, begins.	1570 B.C. New Kingdom of Egypt begins.	563 B.C. Siddhartha Gautama (Buddha) is born.	212 B.C. Great Wall of China construction begins.	500 A.D. Gupta Empire collapses after Hun invasions.

2000 B.C.   **1000 B.C.**   B.C. ◄ | ► A.D.   **1000 A.D.**

1000 B.C. Hindus write down world's oldest scriptures.	551 B.C. Confucius is born.	321 B.C. Mauryan Empire begins in India.	350 A.D. Kingdom of Kush falls.

C After the Middle Kingdom broke apart, Egypt was ruled by the Hyksos people of Asia. Then the Egyptians overthrew the Hyksos and began the New Kingdom. This new Egyptian empire became the strongest and wealthiest in the world.

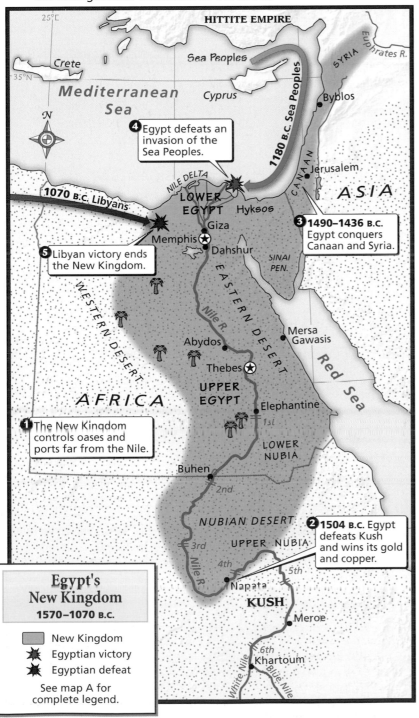

4 Egypt defeats an invasion of the Sea Peoples.

1070 B.C. Libyans

5 Libyan victory ends the New Kingdom.

3 1490–1436 B.C. Egypt conquers Canaan and Syria.

1 The New Kingdom controls oases and ports far from the Nile.

2 1504 B.C. Egypt defeats Kush and wins its gold and copper.

1180 B.C. Sea Peoples

Egypt's New Kingdom
1570–1070 B.C.

New Kingdom
✹ Egyptian victory
✸ Egyptian defeat
See map A for complete legend.

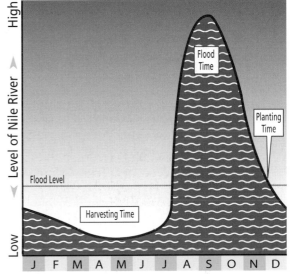

Flooding of the Nile

D Ancient Egypt has been called the "gift of the Nile." The Nile flooded around the same time every year, depositing rich soil for farming.

E Most Egyptians lived in the Nile River Valley. This husband and wife are plowing fields, preparing the soil for planting. Look at graph D. In which months would they be plowing?

Ancient Egypt Under Foreign Rule

At the end of the New Kingdom, nobles and priests began to compete for power. The Egyptian empire weakened and began to lose territory.

▬ Egypt was invaded by neighboring Libyans. The Libyans were among the first foreigners to rule Egypt.

▬ Off and on for more than a thousand years, Egypt was ruled by foreigners: Libya, Kush, Assyria, Persia, Greece, and Rome.

▬ Many of the foreign rulers continued to govern Egypt in an Egyptian manner. Most took the title of pharaoh, the name for an Egyptian king.

A Kush invaded Egypt from the south and gradually conquered Egyptian territory to the Mediterranean Sea. Kushites ruled Egypt until they were defeated by Assyrians.

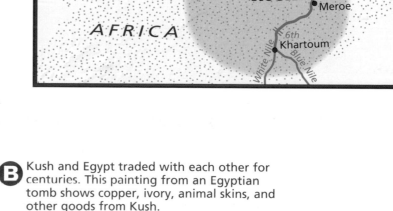

Area shown in maps A and C

❸ Assyrians force Kushites out of Egypt.

❷ Kush invades Lower Egypt.

❶ Kush invades Upper Egypt.

Capital of Kush

Kush Conquers Egypt
750–664 B.C.

- ▨ Egypt under Kushite rule, 750–664 B.C.
- ▨ Kush homelands
- ⠿ Desert
- ╫ Cataract (waterfall)
- 🌴 Oasis
- ★ Capital
- **LOWER EGYPT** Culture region
- — Egypt's boundary today

0   100   200 miles
0   100   200 kilometers

B Kush and Egypt traded with each other for centuries. This painting from an Egyptian tomb shows copper, ivory, animal skins, and other goods from Kush.

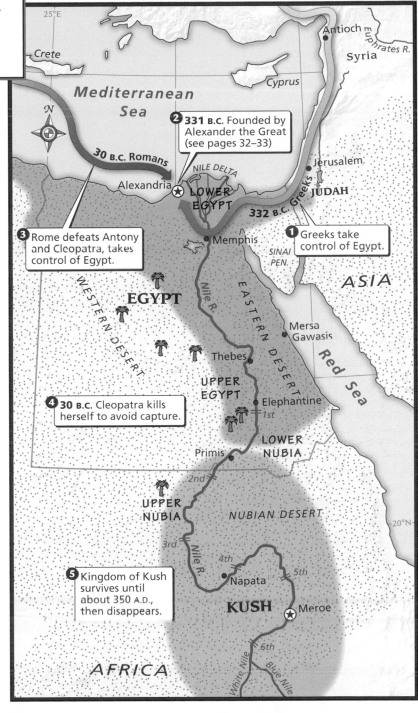

Greeks Rule Egypt
332–30 B.C.

Egypt under Greek rule, 332–30 B.C.

Kingdom of Kush

See map A for complete legend.

C Alexander the Great conquered Egypt in 332 B.C. For the next 300 years, Greek pharaohs ruled Egypt and spread Greek culture.

Map labels:
- 25°E
- Antioch
- Crete
- Syria
- Euphrates R.
- Cyprus
- Mediterranean Sea
- **2** 331 B.C. Founded by Alexander the Great (see pages 32–33)
- 30 B.C. Romans
- NILE DELTA
- Jerusalem
- Alexandria
- LOWER EGYPT
- 332 B.C. Greeks
- JUDAH
- **3** Rome defeats Antony and Cleopatra, takes control of Egypt.
- Memphis
- **1** Greeks take control of Egypt.
- SINAI PEN.
- ASIA
- WESTERN DESERT
- EGYPT
- Nile R.
- EASTERN DESERT
- Mersa Gawasis
- Red Sea
- Thebes
- UPPER EGYPT
- **4** 30 B.C. Cleopatra kills herself to avoid capture.
- Elephantine
- 1st
- LOWER NUBIA
- Primis
- 2nd
- UPPER NUBIA
- NUBIAN DESERT
- 20°N
- 3rd
- Nile R.
- 4th
- Napata
- 5th
- **5** Kingdom of Kush survives until about 350 A.D., then disappears.
- KUSH
- Meroe
- 6th
- White Nile
- Blue Nile
- AFRICA

D Cleopatra was the last of the Greek pharaohs. She married Mark Antony, a Roman leader, and they joined forces in a war with Rome. They lost and Rome took control of Egypt.

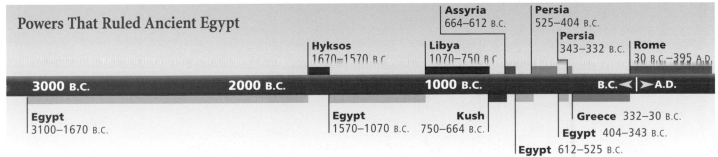

Powers That Ruled Ancient Egypt

Assyria 664–612 B.C.	Persia 525–404 B.C.
Hyksos 1670–1570 B.C.	Libya 1070–750 B.C.
	Persia 343–332 B.C.
	Rome 30 B.C.–395 A.D.

3000 B.C.   2000 B.C.   1000 B.C.   B.C. ◄ | ► A.D.

Egypt 3100–1670 B.C.

Egypt 1570–1070 B.C.   Kush 750–664 B.C.

Greece 332–30 B.C.

Egypt 404–343 B.C.

Egypt 612–525 B.C.

E Compare the amount of time that Egyptians ruled Egypt with the amount of time that foreign powers ruled. Which foreign power ruled Egypt the longest?

Civilization in Ancient China

China has one of the oldest continuous civilizations in the world. Chinese civilization developed from two early cultures living in two river valleys.

- The earliest Chinese culture was the Yangshao. It developed 7,000 years ago in the Huang He Valley, in what is now northern China.

- The Longshan culture developed about 2,000 years later and eventually replaced the Yangshao.

- China's first **dynasty** or family of rulers emerged from the Longshan culture. It is known as the Shang dynasty.

- The Shang dynasty ruled a portion of what is now China for more than 600 years.

A Rice was first grown in the Yangtze Valley around 5000 B.C. It became the main crop of southern China.

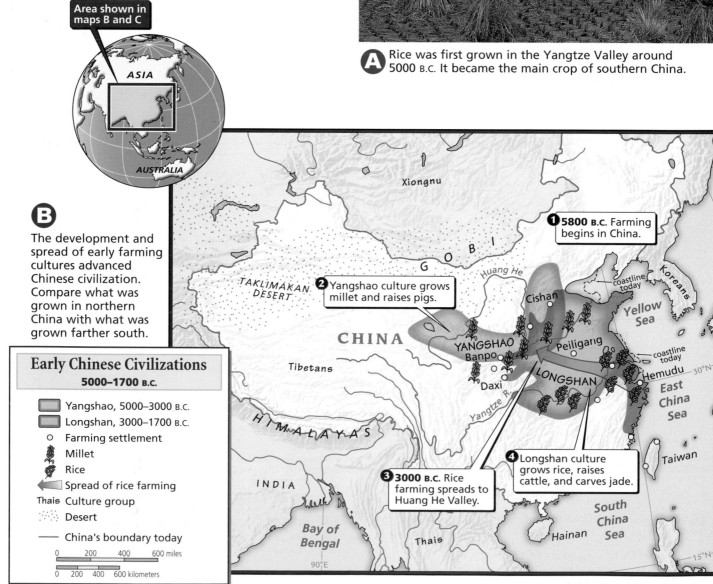

B

The development and spread of early farming cultures advanced Chinese civilization. Compare what was grown in northern China with what was grown farther south.

Early Chinese Civilizations
5000–1700 B.C.

- Yangshao, 5000–3000 B.C.
- Longshan, 3000–1700 B.C.
- ○ Farming settlement
- Millet
- Rice
- → Spread of rice farming
- Thais Culture group
- ⋯ Desert
- — China's boundary today

0   200   400   600 miles
0 200 400 600 kilometers

Area shown in maps B and C

ASIA

AUSTRALIA

Xiongnu

❶ **5800 B.C.** Farming begins in China.

❷ Yangshao culture grows millet and raises pigs.

❸ **3000 B.C.** Rice farming spreads to Huang He Valley.

❹ Longshan culture grows rice, raises cattle, and carves jade.

TAKLIMAKAN DESERT

GOBI

Huang He

Cishan

coastline today

Koreans

Yellow Sea

coastline today

CHINA

YANGSHAO

Banpo

Peiligang

Hemudu

30°N

Tibetans

Daxi

LONGSHAN

East China Sea

Yangtze R.

HIMALAYAS

Taiwan

INDIA

Bay of Bengal

Thais

Hainan

South China Sea

15°N

90°E

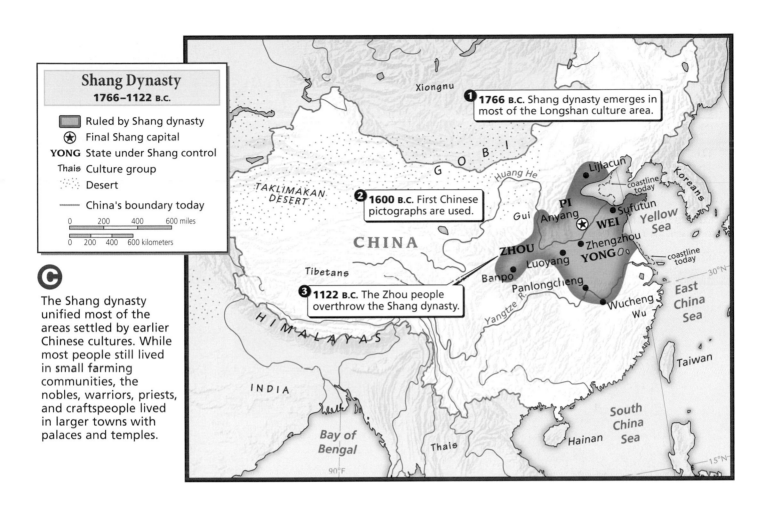

Shang Dynasty
1766–1122 B.C.

- ▨ Ruled by Shang dynasty
- ✪ Final Shang capital
- **YONG** State under Shang control
- Thais Culture group
- ⋯ Desert
- — China's boundary today

0   200   400   600 miles
0   200   400   600 kilometers

❶ 1766 B.C. Shang dynasty emerges in most of the Longshan culture area.

❷ 1600 B.C. First Chinese pictographs are used.

❸ 1122 B.C. The Zhou people overthrow the Shang dynasty.

C The Shang dynasty unified most of the areas settled by earlier Chinese cultures. While most people still lived in small farming communities, the nobles, warriors, priests, and craftspeople lived in larger towns with palaces and temples.

Development of Writing: Chinese Characters
1600 B.C.–Today

Object	Pictograph 1600 B.C.	Ancient Character 200 B.C.	Present Character 200 A.D.
Ear	)		
Moon	D		
Rain	⫶		

D Writing developed during the Shang dynasty. Chinese characters represented ideas, not sounds. Everyone used the same characters so people could communicate through writing even if they spoke different languages.

E The Shang dynasty is known for its use of bronze. Bronze, made from copper and tin, was used for decorative objects, such as this water buffalo, as well as for tools and weapons.

Can we keep it in the family?
When the rule of a kingdom or an empire is passed down from one family member to another, usually from a father to a son, it is sometimes called a **dynasty**. Ancient China was ruled by a series of dynasties, as was ancient Egypt.

21

Dynasties of Ancient China

After the Shang dynasty was overthrown, three other dynasties helped expand, unify, and develop ancient China.

- The Zhou dynasty ruled for 900 years. However, the Zhou had difficulty controlling their territory.

- The Qin established China's first unified empire. The name **China** comes from **Qin**, which is also spelled **Chin**.

- The Qin were overthrown, and the Han dynasty rose to power. The first Han emperor reduced taxes and changed harsh laws.

What did Confucius say?

The ancient Chinese philosopher Confucius (born about 551 B.C.) developed a guide to living a moral life. However, Confucianism is not a religion. The teachings of Confucius apply to everyday life as well as to political rule.

B The Great Wall of China was built and rebuilt by several dynasties. This massive building project was begun by the Qin dynasty to keep out barbarian invaders. The Great Wall still stands and is over 4,000 miles long.

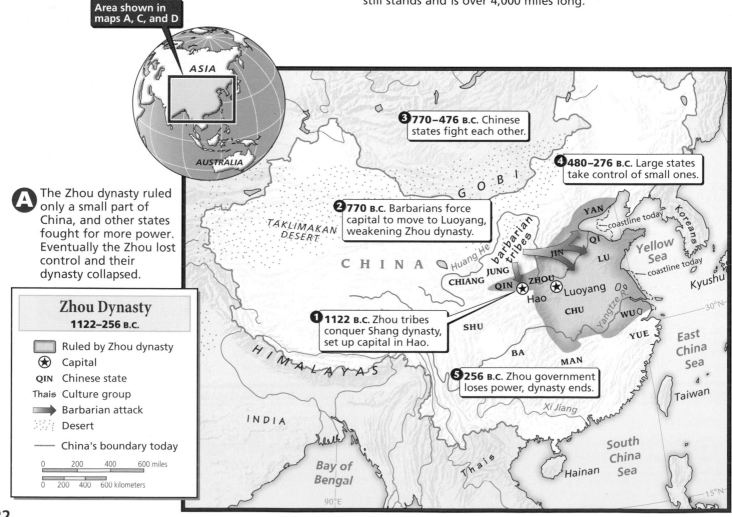

Area shown in maps A, C, and D

❸ 770–476 B.C. Chinese states fight each other.

❹ 480–276 B.C. Large states take control of small ones.

❷ 770 B.C. Barbarians force capital to move to Luoyang, weakening Zhou dynasty.

❶ 1122 B.C. Zhou tribes conquer Shang dynasty, set up capital in Hao.

❺ 256 B.C. Zhou government loses power, dynasty ends.

A The Zhou dynasty ruled only a small part of China, and other states fought for more power. Eventually the Zhou lost control and their dynasty collapsed.

Zhou Dynasty
1122–256 B.C.

- Ruled by Zhou dynasty
- ★ Capital
- QIN Chinese state
- Thais Culture group
- ➡ Barbarian attack
- Desert
- China's boundary today

| 0 | 200 | 400 | 600 miles |
| 0 | 200 | 400 | 600 kilometers |

22

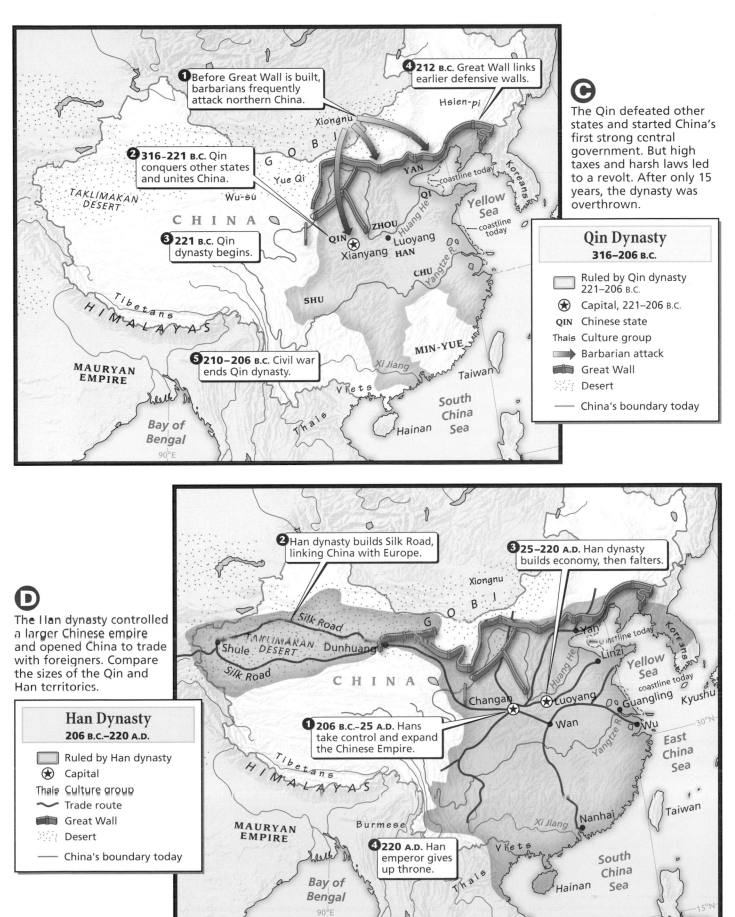

❶ Before Great Wall is built, barbarians frequently attack northern China.

❹ 212 B.C. Great Wall links earlier defensive walls.

Hsien-pi

Xiongnu

❷ 316–221 B.C. Qin conquers other states and unites China.

GOBI

Yue Qi

Wu-su

TAKLIMAKAN DESERT

YAN

coastline today

Koreans

CHINA

QI

Yellow Sea

coastline today

Tibetans

HIMALAYAS

❸ 221 B.C. Qin dynasty begins.

QIN ⊛ Xianyang

ZHOU

HAN

Luoyang

Huang He

CHU

Yangtze R.

SHU

MAURYAN EMPIRE

❺ 210–206 B.C. Civil war ends Qin dynasty.

MIN-YUE

Xi Jiang

Viets

Thais

Taiwan

Hainan

South China Sea

Bay of Bengal

90°E

C

The Qin defeated other states and started China's first strong central government. But high taxes and harsh laws led to a revolt. After only 15 years, the dynasty was overthrown.

Qin Dynasty
316–206 B.C.

▢ Ruled by Qin dynasty 221–206 B.C.

⊛ Capital, 221–206 B.C.

QIN Chinese state

Thais Culture group

➡ Barbarian attack

▰ Great Wall

░ Desert

— China's boundary today

D

The Han dynasty controlled a larger Chinese empire and opened China to trade with foreigners. Compare the sizes of the Qin and Han territories.

❷ Han dynasty builds Silk Road, linking China with Europe.

❸ 25–220 A.D. Han dynasty builds economy, then falters.

Xiongnu

Silk Road

TAKLIMAKAN DESERT

Shule

Dunhuang

GOBI

Yan

coastline today

Koreans

Silk Road

CHINA

Linzi

Yellow Sea

coastline today

Changan ⊛

Huang He

Luoyang ⊛

Guangling

Kyushu

❶ 206 B.C.–25 A.D. Hans take control and expand the Chinese Empire.

Wan

Wu

30°N

Tibetans

HIMALAYAS

Yangtze R.

East China Sea

MAURYAN EMPIRE

Burmese

Nanhai

Taiwan

Han Dynasty
206 B.C.–220 A.D.

▢ Ruled by Han dynasty

⊛ Capital

Thais Culture group

∿ Trade route

▰ Great Wall

░ Desert

— China's boundary today

❹ 220 A.D. Han emperor gives up throne.

Xi Jiang

Viets

Thais

Hainan

South China Sea

Bay of Bengal

90°E

15°N

23

Ancient India and the Spread of Hinduism

One of the first civilizations and one of the world's oldest religions developed in ancient India.

- People began to settle in the Indus River Valley in south Asia about 6,000 years ago. Farming and herding communities developed.

- An advanced civilization with carefully planned cities developed in the valley. The Indus Valley Civilization thrived for 900 years.

- A large group of nomads, the Aryans, migrated to India. Their religious beliefs helped form a new religion called **Hinduism**.

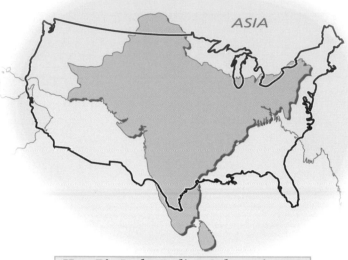

ASIA

What do Hindus believe?

Hindus believe that all living things have many lives. If you do good things in this life, you will come back as someone wiser and better in your next life. If you do bad things in this life, you could come back as a rat or even a gnat!

How Big Is the Indian Subcontinent?

A India is part of a subcontinent that includes the modern countries of India, Pakistan, Bangladesh, Nepal, Sri Lanka, and Bhutan. (See their boundaries on page 129.)

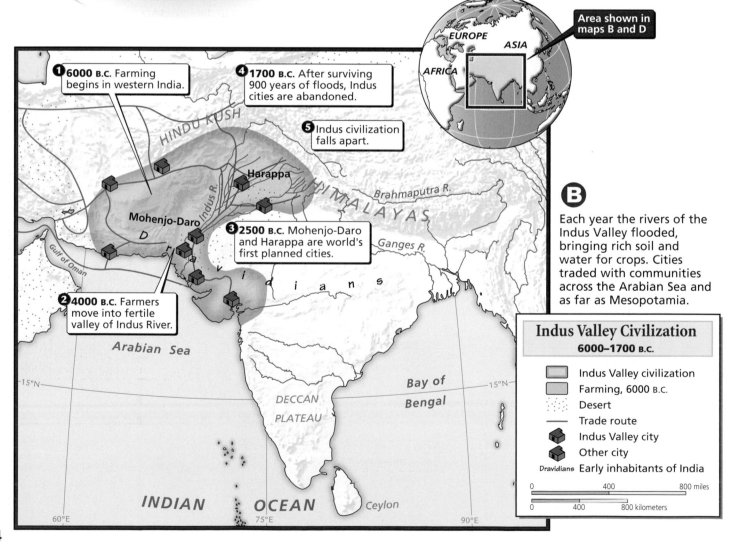

① **6000 B.C.** Farming begins in western India.

④ **1700 B.C.** After surviving 900 years of floods, Indus cities are abandoned.

⑤ Indus civilization falls apart.

HINDU KUSH

Harappa

HIMALAYAS

Brahmaputra R.

Mohenjo-Daro

③ **2500 B.C.** Mohenjo-Daro and Harappa are world's first planned cities.

Indus R.

Ganges R.

D r a v i d i a n s

Gulf of Oman

② **4000 B.C.** Farmers move into fertile valley of Indus River.

Arabian Sea

DECCAN PLATEAU

Bay of Bengal

15°N

15°N

INDIAN OCEAN

Ceylon

60°E

75°E

90°E

Area shown in maps B and D

EUROPE
ASIA
AFRICA

B

Each year the rivers of the Indus Valley flooded, bringing rich soil and water for crops. Cities traded with communities across the Arabian Sea and as far as Mesopotamia.

Indus Valley Civilization
6000–1700 B.C.

☐	Indus Valley civilization
☐	Farming, 6000 B.C.
∵	Desert
—	Trade route
⬢	Indus Valley city
⬢	Other city
Dravidians	Early inhabitants of India

0   400   800 miles
0   400   800 kilometers

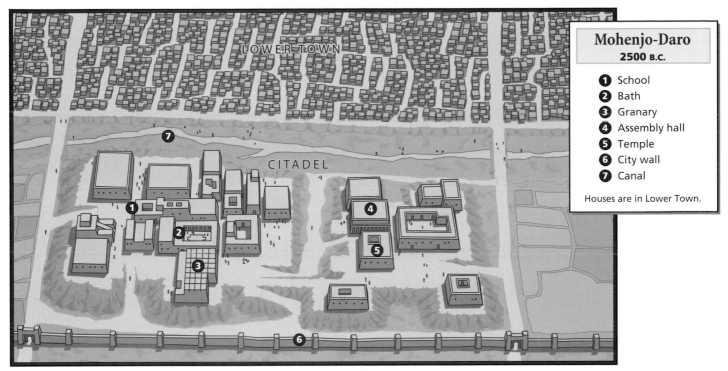

Mohenjo-Daro
2500 B.C.

1 School
2 Bath
3 Granary
4 Assembly hall
5 Temple
6 City wall
7 Canal

Houses are in Lower Town.

C Mohenjo-Daro had straight streets and large public buildings and meeting places. Its two-story houses were built of baked bricks, and many included rooms for bathing.

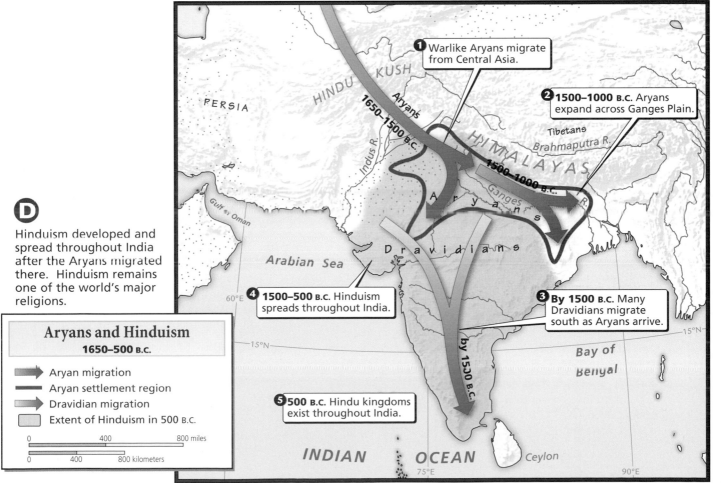

D Hinduism developed and spread throughout India after the Aryans migrated there. Hinduism remains one of the world's major religions.

1 Warlike Aryans migrate from Central Asia.

2 1500–1000 B.C. Aryans expand across Ganges Plain.

3 By 1500 B.C. Many Dravidians migrate south as Aryans arrive.

4 1500–500 B.C. Hinduism spreads throughout India.

5 500 B.C. Hindu kingdoms exist throughout India.

Aryans and Hinduism
1650–500 B.C.

➡ Aryan migration
— Aryan settlement region
➡ Dravidian migration
▢ Extent of Hinduism in 500 B.C.

0   400   800 miles
0   400   800 kilometers

Ancient India and the Spread of Buddhism

In addition to Hinduism, another major world religion developed in ancient India—**Buddhism**.

- Buddhism was based on the teachings of Siddhartha Gautama. He preached a new way of life to end suffering.

- The Mauryas united India and created the first Indian empire. During their reign, Buddhism spread throughout India.

- Later the Gupta Empire emerged. They started a golden age in India when culture and science thrived.

What's nirvana?

Imagine having great wisdom and compassion and being free from suffering. This state of peacefulness is called **nirvana**. Reaching nirvana is the goal of Buddhism.

A The name **Buddha** means "the Enlightened One." Siddhartha Gautama was called Buddha because of his wise teachings on how to live a good life.

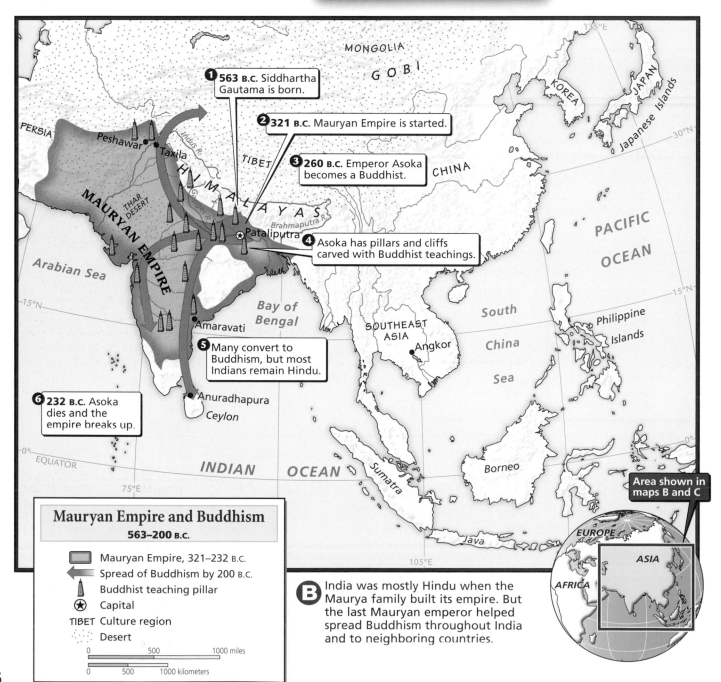

1 **563 B.C.** Siddhartha Gautama is born.

2 **321 B.C.** Mauryan Empire is started.

3 **260 B.C.** Emperor Asoka becomes a Buddhist.

4 Asoka has pillars and cliffs carved with Buddhist teachings.

5 Many convert to Buddhism, but most Indians remain Hindu.

6 **232 B.C.** Asoka dies and the empire breaks up.

Mauryan Empire and Buddhism
563–200 B.C.

- Mauryan Empire, 321–232 B.C.
- Spread of Buddhism by 200 B.C.
- Buddhist teaching pillar
- ★ Capital
- TIBET Culture region
- Desert

0   500   1000 miles
0   500   1000 kilometers

B India was mostly Hindu when the Maurya family built its empire. But the last Mauryan emperor helped spread Buddhism throughout India and to neighboring countries.

Area shown in maps B and C

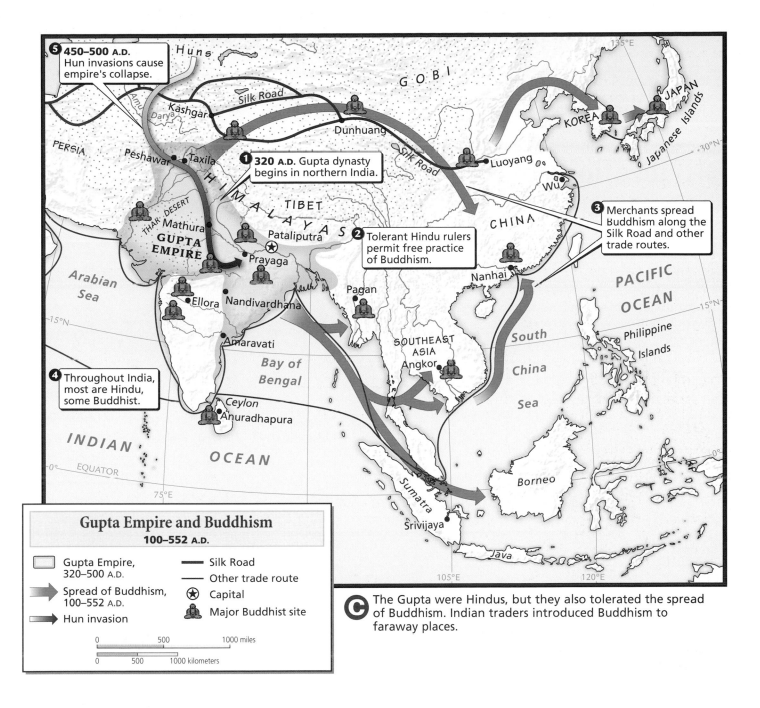

5 **450–500 A.D.** Hun invasions cause empire's collapse.

1 **320 A.D.** Gupta dynasty begins in northern India.

2 Tolerant Hindu rulers permit free practice of Buddhism.

3 Merchants spread Buddhism along the Silk Road and other trade routes.

4 Throughout India, most are Hindu, some Buddhist.

Gupta Empire and Buddhism
100–552 A.D.

- ▢ Gupta Empire, 320–500 A.D.
- ➡ Spread of Buddhism, 100–552 A.D.
- ➡ Hun invasion
- — Silk Road
- — Other trade route
- ✪ Capital
- 🧘 Major Buddhist site

0   500   1000 miles
0 500 1000 kilometers

C The Gupta were Hindus, but they also tolerated the spread of Buddhism. Indian traders introduced Buddhism to faraway places.

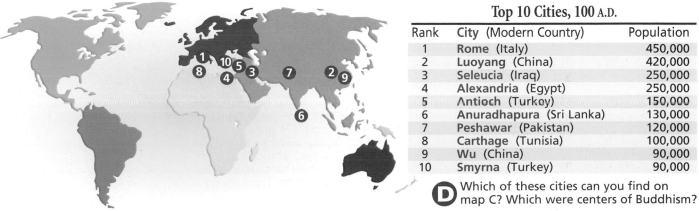

Top 10 Cities, 100 A.D.

Rank	City (Modern Country)	Population
1	Rome (Italy)	450,000
2	Luoyang (China)	420,000
3	Seleucia (Iraq)	250,000
4	Alexandria (Egypt)	250,000
5	Antioch (Turkey)	150,000
6	Anuradhapura (Sri Lanka)	130,000
7	Peshawar (Pakistan)	120,000
8	Carthage (Tunisia)	100,000
9	Wu (China)	90,000
10	Smyrna (Turkey)	90,000

D Which of these cities can you find on map C? Which were centers of Buddhism?

	1200–800 B.C. Early Greek civilizations are destroyed.

3000 B.C.	1500 B.C.	1000 B.C.
3000 B.C. Minoan civilization emerges in Crete.	**1600 B.C.** Mycenaean civilization develops in Greece.	

Civilizations of Ancient Greece

The Minoans and the Mycenaeans developed civilizations in the region of present-day Greece. Their achievements became the foundation of Greek culture.

- The Minoans were known as great artisans. Legends of their cleverness became part of Greek myths.

- The Mycenaeans were fierce warriors. Through conquest, they spread their culture around the Aegean Sea.

- The Minoans and the Mycenaeans were expert sailors. Both civilizations became wealthy from sea trade.

- Invasions destroyed the civilizations surrounding the Aegean Sea.

Find Crete on maps B and D.

❶ **2000 B.C.** Minoans become sea traders.

❷ **1600 B.C.** Knossos becomes capital.

Khania • Mallia • Knossos Crete Zakro Monastiraki • Gournia Phaistos • Pyrgos
Mediterranean Sea

A Large buildings called palaces were used for religious rituals and storing food. The cities that developed around these places were known as palace cities.

Minoan Crete
3000–1450 B.C.

🏛 Palace city

0   25   50 miles
0   25   50 kilometers

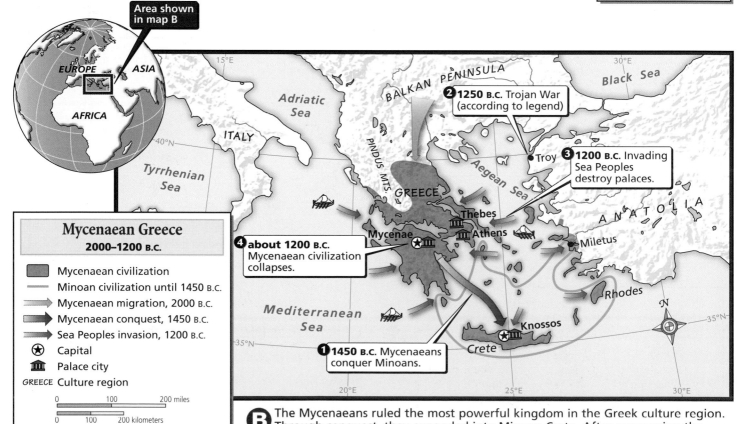

Area shown in map B

EUROPE   ASIA
AFRICA

15°E   30°E
Adriatic Sea   BALKAN PENINSULA   Black Sea

❷ **1250 B.C.** Trojan War (according to legend)

ITALY
Tyrrhenian Sea
PINDUS MTS.   Aegean Sea   • Troy   ❸ **1200 B.C.** Invading Sea Peoples destroy palaces.

GREECE   ANATOLIA
Thebes
Mycenae ★   Athens   • Miletus

❹ **about 1200 B.C.** Mycenaean civilization collapses.

Mediterranean Sea
Rhodes

Knossos ★
❶ **1450 B.C.** Mycenaeans conquer Minoans.   Crete

20°E   25°E   30°E   35°N

Mycenaean Greece
2000–1200 B.C.

- ▇ Mycenaean civilization
- — Minoan civilization until 1450 B.C.
- ⇨ Mycenaean migration, 2000 B.C.
- ⇨ Mycenaean conquest, 1450 B.C.
- ⇨ Sea Peoples invasion, 1200 B.C.
- ✪ Capital
- 🏛 Palace city
- GREECE Culture region

0   100   200 miles
0   100   200 kilometers

B The Mycenaeans ruled the most powerful kingdom in the Greek culture region. Through conquest, they expanded into Minoan Crete. After conquering the Minoans, the Mycenaeans adopted Minoan culture.

| 509–508 B.C.
Rome becomes
a republic.
Democracy begins
in **Athens**. | 399 B.C.
Socrates
dies. | 336–323 B.C.
Alexander the Great
conquers the
Persian Empire. | 27 B.C.
Rome becomes
an empire. | 117 A.D.
Roman Empire reaches
its greatest extent. | 476 A.D.
Western
Roman
Empire falls. |

500 B.C.   B.C. ◄│► A.D.   **500**

| 431 B.C.
Athens and **Sparta**
go to war. | 146 B.C.
Romans conquer **Greeks**. | 392 A.D.
Christianity becomes
the official religion of
the Roman Empire. |

How did you get that?

Through **trade**, people can exchange goods they have for goods they need or want. At first, people exchanged goods directly. After money was invented, people usually sold goods and used money to buy what they needed.

C Olive trees, shown in this photo, grow well in the rocky soil of Greece. Olive oil produced by early Greeks was a valuable trade good. Today, olives are still a major crop in Greece.

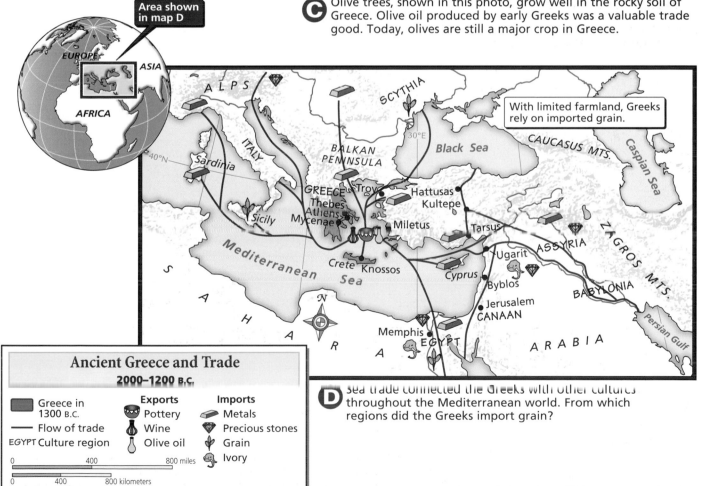

Area shown in map D

With limited farmland, Greeks rely on imported grain.

D Sea trade connected the Greeks with other cultures throughout the Mediterranean world. From which regions did the Greeks import grain?

Ancient Greece and Trade
2000–1200 B.C.

Greece in 1300 B.C.
Flow of trade
EGYPT Culture region

Exports
Pottery
Wine
Olive oil

Imports
Metals
Precious stones
Grain
Ivory

0   400   800 miles
0   400   800 kilometers

Growth of Greek City-States

Ancient Greece was a culture region, not a country. It was made up of independent city-states.

- Although Greek city-states shared the same language and religion, they had different forms of government.

- As city-states grew, they established colonies along the seacoasts. Conflicts over land led to wars with neighbors.

- Wars between the two most powerful city-states, Athens and Sparta, nearly destroyed Greece.

Who's in charge?

Before **democracy** developed, only people who were rich or royal could govern. Democracy let all adult male citizen, whether rich or poor, vote on decisions.

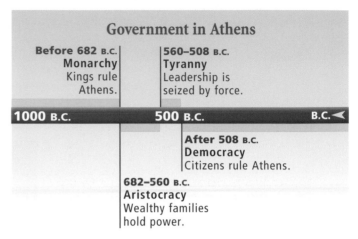

Government in Athens

Before 682 B.C.
Monarchy
Kings rule Athens.

560–508 B.C.
Tyranny
Leadership is seized by force.

1000 B.C.   **500 B.C.**   B.C. ◀

After 508 B.C.
Democracy
Citizens rule Athens.

682–560 B.C.
Aristocracy
Wealthy families hold power.

A Athens was the first city state to have a democracy. Monarchy, aristocracy, and tyranny remained common types of government in other city-states.

750 B.C. Greeks begin forming colonies to increase farmland and expand trade.

Ten city-states start most Greek colonies.

Greece and Its Colonies
750–550 B.C.

- ▨ Greece, 750 B.C.
- ▨ Greek colonial area, 550 B.C.
- ▨ Phoenician lands, 750 B.C.
- ● City-state with colonies
- ○ Other city-state
- — Trade route
- GREECE Culture region

```
0        250        500 miles
0      250      500 kilometers
```

B The Greeks and the Phoenicians were trading partners and rivals. Compare this map with map C on page 15. Which areas did both Greeks and Phoenicians settle?

C In the 400s B.C., the expanding Persian Empire invaded Greece twice. Greek city-states, including Athens and Sparta, united to defeat the Persians.

What didn't the Persians expect?

The conquering Persians had built a vast empire in southwest Asia (see map C, page 33) before they headed west toward Greece. The Greek victories over the Persians surprised everyone, even the Greeks.

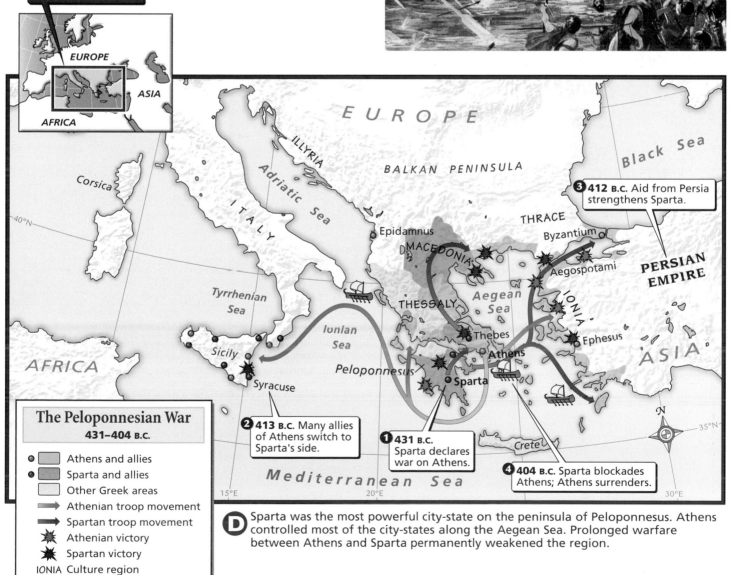

Area shown in map D

3 412 B.C. Aid from Persia strengthens Sparta.

2 413 B.C. Many allies of Athens switch to Sparta's side.

1 431 B.C. Sparta declares war on Athens.

4 404 B.C. Sparta blockades Athens; Athens surrenders.

The Peloponnesian War
431–404 B.C.

- Athens and allies
- Sparta and allies
- Other Greek areas
- → Athenian troop movement
- → Spartan troop movement
- ✸ Athenian victory
- ✸ Spartan victory
- IONIA Culture region

```
0        100        200 miles
0    100    200 kilometers
```

D Sparta was the most powerful city-state on the peninsula of Peloponnesus. Athens controlled most of the city-states along the Aegean Sea. Prolonged warfare between Athens and Sparta permanently weakened the region.

The Conquests of Alexander the Great

Alexander the Great, king of ancient Macedonia, built an empire that stretched from Greece to India.

- Years of fighting had weakened the Greek city-states. Macedonia, a kingdom in northern Greece, conquered the entire region.

- Then Alexander turned to the east and conquered the Persian Empire.

- When Alexander died, his generals divided his empire into separate kingdoms.

- Alexander's conquests led to the mixing of Greek culture with the cultures of conquered lands.

A Alexander encouraged cultural exchange between Greeks and Persians and adopted many Persian customs himself. This illustration shows Alexander as a great Persian hero.

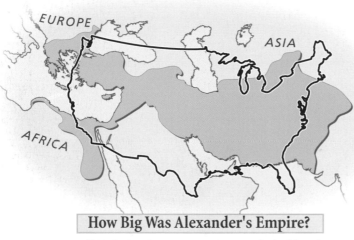

How Big Was Alexander's Empire?

B Alexander's vast empire included land on Europe, Africa, and Asia.

How do you show your culture?

Culture is what makes a group of people unique, or different from other groups. The religion we follow, the language we speak, even what we eat or drink, can all be part of our culture.

1 336 B.C. Alexander becomes ruler of Greece.

MACEDONIA
Pella THRACE
GREECE
334 B.C. Granicus
334–333 B.C.

Mediterranean Sea

CYRENAICA
Alexandria
333–332 B.C.

EGYPT

SAHARA

Nile R.

Alexander Conquers Persia
336–323 B.C.

- Alexander's Empire, 323 B.C.
- → Route of conquest
- ── Persian road
- ✸ Major battle
- ✪ Capital
- PERSIA Culture region
- Desert area

| 0 | 300 | 600 miles |
| 0 | 300 | 600 kilometers |

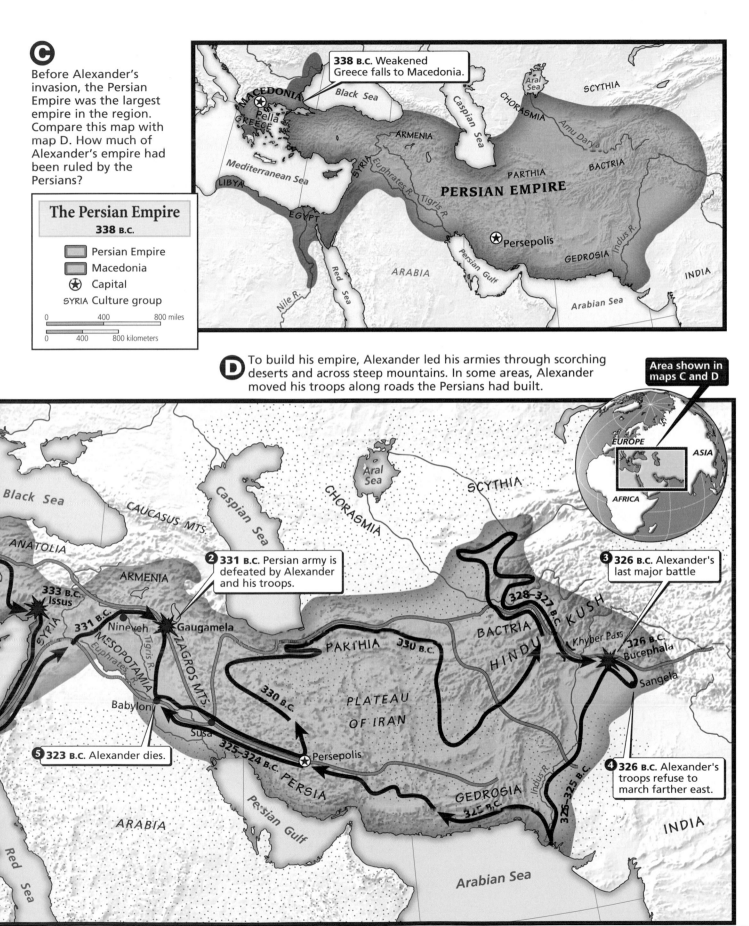

C

Before Alexander's invasion, the Persian Empire was the largest empire in the region. Compare this map with map D. How much of Alexander's empire had been ruled by the Persians?

338 B.C. Weakened Greece falls to Macedonia.

MACEDONIA
Pella
GREECE
Black Sea
Caspian Sea
Aral Sea
SCYTHIA
CHORASMIA
ARMENIA
Amu Darya
SYRIA
Euphrates R.
Tigris R.
PARTHIA
BACTRIA
Mediterranean Sea
LIBYA
EGYPT
Nile R.
Red Sea
PERSIAN EMPIRE
Persepolis
ARABIA
Persian Gulf
GEDROSIA
Indus R.
INDIA
Arabian Sea

The Persian Empire
338 B.C.

☐ Persian Empire
☐ Macedonia
★ Capital
SYRIA Culture group

0   400   800 miles
0   400   800 kilometers

D To build his empire, Alexander led his armies through scorching deserts and across steep mountains. In some areas, Alexander moved his troops along roads the Persians had built.

Area shown in maps C and D

EUROPE
ASIA
AFRICA

Black Sea
CAUCASUS MTS.
Caspian Sea
Aral Sea
CHORASMIA
SCYTHIA
ANATOLIA
ARMENIA
333 B.C. Issus
2 331 B.C. Persian army is defeated by Alexander and his troops.
331 B.C.
Nineveh
Gaugamela
Tigris R.
ZAGROS MTS.
MESOPOTAMIA
Euphrates
SYRIA
330 B.C.
PARTHIA
328–327 B.C.
BACTRIA
HINDU KUSH
Khyber Pass
3 326 B.C. Alexander's last major battle
326 B.C. Bucephala
Sangela
PLATEAU OF IRAN
330 B.C.
Babylon
Susa
325–324 B.C.
Persepolis
PERSIA
5 323 B.C. Alexander dies.
GEDROSIA
325 B.C.
325–325 B.C.
Indus R.
4 326 B.C. Alexander's troops refuse to march farther east.
ARABIA
Persian Gulf
INDIA
Red Sea
Arabian Sea

From Roman Republic to Roman Empire

Rome was founded as a small city-state, then became a republic, and eventually grew into a powerful empire.

- Rome became a republic in 509 B.C. The Republic came to have a democratic government.

- The Roman Republic gained land through conquest. As the Republic grew, so did its army.

- Civil wars destroyed the Roman Republic. The Republic became an empire, led by a single ruler.

- The capital of the Republic and the Empire was the city of Rome.

How is our country like ancient Rome?

Beginning in 509 B.C., Rome was a **republic**. In a republic, people choose leaders to make decisions for them. The United States and most other modern countries are republics.

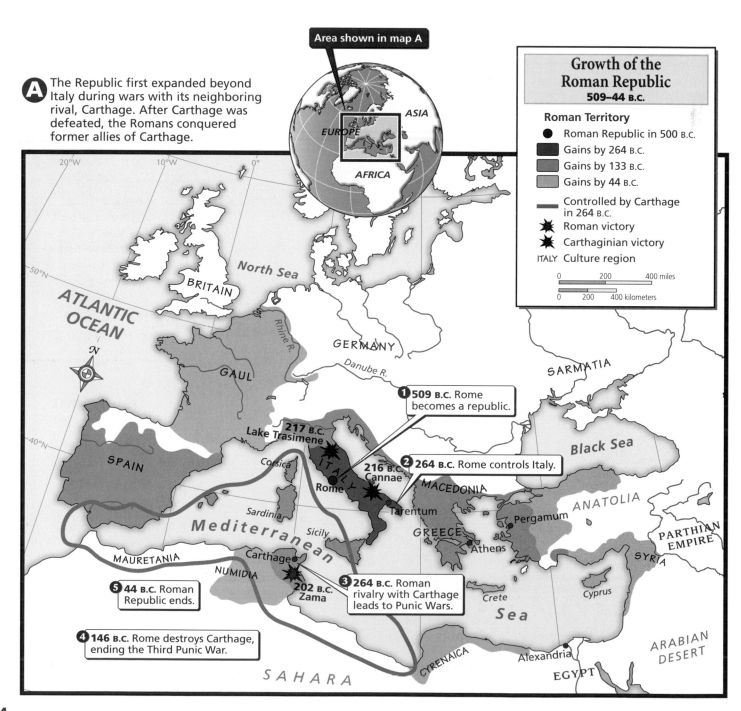

Area shown in map A

A The Republic first expanded beyond Italy during wars with its neighboring rival, Carthage. After Carthage was defeated, the Romans conquered former allies of Carthage.

Growth of the Roman Republic
509–44 B.C.

Roman Territory
- ● Roman Republic in 500 B.C.
- Gains by 264 B.C.
- Gains by 133 B.C.
- Gains by 44 B.C.
- ─── Controlled by Carthage in 264 B.C.
- ✶ Roman victory
- ✶ Carthaginian victory
- ITALY Culture region

0   200   400 miles
0   200   400 kilometers

❶ **509 B.C.** Rome becomes a republic.

❷ **264 B.C.** Rome controls Italy.

❸ **264 B.C.** Roman rivalry with Carthage leads to Punic Wars.

❹ **146 B.C.** Rome destroys Carthage, ending the Third Punic War.

❺ **44 B.C.** Roman Republic ends.

217 B.C. Lake Trasimene

216 B.C. Cannae

202 B.C. Zama

34

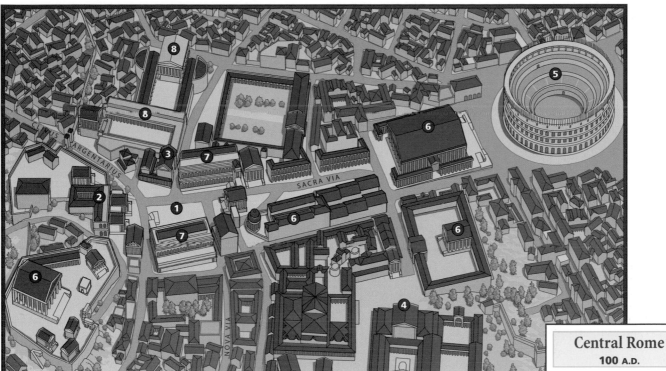

Central Rome
100 A.D.

1 Forum
2 Hall of Records
3 Senate
4 Imperial Palace
5 Colosseum
6 temple
7 court
8 meeting hall

Smaller buildings are shops and houses.

B The Forum, an open area reserved for public gatherings, was the original center of Rome. Later, Roman emperors expanded the city center by building temples, government offices, and entertainment centers.

C By 270 B.C. the Roman Republic had the largest army in the Mediterranean region. Roman soldiers were the most highly trained in the ancient world.

From Republic to Empire

Roman REPUBLIC	Roman EMPIRE
Who leads?	
Elected officials	Emperor
How long do they rule?	
One year	For life, although many were assassinated
How do new leaders take power?	
Appointed by Senate	By inheritance or by force

D The Republic ended when powerful generals seized control of the government. After about 20 years of civil war, a new government was established. The Roman Empire had begun.

Height of the Roman Empire

After the change from republic to empire, Roman territory continued to expand. At its height, the Roman Empire ruled the entire Mediterranean region.

- Strong Roman rulers brought peace and wealth to the region during a period called "Pax Romana."

- Roman roads and sea routes connected the Empire. Long-distance trade thrived.

- The Roman Empire included many different cultures. Trade and a common language helped unite the Empire.

A Roman coins were used throughout the Empire, making trade easier. Coins also announced an emperor's achievements, similar to newspaper headlines.

B The Roman Empire was rich with important resources, such as grain and metal. As the Empire grew, the variety of trade goods increased.

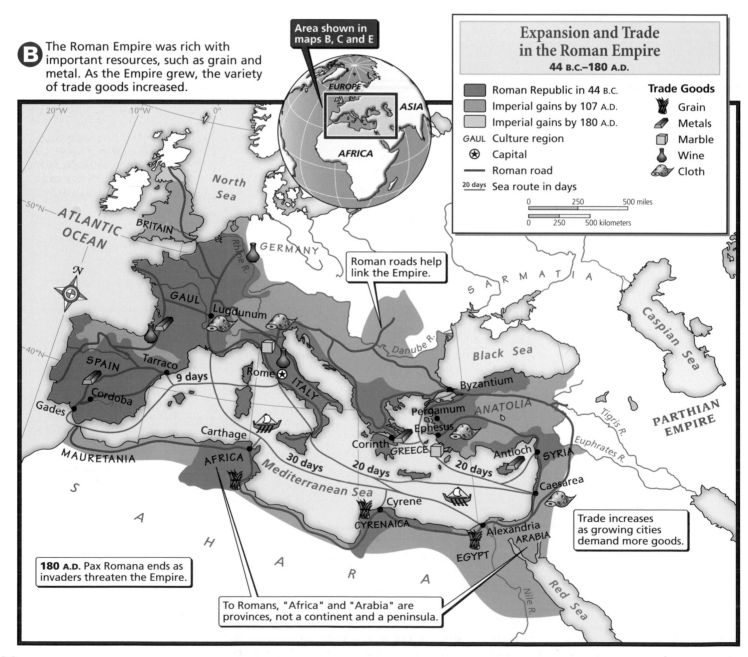

Area shown in maps B, C and E

Expansion and Trade in the Roman Empire
44 B.C.–180 A.D.

- Roman Republic in 44 B.C.
- Imperial gains by 107 A.D.
- Imperial gains by 180 A.D.
- GAUL Culture region
- ✪ Capital
- —— Roman road
- 20 days Sea route in days

Trade Goods
- Grain
- Metals
- Marble
- Wine
- Cloth

0   250   500 miles
0   250   500 kilometers

Roman roads help link the Empire.

Trade increases as growing cities demand more goods.

180 A.D. Pax Romana ends as invaders threaten the Empire.

To Romans, "Africa" and "Arabia" are provinces, not a continent and a peninsula.

36

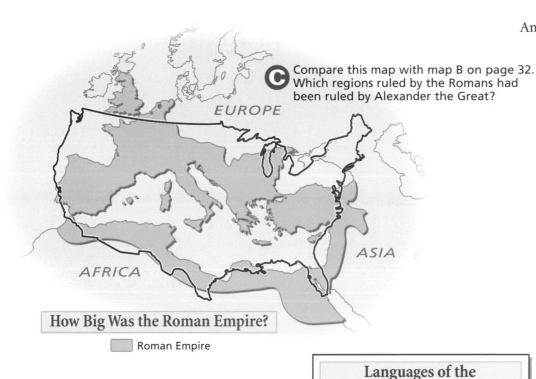

C Compare this map with map B on page 32. Which regions ruled by the Romans had been ruled by Alexander the Great?

EUROPE

AFRICA

ASIA

How Big Was the Roman Empire?

Roman Empire

Languages of the Roman Empire

Roman Empire, 120 A.D.
Mainly Latin-speaking
Mainly Greek-speaking
GAUL Culture region

Languages Used Today
FRENCH Romance language (from Latin)
GREEK Greek language
GERMAN Other language

D In 27 B.C. Augustus became emperor. His reign brought peace to the Empire after years of civil war.

20°W 10°W 0° 20°E

North Sea

ATLANTIC OCEAN

50°N

ENGLISH
BRITAIN
GERMANY

FRENCH
GAUL
GERMAN

SARMATIA

Caspian Sea

PORTUGUESE
SPANISH
SPAIN

40°N

ITALY
ITALIAN

ROMANIAN

Black Sea

THRACE

MAURETANIA
ARABIC
AFRICA

Mediterranean Sea

GREECE
GREEK

TURKISH

SYRIA
ARABIC

ARABIA

CYRENAICA

ARABIC

EGYPT

Red Sea

Latin replaces other languages in the western part of the Roman Empire.

Greek remains the main language in the eastern part of the Roman Empire.

E Latin was the official language of the Roman Empire. Languages that developed from Latin are known as Romance languages. What other language was widely spoken in the Roman Empire?

Latin Origins of Modern Languages

LATIN	MODERN ROMANCE LANGUAGES					MODERN ENGLISH
	Portuguese	Spanish	French	Italian	Romanian	
tres	tres	tres	trois	tre	trei	three
nota	nota	nota	note	notazione	nota	note
ferrum	ferro	hierro	fer	ferro	fier	iron

F Latin is no longer spoken, but modern Romance languages are based on Latin. English is not a Romance language. Many of its words have Latin roots, but many others do not.

Judaism and Christianity in the Roman Empire

Followers of Judaism and Christianity settled in many regions of the Roman Empire. Both religions spread far beyond where they first developed.

- Both Judaism and Christianity began in the Middle East.

- Jews migrated from their homeland to settle in other parts of the Roman Empire.

- Christianity, a new religion, began to spread throughout the Empire. It attracted many followers, called Christians.

Jews and Christians Under Roman Rule

63 B.C. Rome conquers Jewish kingdom of Judea.	**135** After revolts, Jews forbidden to live in Jerusalem.	**392** Christianity becomes the official religion of Rome.

100	B.C. ◄ ▷ A.D.	100	200	300	400

About 4 B.C. Jesus, the central figure of Christianity, is born.	**45–62** Paul spreads Christianity among non-Jews.	**303–312** Persecution of Christians intensifies.

A Roman leaders persecuted both Jews and Christians, but Jewish and Christian communities continued to spread. Eventually Christianity became the main religion in the Roman Empire.

B Many Jews fled the harsh Roman rule of their homeland, Judea, to settle in other regions. The movement of Jews from their homeland is known as the Jewish Diaspora.

Area shown in maps B and C.

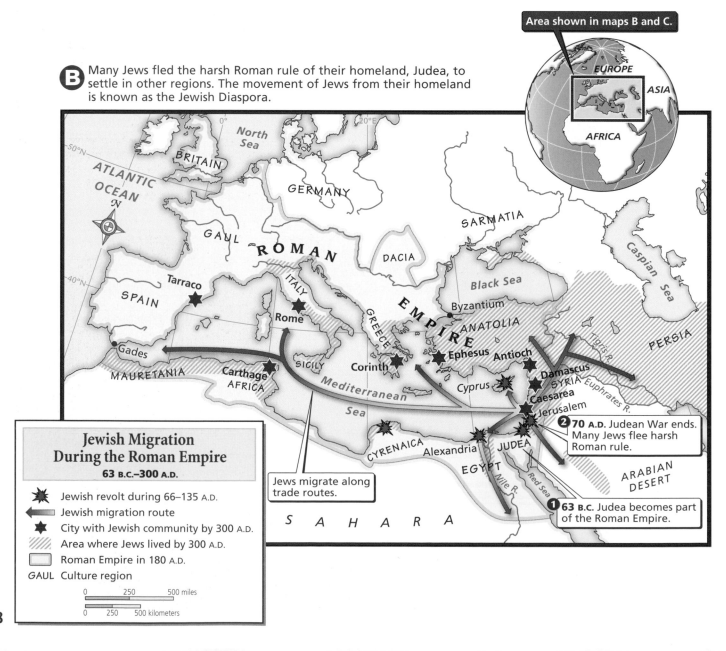

Jewish Migration During the Roman Empire
63 B.C.–300 A.D.

- ✸ Jewish revolt during 66–135 A.D.
- ← Jewish migration route
- ★ City with Jewish community by 300 A.D.
- ▨ Area where Jews lived by 300 A.D.
- ▭ Roman Empire in 180 A.D.
- GAUL Culture region

0   250   500 miles
0   250   500 kilometers

Jews migrate along trade routes.

2 70 A.D. Judean War ends. Many Jews flee harsh Roman rule.

1 63 B.C. Judea becomes part of the Roman Empire.

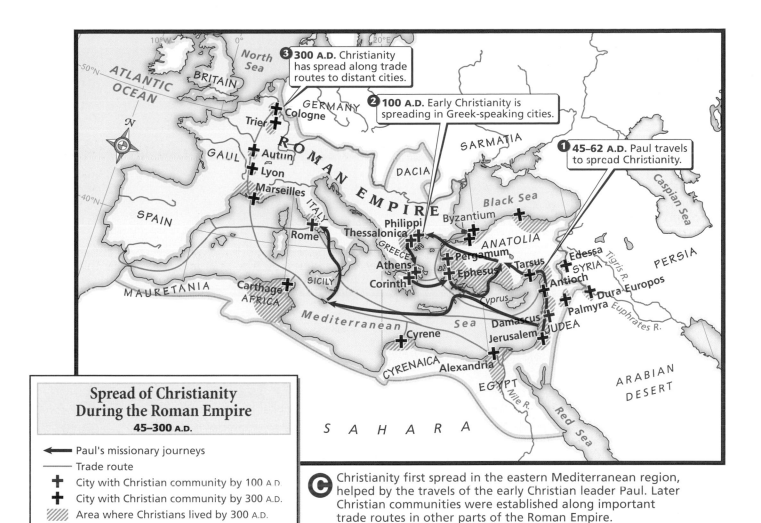

③ **300 A.D.** Christianity has spread along trade routes to distant cities.

② **100 A.D.** Early Christianity is spreading in Greek-speaking cities.

① **45–62 A.D.** Paul travels to spread Christianity.

Spread of Christianity During the Roman Empire
45–300 A.D.

⬅ Paul's missionary journeys

— Trade route

✝ City with Christian community by 100 A.D.

✝ City with Christian community by 300 A.D.

▨ Area where Christians lived by 300 A.D.

▢ Roman Empire in 180 A.D.

GAUL Culture region

0   250   500 miles

0   250   500 kilometers

C Christianity first spread in the eastern Mediterranean region, helped by the travels of the early Christian leader Paul. Later Christian communities were established along important trade routes in other parts of the Roman Empire.

What Is Christianity?

Christianity is based on the teachings of Jesus, whom Christians believe is the son of God. Today Christianity, which began as a branch of Judaism, has more followers than any other religion in the world.

D Paul was a Jew who converted to Christianity. He traveled from city to city preaching Christian ideas and helped establish many early Christian communities.

Decline of the Roman Empire

Corrupt rulers and constant wars weakened the Roman Empire. By the end of the 400s, only the eastern half of the Empire had survived.

- Civil wars, disease, and famine created disorder throughout the Empire.
- At the same time, migrating barbarians from Europe and Asia invaded the Empire. They claimed land for their own kingdoms.
- In 395 Roman territory was divided into the Western Empire and the Eastern Empire.
- By 476 the western lands were no longer under Roman control. The Eastern Empire continued to thrive.

What is a barbarian?

The word **barbarian** comes from a Greek insult to non-Greek speakers. To the Greeks, other languages were just "bar-bar," or nonsense. The Romans used the word to describe people who were uncivilized, which is how we use it today.

A Constantine, shown here being baptized, is known as the first Christian emperor. He was the last major emperor to rule the united Roman Empire.

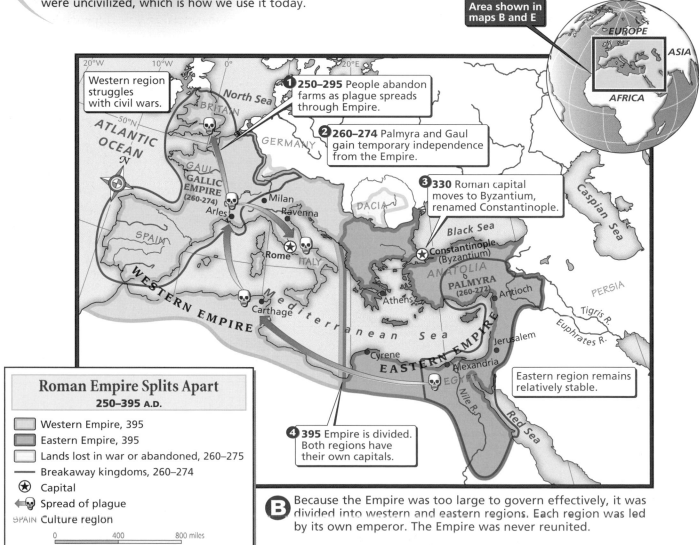

Area shown in maps B and E

EUROPE
ASIA
AFRICA

Western region struggles with civil wars.

1 **250–295** People abandon farms as plague spreads through Empire.

2 **260–274** Palmyra and Gaul gain temporary independence from the Empire.

3 **330** Roman capital moves to Byzantium, renamed Constantinople.

Eastern region remains relatively stable.

4 **395** Empire is divided. Both regions have their own capitals.

Roman Empire Splits Apart
250–395 A.D.

- Western Empire, 395
- Eastern Empire, 395
- Lands lost in war or abandoned, 260–275
- — Breakaway kingdoms, 260–274
- ⊛ Capital
- Spread of plague
- SPAIN Culture region

0   400   800 miles
0   400   800 kilometers

B Because the Empire was too large to govern effectively, it was divided into western and eastern regions. Each region was led by its own emperor. The Empire was never reunited.

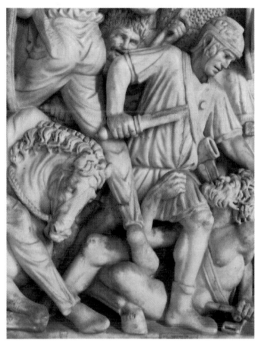

C The barbarian migrations were the greatest military challenge the Empire had ever faced. The Romans fought fiercely against the invaders.

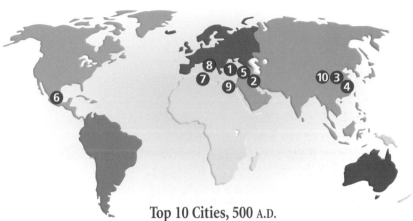

Top 10 Cities, 500 A.D.

Rank	City (Modern Country)	Population
1	**Constantinople** (Turkey)	900,000
2	**Ctesiphon** (Iraq)	500,000
3	**Luoyang** (China)	300,000
4	**Nanjing** (China)	200,000
5	**Antioch** (Turkey)	200,000
6	**Teotihuacan** (Mexico)	175,000
7	**Carthage** (Tunisia)	150,000
8	**Rome** (Italy)	150,000
9	**Alexandria** (Egypt)	100,000
10	**Changan** (China)	100,000

D By 500 Constantinople had become one of the world's great cities.

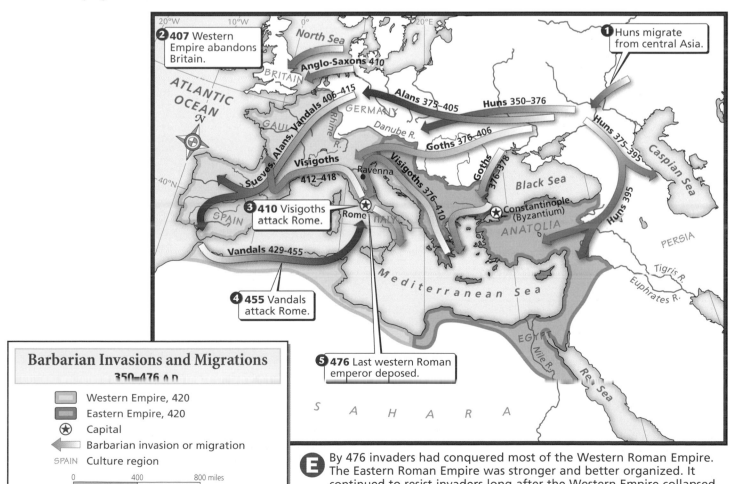

1 Huns migrate from central Asia.

2 407 Western Empire abandons Britain.

3 410 Visigoths attack Rome.

4 455 Vandals attack Rome.

5 476 Last western Roman emperor deposed.

Anglo-Saxons 410
Alans 375–405
Huns 350–376
Huns 375–395
Vandals 406–415
Goths 376–406
Visigoths 376–410
Goths 376–378
Huns 395
Visigoths 412–418
Sueves, Alans, Vandals
Vandals 429–455

North Sea
ATLANTIC OCEAN
BRITAIN
GERMANY
GAUL
Rhine R.
Danube R.
SPAIN
ITALY
Ravenna
Rome
Black Sea
Constantinople (Byzantium)
ANATOLIA
PERSIA
Caspian Sea
Tigris R.
Euphrates R.
Mediterranean Sea
EGYPT
Nile R.
Red Sea
SAHARA

Barbarian Invasions and Migrations
350–476 A.D.

- Western Empire, 420
- Eastern Empire, 420
- ⊛ Capital
- ← Barbarian invasion or migration
- SPAIN Culture region

0 400 800 miles
0 400 800 kilometers

E By 476 invaders had conquered most of the Western Roman Empire. The Eastern Roman Empire was stronger and better organized. It continued to resist invaders long after the Western Empire collapsed.

Empires and Cultures of Asia

395 to 1818

622 Islam begins to spread.	**800–1400** Khmer kingdoms flourish in Southeast Asia.

B.C. ◄ | ► A.D.   500

395 Byzantine Empire separates from Western Roman Empire.	**751** Chinese expansion into Islamic lands is halted.

Cultures and Trade In and Around Asia

Between 400 A.D. and 1500, cultures of Asia, Africa, and Europe came into closer contact with one another.

- Land and sea trade routes helped link distant areas. Trade and travel increased.

- Conquering armies spread cultures from one region to another.

- The spread of religions such as Christianity, Islam, and Buddhism united large regions.

Religious Change

		500 A.D.	1500 A.D.
CENTRAL ASIA		local religions	Islam
ARABIA		local religions	Islam
PERSIA		Zoroastrianism	Islam
INDIA		Hinduism and Buddhism	Hinduism and Islam
CHINA		Confucianism and Taoism	Confucianism, Taoism, and Buddhism
JAPAN		Shinto	Shinto and Buddhism

A Outside influences often changed the main religion of a region. Which regions had become Islamic by 1500?

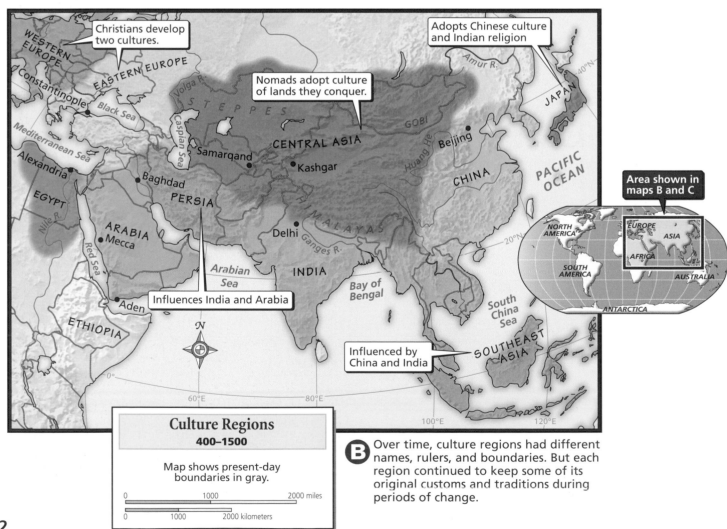

Culture Regions

400–1500

Map shows present-day boundaries in gray.

0   1000   2000 miles

0   1000   2000 kilometers

B Over time, culture regions had different names, rulers, and boundaries. But each region continued to keep some of its original customs and traditions during periods of change.

1054	1398	1453	1803
Eastern and Western Christianity split into two separate churches.	**Mongol ruler Timur** invades Delhi.	**Ottoman Turks** conquer Byzantine Empire.	**Mughal Empire** comes under British control.

1000   **1500**   **2000**

1180–1603	1279–1368	1640
Japan is engulfed by civil wars.	**Mongols** conquer and rule China.	**Japan** expels European traders.

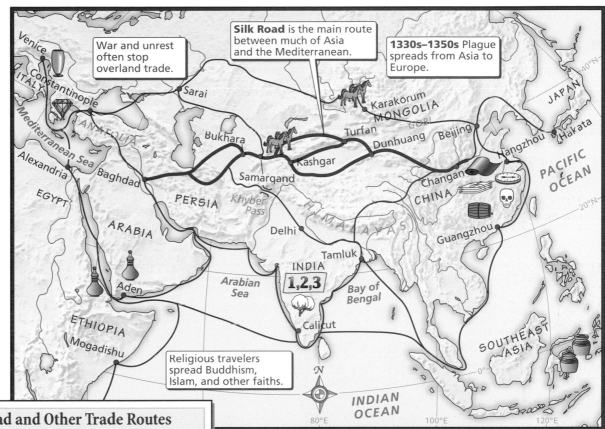

Silk Road is the main route between much of Asia and the Mediterranean.

War and unrest often stop overland trade.

1330s–1350s Plague spreads from Asia to Europe.

Religious travelers spread Buddhism, Islam, and other faiths.

Silk Road and Other Trade Routes
400–1500

— Silk Road   — Other trade route

Sources of Trade and Cultural Exchange

- Frankincense
- Gems
- Spices
- 1,2,3 Arabic numerals
- Cotton
- Silk
- Horses
- Plague
- Compass
- Glassware
- Gunpowder
- Paper

0   1000   2000 miles
0   1000   2000 kilometers

C Ideas, goods, and even disease were carried along the trade routes of Asia. Many empires and kingdoms competed for control of the main route, called the Silk Road.

D Today silk is made in several countries, but for hundreds of years it could be gotten only from China. Silk was one of China's main exports.

43

The Spread of Islam

Islam emerged in Arabia in the 600s A.D. and grew into a major world religion.

- Muhammad was the founder of Islam. He was both a political and a religious leader.

- The early leaders of Islam built large empires. Many of the people they conquered became followers of Islam, or **Muslims**.

- Later, through trade, Islam spread into regions that were not ruled by Muslims.

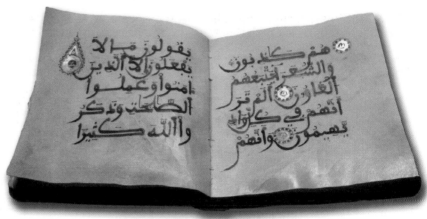

A The **Quran**, (also spelled *Koran*) is the holy book of Islam. It includes basic religious duties of all Muslims.

What's Islam?

Islam is a religion based on the teachings of Muhammad, whom Muslims believe was the messenger of God (called Allah in Arabic). Today Islam is one of the world's most widespread religions.

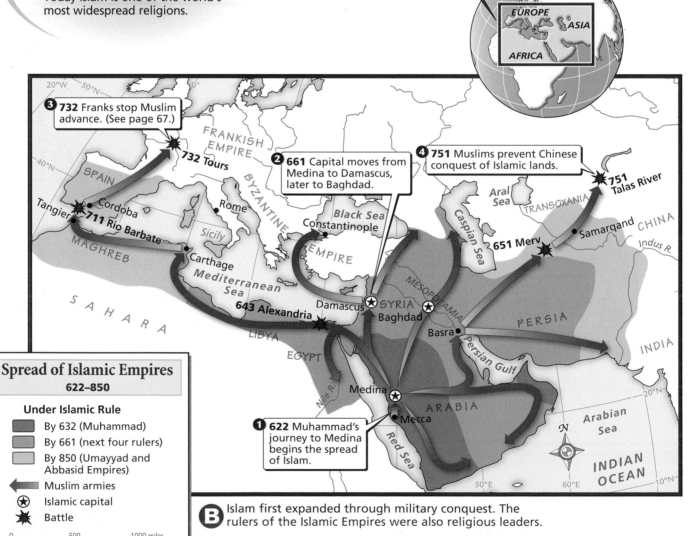

Area shown in map B

3 **732** Franks stop Muslim advance. (See page 67.)

2 **661** Capital moves from Medina to Damascus, later to Baghdad.

4 **751** Muslims prevent Chinese conquest of Islamic lands.

732 Tours

711 Rio Barbate

643 Alexandria

651 Merv

751 Talas River

1 **622** Muhammad's journey to Medina begins the spread of Islam.

Spread of Islamic Empires
622–850

Under Islamic Rule

- By 632 (Muhammad)
- By 661 (next four rulers)
- By 850 (Umayyad and Abbasid Empires)
- ← Muslim armies
- ✪ Islamic capital
- ✸ Battle

0   500   1000 miles

0   500   1000 kilometers

B Islam first expanded through military conquest. The rulers of the Islamic Empires were also religious leaders.

C After 850 the Islamic Empire had begun to lose power, but Islam continued to spread. Muslim traders introduced Islamic culture into China, Southeast Asia, and Africa.

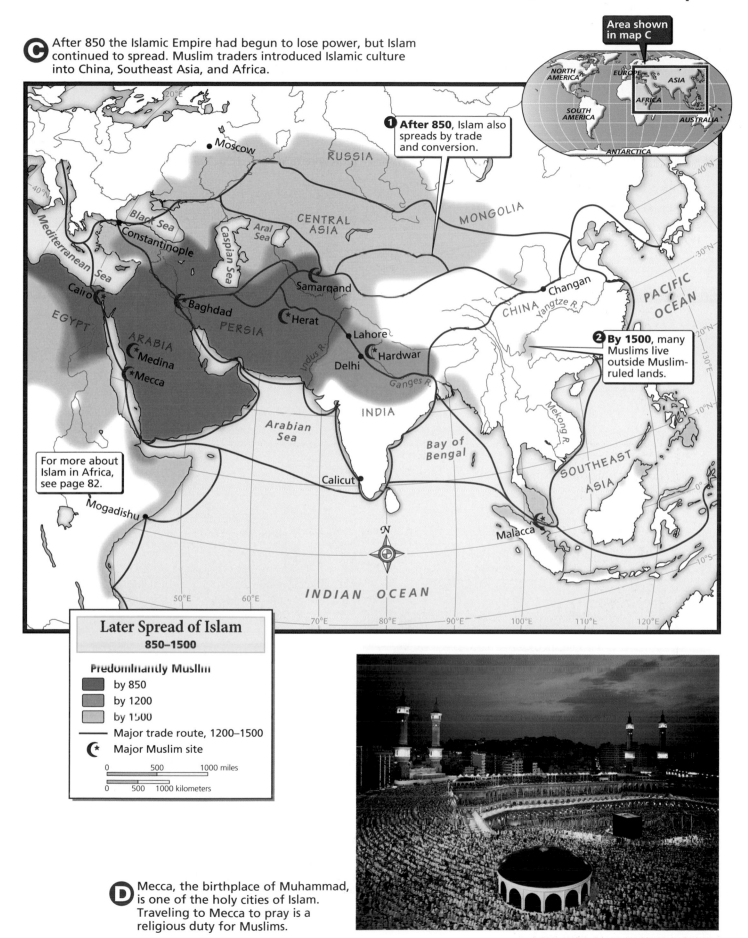

Area shown in map C

1 **After 850**, Islam also spreads by trade and conversion.

2 **By 1500**, many Muslims live outside Muslim-ruled lands.

For more about Islam in Africa, see page 82.

Later Spread of Islam
850–1500

Predominantly Muslim
- by 850
- by 1200
- by 1500
- —— Major trade route, 1200–1500
- ☪ Major Muslim site

0   500   1000 miles
0   500   1000 kilometers

D Mecca, the birthplace of Muhammad, is one of the holy cities of Islam. Traveling to Mecca to pray is a religious duty for Muslims.

Growth and Decline of the Byzantine Empire

The Eastern Roman Empire became known as the **Byzantine Empire**. It outlasted the Western Empire by nearly 1000 years.

- ■ The Byzantine Empire had many enemies. Islamic empires, led by Arabs and Turks, conquered much of Byzantine territory.

- ■ Constantinople, the capital, was a major trade center. Wealth from trade was spent to keep the army strong.

- ■ After 400 years of fighting, Turkish invaders conquered the Empire.

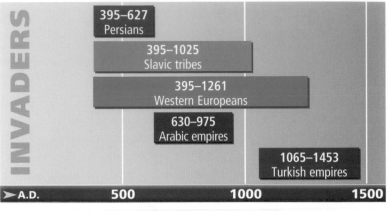

INVADERS

395–627 Persians	
395–1025 Slavic tribes	
395–1261 Western Europeans	
630–975 Arabic empires	
1065–1453 Turkish empires	

A.D.   500   1000   1500

Byzantine Wars, 395–1453

A The Byzantine Empire was constantly threatened with invasion. Religious differences and competition for land were the main reasons for these attacks.

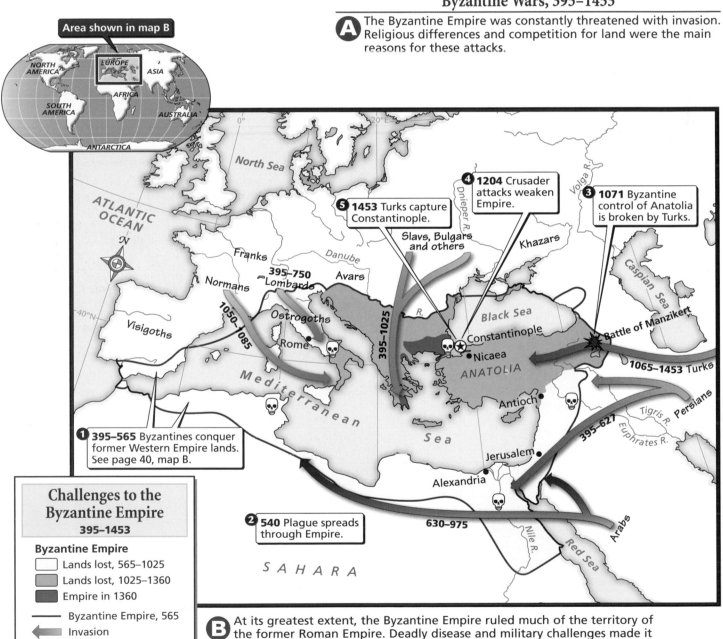

Area shown in map B

1 **395–565** Byzantines conquer former Western Empire lands. See page 40, map B.

2 **540** Plague spreads through Empire.

3 **1071** Byzantine control of Anatolia is broken by Turks.

4 **1204** Crusader attacks weaken Empire.

5 **1453** Turks capture Constantinople.

Challenges to the Byzantine Empire
395–1453

Byzantine Empire
- ☐ Lands lost, 565–1025
- ▨ Lands lost, 1025–1360
- ▨ Empire in 1360

— Byzantine Empire, 565
← Invasion
☠ Plague outbreak, 540
Persians Culture group

0   300   600 miles
0   300   600 kilometers

B At its greatest extent, the Byzantine Empire ruled much of the territory of the former Roman Empire. Deadly disease and military challenges made it difficult to hold on to land gains.

Tang and Sung Dynasties of China

During the Tang and Sung dynasties, trade as well as conflict between China and neighboring cultures increased.

▬ Under the control of the Tang dynasty, trade along the Silk Road flourished.

▬ Like the Byzantine emperors, Tang and Sung rulers defended their realm against many invasions by neighbors.

▬ By the end of the Sung dynasty, the Mongols had conquered all of China.

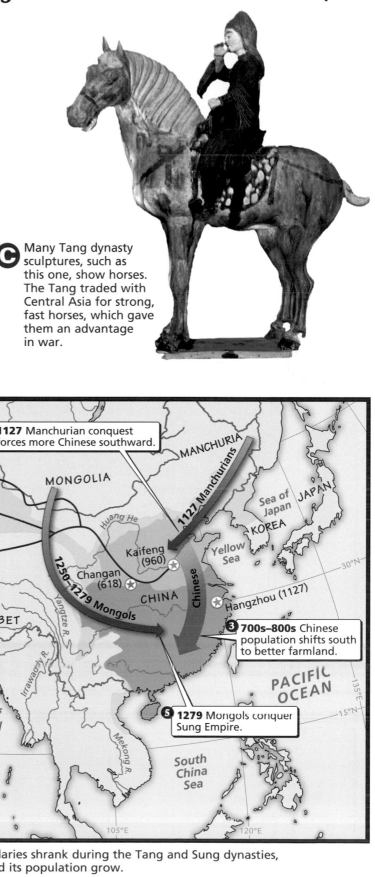

C Many Tang dynasty sculptures, such as this one, show horses. The Tang traded with Central Asia for strong, fast horses, which gave them an advantage in war.

Area shown in map D

4 **1127** Manchurian conquest forces more Chinese southward.

1 **660** Tang dynasty controls Silk Road east of the Caspian Sea.

2 **791** Tibet ends Tang control of central Asia.

3 **700s–800s** Chinese population shifts south to better farmland.

5 **1279** Mongols conquer Sung Empire.

650–800 Tibetans

1250–1279 Mongols

1127 Manchurians

Chinese

Kaifeng (960)

Changan (618)

Hangzhou (1127)

Tang and Sung China
618–1279

- ▢ Tang lands lost, 660–960
- ▢ Sung lands lost by 1127
- ▢ Sung Empire, 1127–1279
- ◀ Chinese migration
- ◀ Invasion
- — Silk Road
- ✪ Tang capital
- ✪ Sung capital
- TIBET Culture region
- — China's boundary today

| 0 | 1000 | 2000 miles |
| 0 | 1000 | 2000 kilometers |

D Although China's boundaries shrank during the Tang and Sung dynasties, farming advances helped its population grow.

The Mongol Empire Spans Eurasia

Mongol tribes swept across Asia and Europe, creating one of the largest empires in world history.

- The Mongols were nomads who originally lived in the dry grasslands of Central Asia. They were excellent horsemen and ruthless warriors.

- The Mongols conquered Muslim and Chinese empires and destroyed major cities along the Silk Road.

- During Mongol rule, trade and cultural exchange in Europe and Asia increased.

- Mongol rulers spread Islamic and Chinese culture throughout their kingdoms.

B This illustration shows a Mongol attack on a neighboring kingdom. Mongol battles often ended in destruction and brutal massacres.

A The Mongols rapidly expanded their territory. Their speed of travel and military skill made them difficult to defeat.

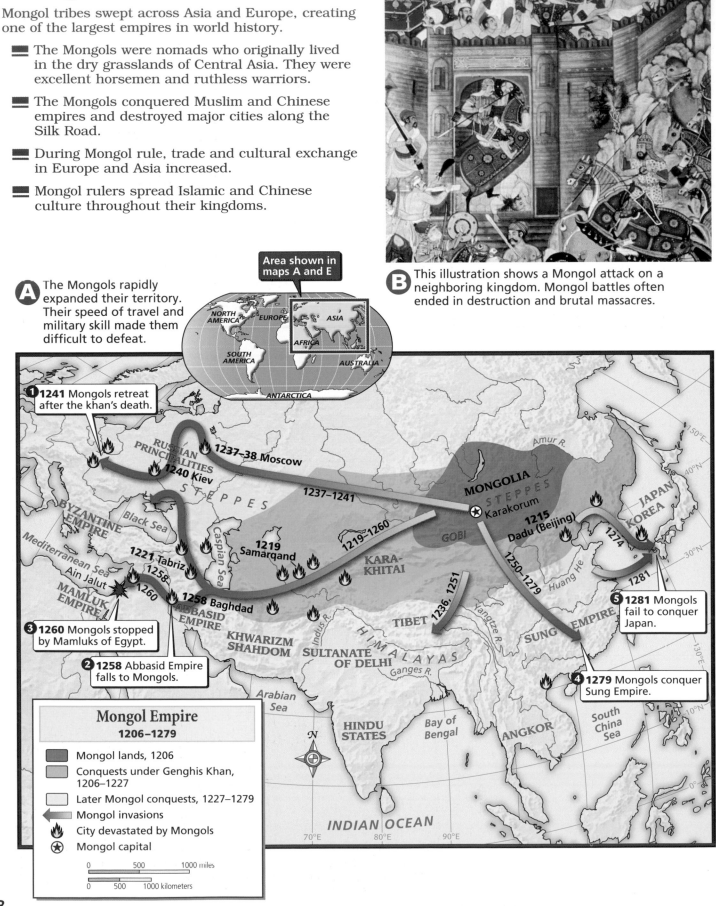

Area shown in maps A and E

①1241 Mongols retreat after the khan's death.

RUSSIAN PRINCIPALITIES
1237–38 Moscow
1240 Kiev
STEPPES
1237–1241

BYZANTINE EMPIRE
Black Sea
Mediterranean Sea
Ain Jalut
1221 Tabriz
1258
Caspian Sea
1219 Samarqand
1219–1260

Amur R.
MONGOLIA
STEPPES
Karakorum
1215 Dadu (Beijing)
GOBI
KARA-KHITAI
1250–1279
Huang He
1274
JAPAN
KOREA
1281

③1260 Mongols stopped by Mamluks of Egypt.

MAMLUK EMPIRE
1260
1258 Baghdad
ABBASID EMPIRE
KHWARIZM SHAHDOM
SULTANATE OF DELHI
Indus R.
Ganges R.

②1258 Abbasid Empire falls to Mongols.

TIBET **1236, 1251**
HIMALAYAS
Yangtze R.
SUNG EMPIRE

⑤1281 Mongols fail to conquer Japan.

④1279 Mongols conquer Sung Empire.

Arabian Sea
HINDU STATES
Bay of Bengal
ANGKOR
South China Sea

Mongol Empire
1206–1279

- Mongol lands, 1206
- Conquests under Genghis Khan, 1206–1227
- Later Mongol conquests, 1227–1279
- Mongol invasions
- City devastated by Mongols
- Mongol capital

0   500   1000 miles
0   500   1000 kilometers

INDIAN OCEAN

C Genghis was the khan, or ruler, who united the Mongol tribes. Although he is best known for his brutality, he also introduced law and written language into Mongol culture.

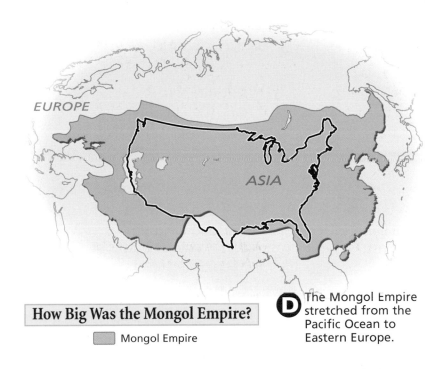

How Big Was the Mongol Empire?

☐ Mongol Empire

D The Mongol Empire stretched from the Pacific Ocean to Eastern Europe.

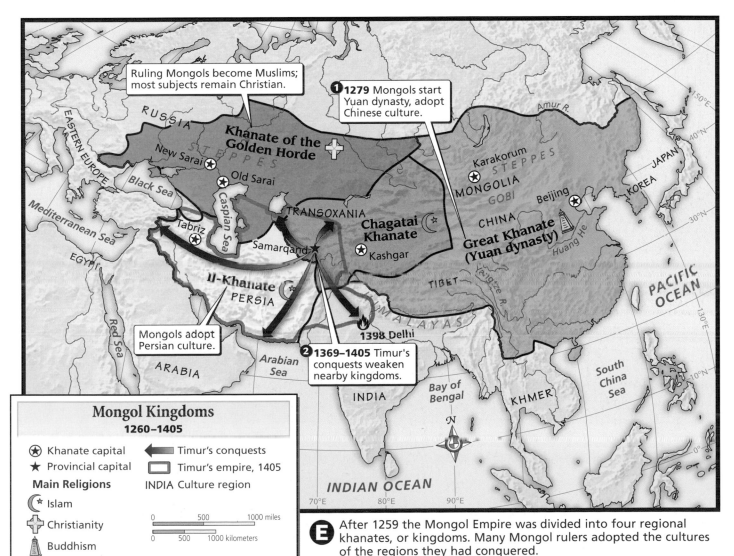

Ruling Mongols become Muslims; most subjects remain Christian.

①1279 Mongols start Yuan dynasty, adopt Chinese culture.

RUSSIA

Khanate of the Golden Horde

New Sarai · Old Sarai

Black Sea · Caspian Sea

TRANSOXANIA

Tabriz · Samarqand

Chagatai Khanate · Kashgar

Karakorum · MONGOLIA · GOBI · Beijing

STEPPES · CHINA

Great Khanate (Yuan dynasty) · Huang He

JAPAN · KOREA

Mediterranean Sea · EGYPT

Il-Khanate PERSIA

Mongols adopt Persian culture.

1398 Delhi

②1369–1405 Timur's conquests weaken nearby kingdoms.

Red Sea · ARABIA · Arabian Sea · INDIA · Bay of Bengal · KHMER · South China Sea

TIBET · HIMALAYAS · Yangtze R.

PACIFIC OCEAN

INDIAN OCEAN

70°E · 80°E · 90°E

Mongol Kingdoms 1260–1405

⊛ Khanate capital — Timur's conquests
★ Provincial capital ☐ Timur's empire, 1405
Main Religions INDIA Culture region
☪ Islam
✚ Christianity
🔔 Buddhism

0 500 1000 miles
0 500 1000 kilometers

E After 1259 the Mongol Empire was divided into four regional khanates, or kingdoms. Many Mongol rulers adopted the cultures of the regions they had conquered.

49

Ming Dynasty of China

After almost 100 years of foreign rule in China, the Ming dynasty restored Chinese control. Ming rulers brought political and economic growth to China.

- Ming emperors ended Mongol rule. They rebuilt regions of the empire damaged from years of war.

- To rebuild northern China, Ming rulers moved the capital to Beijing and encouraged people to move back north.

- In the 1600s rebellions and war weakened the Ming dynasty. Northern invaders then conquered China.

A Porcelain, also known as china, was invented during the Tang dynasty. This porcelain vase shows the unique Ming style.

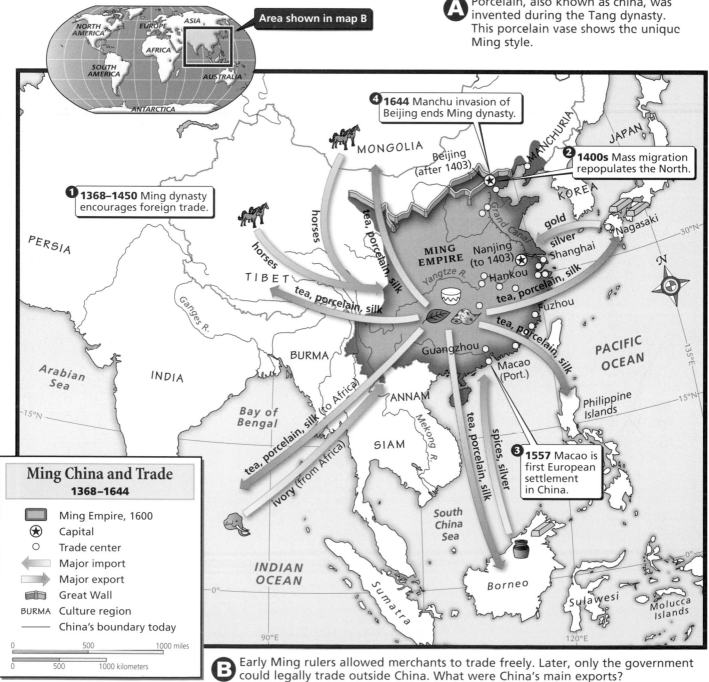

Area shown in map B

4 1644 Manchu invasion of Beijing ends Ming dynasty.

2 1400s Mass migration repopulates the North.

1 1368–1450 Ming dynasty encourages foreign trade.

3 1557 Macao is first European settlement in China.

Ming China and Trade
1368–1644

- Ming Empire, 1600
- ★ Capital
- ○ Trade center
- ← Major import
- → Major export
- Great Wall
- BURMA Culture region
- China's boundary today

0   500   1000 miles
0   500   1000 kilometers

B Early Ming rulers allowed merchants to trade freely. Later, only the government could legally trade outside China. What were China's main exports?

Kingdoms of Southeast Asia

Unlike its neighbors India and China, Southeast Asia did not develop large empires. The region was ruled by many small kingdoms.

- Many culture groups lived in Southeast Asia. Their kingdoms were often at war.

- Kingdoms were influenced by Indian and Chinese cultures. Hinduism and Buddhism spread through the region.

- The Khmer kingdom of Angkor developed one of the region's longest-lasting civilizations.

C Angkor Wat, built in the 1100s, is located in the ancient city of Angkor. This religious monument is part of the region's largest temple complex, which includes more than 100 temples.

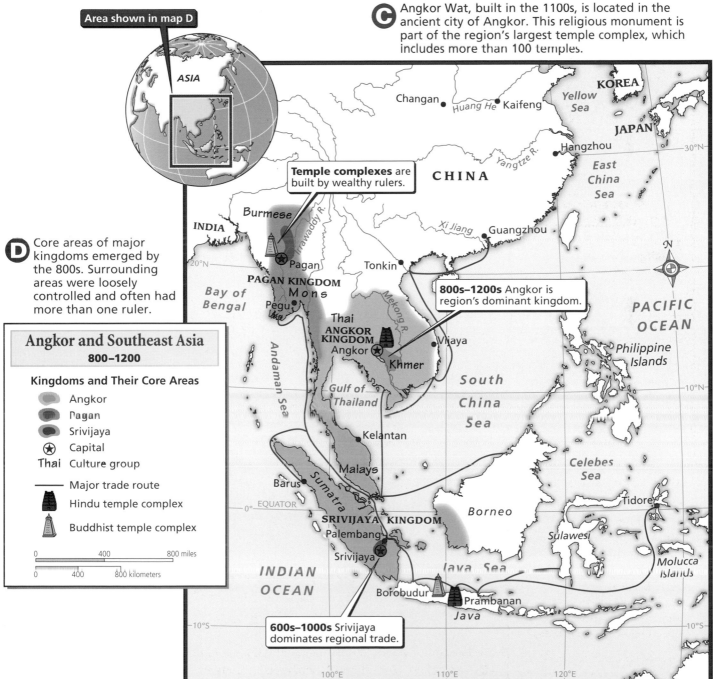

D Core areas of major kingdoms emerged by the 800s. Surrounding areas were loosely controlled and often had more than one ruler.

Area shown in map D

Temple complexes are built by wealthy rulers.

800s–1200s Angkor is region's dominant kingdom.

600s–1000s Srivijaya dominates regional trade.

Angkor and Southeast Asia
800–1200

Kingdoms and Their Core Areas

- Angkor
- Pagan
- Srivijaya
- ⊛ Capital
- Thai Culture group
- —— Major trade route
- Hindu temple complex
- Buddhist temple complex

```
0        400        800 miles
0      400    800 kilometers
```

ASIA

KOREA
Yellow Sea
JAPAN
Changan
Huang He
Kaifeng
Hangzhou
CHINA
Yangtze R.
East China Sea
30°N
INDIA
Burmese
Irrawaddy R.
Pagan
PAGAN KINGDOM
Mons
Xi Jiang
Guangzhou
Tonkin
Pegu
Bay of Bengal
Thai
ANGKOR KINGDOM
Angkor
Khmer
Mekong R.
Vijaya
PACIFIC OCEAN
Philippine Islands
Andaman Sea
Gulf of Thailand
South China Sea
10°N
Kelantan
Malays
Barus
Sumatra
Celebes Sea
Tidore
EQUATOR
0°
Borneo
Sulawesi
Molucca Islands
SRIVIJAYA KINGDOM
Palembang
Srivijaya
INDIAN OCEAN
Java Sea
Borobudur
Prambanan
Java
10°S
10°S
100°E   110°E   120°E

From Imperial to Feudal Japan

Unlike mainland Asian civilizations, Japan was rarely threatened by invaders. However, it was influenced by neighboring cultures.

■ Japan's religion, written language, and government were based on ideas from China and Korea.

■ Strong emperors ruled early Japan. Over time, civil wars divided Japan into tiny kingdoms with their own rulers.

■ As internal conflict decreased, a more unified Japan increased trade with neighboring regions.

Emperor
Ruler in name only

Shogun | **Daimyo**
Military leader | Warlord

Samurai
Warriors serving shogun and daimyo

Merchants and Artisans
Low status, although some were wealthy

Peasants
Largest and poorest group

Japanese Feudal Structure, 1467–1867

B After years of civil war, a new social structure emerged in Japan. Local military leaders, called daimyo, challenged the power of the shoguns.

A Conflicts between land-owning families weakened the emperor's political power. By 1192 **shoguns** (military commanders) took over as the true rulers of Japan.

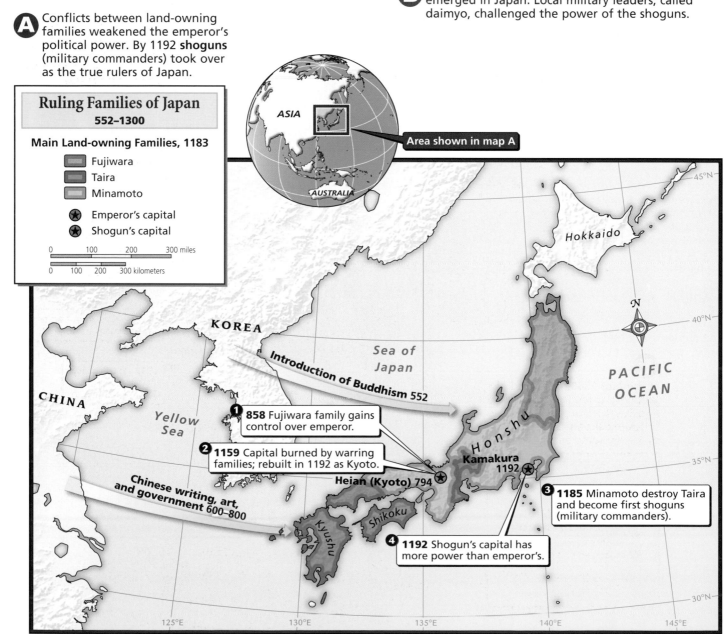

Ruling Families of Japan
552–1300

Main Land-owning Families, 1183

- Fujiwara
- Taira
- Minamoto

- ★ Emperor's capital
- ★ Shogun's capital

```
0    100    200    300 miles
0  100   200   300 kilometers
```

ASIA

AUSTRALIA

Area shown in map A

Hokkaido

KOREA

Sea of Japan

PACIFIC OCEAN

Introduction of Buddhism 552

CHINA

Yellow Sea

Honshu

Kamakura 1192

Heian (Kyoto) 794

Chinese writing, art, and government 600–800

Kyushu

Shikoku

1 **858** Fujiwara family gains control over emperor.

2 **1159** Capital burned by warring families; rebuilt in 1192 as Kyoto.

3 **1185** Minamoto destroy Taira and become first shoguns (military commanders).

4 **1192** Shogun's capital has more power than emperor's.

Top 10 Cities, 900

Rank	City (Modern Country)	Population
1	**Baghdad** (Iraq)	900,000
2	**Changan** (China)	500,000
3	**Constantinople** (Turkey)	300,000
4	**Kyoto** (Japan)	200,000
5	**Cordoba** (Spain)	200,000
6	**Alexandria** (Egypt)	175,000
7	**Luoyang** (China)	150,000
8	**Fustat** (Egypt)	150,000
9	**Manyakheta** (India)	100,000
10	**Kairwan** (Tunisia)	100,000

C Kyoto was the imperial, or the emperor's, capital. Strong imperial power made Kyoto one of the world's great cities.

D Samurai followed a strict honor code called **bushido**, or "way of the warrior." They valued honesty, courage, and fighting skills.

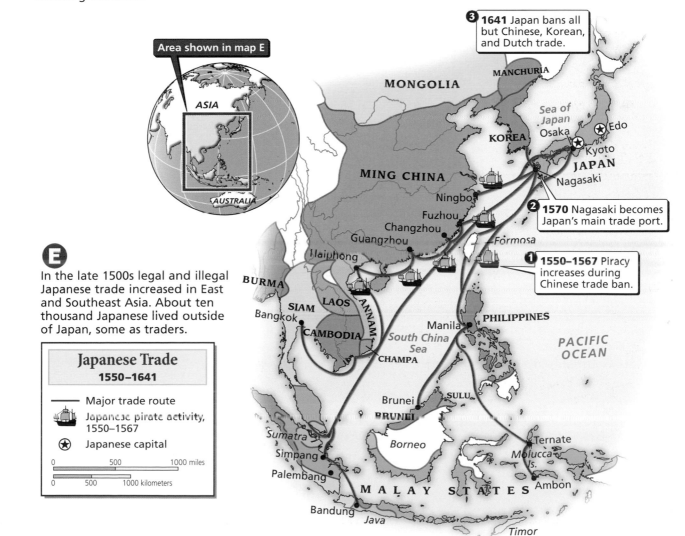

E In the late 1500s legal and illegal Japanese trade increased in East and Southeast Asia. About ten thousand Japanese lived outside of Japan, some as traders.

3 **1641** Japan bans all but Chinese, Korean, and Dutch trade.

2 **1570** Nagasaki becomes Japan's main trade port.

1 **1550–1567** Piracy increases during Chinese trade ban.

Japanese Trade
1550–1641

— Major trade route

Japanese pirate activity, 1550–1567

★ Japanese capital

0   500   1000 miles

0   500   1000 kilometers

53

India and the Mughal Empire

Invasions from Central Asia spread Islam into Hindu India. Mughal invaders ruled the greatest Islamic empire in India.

- As early Islamic rulers weakened, India was divided into many independent states. Some remained Islamic, others were led by Hindus.

- About 100 years later, Mughal rulers restored Islamic rule to nearly all of India.

- Later wars between Muslim and Hindu states allowed European colonizers to gain control in the region.

Area shown in maps A, C, and D

ASIA

AFRICA

A Turks from what is now Afghanistan once ruled most of India and spread the Islamic faith.

B Babur, a descendant of Genghis Khan, founded the Mughal Empire.

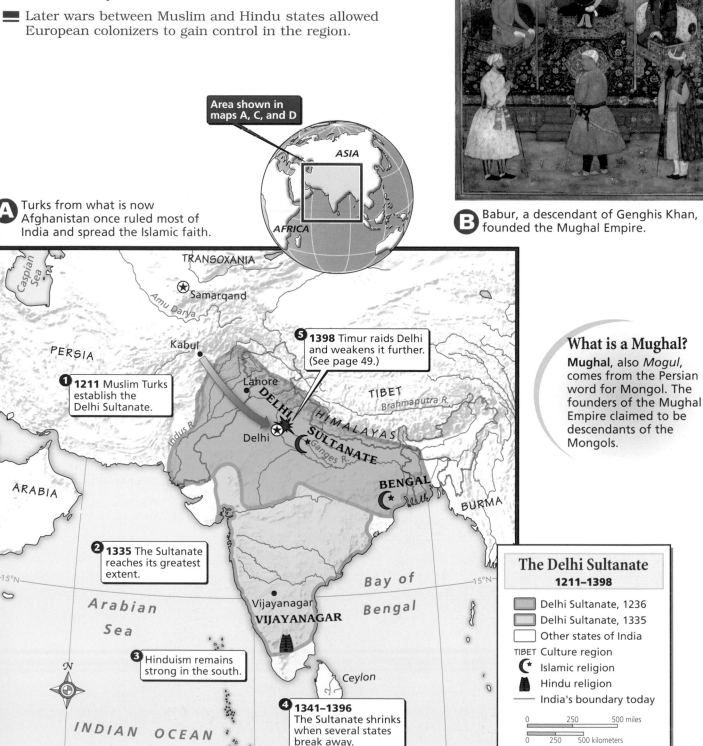

Caspian Sea

TRANSOXANIA

Amu Darya

Samarqand

PERSIA

Kabul

1 **1211** Muslim Turks establish the Delhi Sultanate.

5 **1398** Timur raids Delhi and weakens it further. (See page 49.)

Lahore

DELHI

Indus R.

Delhi

SULTANATE

HIMALAYAS

TIBET

Brahmaputra R.

Ganges R.

BENGAL

BURMA

ARABIA

2 **1335** The Sultanate reaches its greatest extent.

15°N

Arabian Sea

Bay of Bengal

15°N

Vijayanagar

VIJAYANAGAR

3 Hinduism remains strong in the south.

Ceylon

4 **1341–1396** The Sultanate shrinks when several states break away.

INDIAN OCEAN

N

60°E

75°E

90°E

What is a Mughal?

Mughal, also *Mogul*, comes from the Persian word for Mongol. The founders of the Mughal Empire claimed to be descendants of the Mongols.

The Delhi Sultanate
1211–1398

▆	Delhi Sultanate, 1236
▆	Delhi Sultanate, 1335
☐	Other states of India
TIBET	Culture region
☪	Islamic religion
⛩	Hindu religion
—	India's boundary today

0   250   500 miles

0   250   500 kilometers

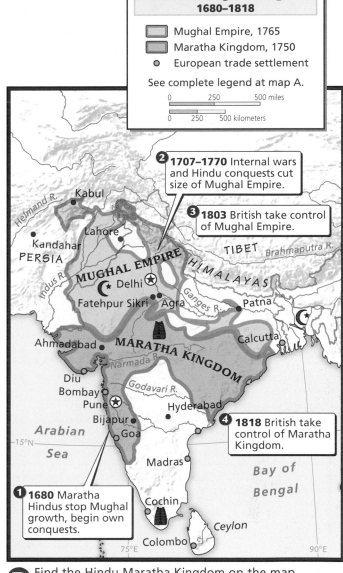

Rise of the Mughal Empire
1526–1707

- Mughal Empire at death of Babur, 1530
- Mughal Empire's greatest extent, 1707
- Maratha Kingdom
- ● European trade settlement

See complete legend at map A.

0   250   500 miles
0   250   500 kilometers

❶ **1526** Babur, a Mughal, conquers Delhi Sultanate.

❷ **1556–1707** Mughal Empire grows to rule most of India.

❸ **1674** Hindus establish the Maratha Kingdom.

❹ **1700** Most European traders are still on coast.

© (C) Early Mughal emperors encouraged peace between Hindus and Muslims. The persecution of Hindus by later Mughal rulers led to uprisings in the south.

The Maratha Kingdom and the Mughal Empire
1680–1818

- Mughal Empire, 1765
- Maratha Kingdom, 1750
- ● European trade settlement

See complete legend at map A.

0   250   500 miles
0   250   500 kilometers

❷ **1707–1770** Internal wars and Hindu conquests cut size of Mughal Empire.

❸ **1803** British take control of Mughal Empire.

❹ **1818** British take control of Maratha Kingdom.

❶ **1680** Maratha Hindus stop Mughal growth, begin own conquests.

(D) Find the Hindu Maratha Kingdom on the map. Compare this area with the same kingdom as shown on map C.

(E) The Taj Mahal, a magnificent tomb in Agra, was built for a Mughal empress. It was completed in 1648, after 22 years of work.

55

Europe in the Middle Ages

418 to 1580

711–1492
Moors rule Spain.

400	600	800

418
Visigoths start a kingdom in Spain.

432
St. Patrick introduces Christianity to Ireland.

789
Vikings' first raid strikes Portland, England.

800
Charlemagne is crowned "Emperor of the West."

Early Kingdoms of Medieval Europe

During the **Middle Ages** or **medieval era**, many Europeans were poor, uneducated, and violent.

- Early in the Middle Ages, barbarian tribes settled in Western Europe and established their own kingdoms.

- Barbarian kings, wanting to be as civilized as the Romans, became Roman Catholic.

- One Frankish king, Charlemagne, conquered much of Western Europe.

Barbarians in Our Language

barbarian—*a brutal or uncultured person*	From **bar bar**, an imitation of how barbarians talked.
frank—*straightforward*	From the **Franks**, who thought violence was more direct than laws or diplomacy.
slave—*person held as property of another*	From the **Slavs**, a tribe that lost many people to slavery in the Roman Empire.
vandalism—*deliberate destruction of property*	From the **Vandals**, the tribe that looted Rome in 455.

B The table above shows some modern-day words, definitions, and histories.

A Compare the barbarian invasions on page 41 with the kingdoms on this map.

2 432 St. Patrick brings Christianity to Ireland.

7 Lombards conquer Ostrogoths and start their own kingdom.

6 Avars force Slavs to migrate.

4 Franks conquer northern lands of Visigoths.

1 418 Visigoths start the first barbarian kingdom.

3 461–644 Barbarian kingdoms become Roman Catholic.

5 534 Byzantine Empire conquers Vandals.

Barbarian Kingdoms
418–644

- Barbarian kingdoms
- Byzantine Empire
- Barbarian invasion and migration
- Slavs Barbarian tribe
- Map shows boundaries of 500

0 400 800 miles
0 400 800 kilometers

Area shown in map A

1066	1095	1347	1498	1519–1522
Normans take control of England.	**First Crusade** is called by Pope Urban II.	**Plague**-infected rats arrive in Sicily.	**Vasco da Gama** reaches the Indies.	**Magellan's crew** circles the earth.

1000 — **1200** — **1400** — **1600**

936 Otto I creates what will be the Holy Roman Empire.

1215 **Magna Carta** gives rights to free men in England.

1337–1453 **Hundred Years' War** fought between England and France.

Area shown in map C

Charlemagne's Frankish Empire
711–814

Expansion Under Charlemagne

- Frankish Empire, 771
- Additions to the Frankish Empire by 814
- Defeated but not taken over
- ✸ Battle
- ✪ Capital

0   200   400 miles
0 200 400 kilometers

❶ 771 Charlemagne becomes sole ruler of the Frankish Empire.

❷ 782 After 30 years of war, Charlemagne defeats the Saxons.

❸ Some conquests pay the Empire but keep their rulers.

❹ 800 Charlemagne is Emperor of the West.

❺ 843 The Empire breaks up 29 years after death of Charlemagne.

778

C Charlemagne's empire extended beyond what is now France into lands that are now Germany, Italy, Switzerland, Belgium and the Netherlands. His empire spread Christianity into new areas.

D The pope (center) crowned Charlemagne "Emperor of the West." Western Europeans hoped Charlemagne's rule would end centuries of chaos.

Who is the pope?
The pope is the Roman Catholic bishop of Rome and is the leader of the entire church. In the Middle Ages, the Catholic Church was very powerful in Western Europe. Today the pope leads over a billion Catholics worldwide.

57

Viking Impact on Europe

Vikings came from Scandinavia—Denmark, Sweden, and Norway. They were fierce warriors and superb sailors.

- Vikings terrorized towns along the coasts and rivers of Europe. They murdered villagers and looted and burned their towns.

- Vikings also built settlements in Europe as well as in Iceland and Greenland.

- One group of Vikings, called Normans, later conquered and ruled England.

A Viking ships used sails and oars to cross open water and move up rivers. Vikings landed quickly and left before defenders could gather.

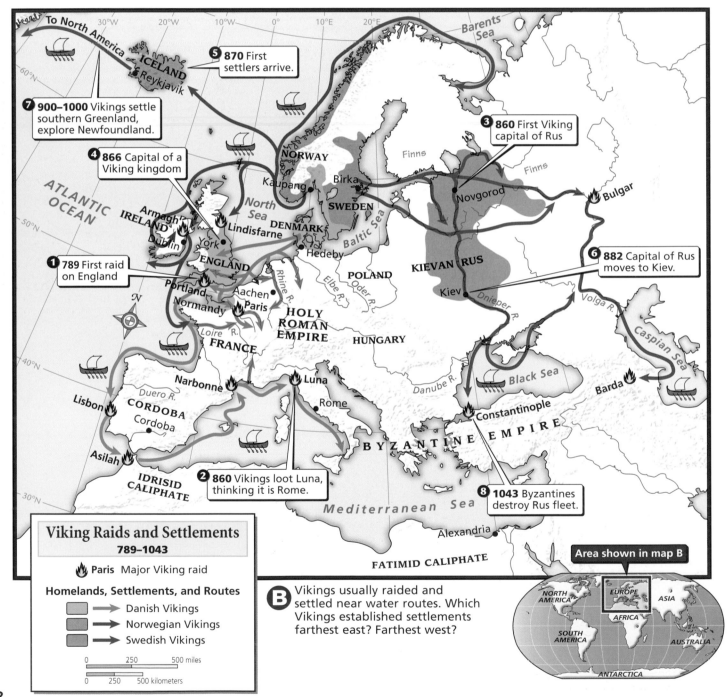

To North America

5 870 First settlers arrive.

ICELAND
Reykjavik

7 900–1000 Vikings settle southern Greenland, explore Newfoundland.

4 866 Capital of a Viking kingdom

3 860 First Viking capital of Rus

Barents Sea

NORWAY
Kaupang
Birka
Finns
Novgorod
Finns
Bulgar

SWEDEN
DENMARK
Hedeby

ATLANTIC OCEAN

IRELAND
Armagh
Dublin
York
ENGLAND
Lindisfarne
North Sea
Baltic Sea

1 789 First raid on England

Portland
Normandy
Aachen
Paris
Rhine R.
Elbe R.
Oder R.
POLAND

KIEVAN RUS
Kiev
Dnieper R.

6 882 Capital of Rus moves to Kiev.

Volga R.
Caspian Sea

Loire R.
FRANCE
HOLY ROMAN EMPIRE
HUNGARY

Narbonne
Luna
Rome
Danube R.
Black Sea
Barda

Lisbon
CORDOBA
Cordoba
Duero R.

Asilah

BYZANTINE EMPIRE

Constantinople

2 860 Vikings loot Luna, thinking it is Rome.

IDRISID CALIPHATE

8 1043 Byzantines destroy Rus fleet.

Mediterranean Sea
Alexandria

FATIMID CALIPHATE

Viking Raids and Settlements
789–1043

🔥 **Paris** Major Viking raid

Homelands, Settlements, and Routes

→	Danish Vikings
→	Norwegian Vikings
→	Swedish Vikings

0   250   500 miles
0   250   500 kilometers

B Vikings usually raided and settled near water routes. Which Vikings established settlements farthest east? Farthest west?

NORTH AMERICA
EUROPE
ASIA
AFRICA
SOUTH AMERICA
AUSTRALIA
ANTARCTICA

Area shown in map B

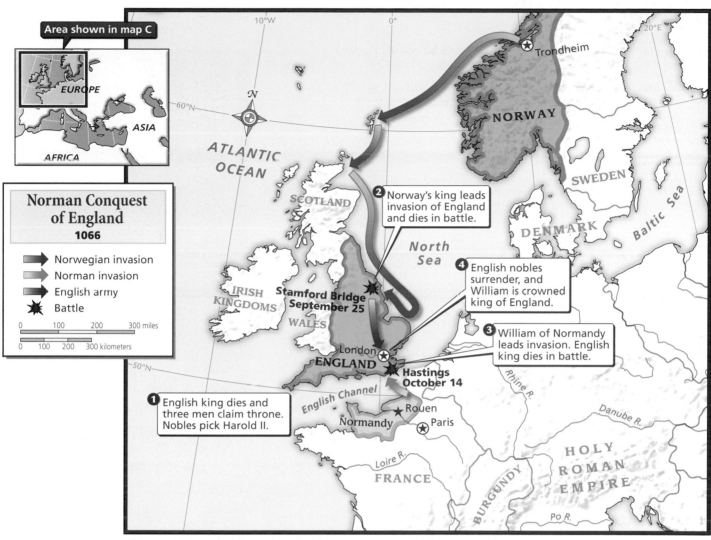

Area shown in map C

EUROPE

ASIA

AFRICA

Norman Conquest of England
1066

- ➡️ Norwegian invasion
- ➡️ Norman invasion
- ➡️ English army
- ✴️ Battle

0   100   200   300 miles

0   100   200   300 kilometers

ATLANTIC OCEAN

NORWAY

Trondheim

SWEDEN

SCOTLAND

DENMARK

Baltic Sea

North Sea

2 Norway's king leads invasion of England and dies in battle.

4 English nobles surrender, and William is crowned king of England.

3 William of Normandy leads invasion. English king dies in battle.

IRISH KINGDOMS

WALES

Stamford Bridge September 25

London

ENGLAND

Hastings October 14

Rhine R.

1 English king dies and three men claim throne. Nobles pick Harold II.

English Channel

Normandy

★ Rouen

Paris

Loire R.

FRANCE

Danube R.

HOLY ROMAN EMPIRE

BURGUNDY

Po R.

C In 1066 England was invaded by two groups of Vikings, one from Norway and the other from Normandy. The Normans were victorious, and their leader became known as William the Conqueror.

D During the Norman Conquest, Norman horsemen defeated Anglo-Saxon foot soldiers. Norman women embroidered a 230-foot long cloth, the Bayeaux Tapestry, depicting the conquest. One section is shown here.

Norman who?

The French king allowed Vikings to settle along his country's northwest coast. A Viking settler was called a **Norman**, short for Norseman or Northman. The region came to be known as Normandy.

Feudalism and the Holy Roman Empire

Although there were kings during the Middle Ages, power was held by local leaders.

- To govern his land and protect it from invaders, each local leader—usually a noble—needed his own soldiers, supplies, and fortified castles. The result was a system known as **feudalism**.

- One leader, Otto I, created a feudal empire later called the Holy Roman Empire. In the Empire, local leaders held the real power.

- The Holy Roman Empire survived over 800 years.

Who were the nobles?

During the middle ages, all the people born into certain families were **nobles**. In theory, they owned land and provided the king with military service. But some nobles lost their lands, and others fought against the king.

A Monks and priests were often the only educated people in a region, because Roman Catholic monasteries often had the only schools and libraries.

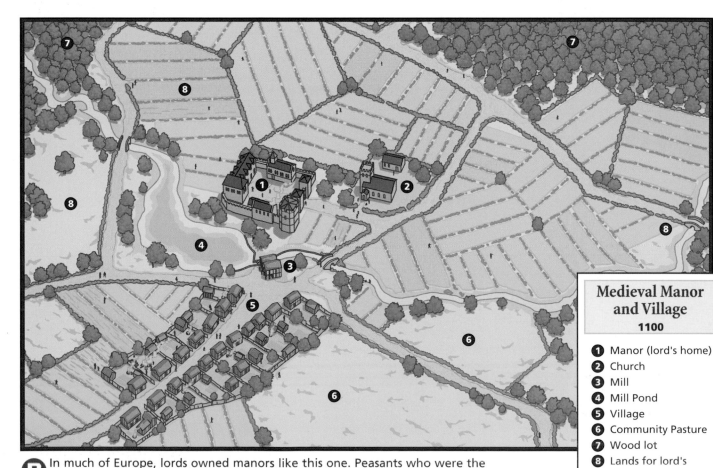

Medieval Manor and Village
1100

1. Manor (lord's home)
2. Church
3. Mill
4. Mill Pond
5. Village
6. Community Pasture
7. Wood lot
8. Lands for lord's personal use

B In much of Europe, lords owned manors like this one. Peasants who were the property of their lords were called **serfs**. Serfs farmed land both for their lords, who were usually nobles, and for themselves.

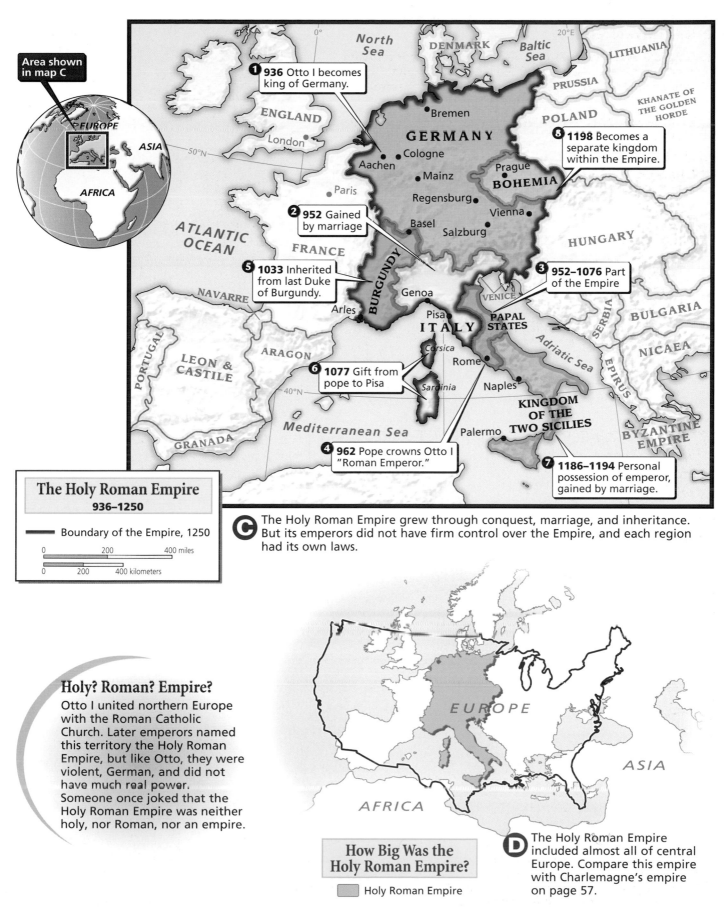

Area shown in map C

1 936 Otto I becomes king of Germany.

8 1198 Becomes a separate kingdom within the Empire.

2 952 Gained by marriage

5 1033 Inherited from last Duke of Burgundy.

3 952–1076 Part of the Empire

6 1077 Gift from pope to Pisa

4 962 Pope crowns Otto I "Roman Emperor."

7 1186–1194 Personal possession of emperor, gained by marriage.

North Sea · DENMARK · Baltic Sea · LITHUANIA
PRUSSIA · POLAND · KHANATE OF THE GOLDEN HORDE
ENGLAND · Bremen · GERMANY
London · Cologne · Mainz · Prague · BOHEMIA
Aachen · Regensburg · Vienna
Paris · Basel · Salzburg · HUNGARY
ATLANTIC OCEAN · FRANCE · BURGUNDY
NAVARRE · Genoa · VENICE · PAPAL STATES · SERBIA · BULGARIA
Arles · Pisa · ITALY · NICAEA
PORTUGAL · LEON & CASTILE · ARAGON · Corsica · Rome · EPIRUS
Sardinia · Naples · KINGDOM OF THE TWO SICILIES · BYZANTINE EMPIRE
GRANADA · Mediterranean Sea · Palermo

EUROPE · ASIA · AFRICA · 50°N · 40°N · 0° · 20°E · Adriatic Sea

The Holy Roman Empire
936–1250

—— Boundary of the Empire, 1250

0 — 200 — 400 miles
0 — 200 — 400 kilometers

C The Holy Roman Empire grew through conquest, marriage, and inheritance. But its emperors did not have firm control over the Empire, and each region had its own laws.

Holy? Roman? Empire?

Otto I united northern Europe with the Roman Catholic Church. Later emperors named this territory the Holy Roman Empire, but like Otto, they were violent, German, and did not have much real power. Someone once joked that the Holy Roman Empire was neither holy, nor Roman, nor an empire.

EUROPE · ASIA · AFRICA

How Big Was the Holy Roman Empire?

☐ Holy Roman Empire

D The Holy Roman Empire included almost all of central Europe. Compare this empire with Charlemagne's empire on page 57.

Crusades to the Holy Land

In 1095 the Byzantine emperor asked the pope for help in defending his empire from Muslim attacks. The pope agreed and called on European Catholics to join in a crusade against the Muslims.

- It was the first of eight crusades in which Europe sent huge armies to drive Muslims from the Holy Land, especially from Jerusalem.

- Thousands of Muslims, Jews, pagans, and Christians died in the brutal fighting.

- The crusades failed to win permanent Christian control over the Holy Land. But they had the accidental benefit of increasing trade and knowledge of other cultures.

B When the First Crusaders captured Jerusalem, they massacred 40,000 Muslims and Jews.

A Disease, hunger, and war along the way killed as many Crusaders as battles with Muslims did. Three of the eight crusades are shown below.

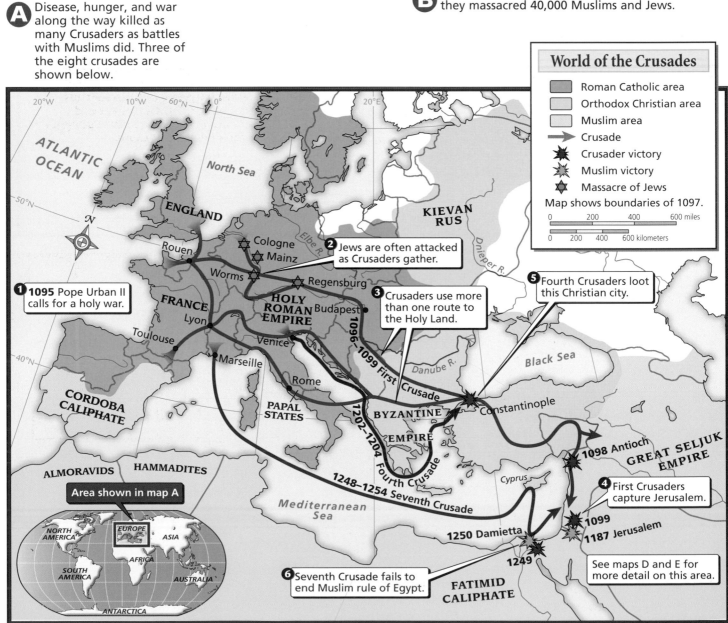

World of the Crusades

- Roman Catholic area
- Orthodox Christian area
- Muslim area
- → Crusade
- ✹ Crusader victory
- ✷ Muslim victory
- ✡ Massacre of Jews

Map shows boundaries of 1097.

0   200   400   600 miles
0   200   400   600 kilometers

ATLANTIC OCEAN

North Sea

ENGLAND

Rouen

Cologne
Mainz
Worms

Regensburg

2 Jews are often attacked as Crusaders gather.

KIEVAN RUS

Elbe R.

Dnieper R.

1 1095 Pope Urban II calls for a holy war.

FRANCE
Lyon

HOLY ROMAN EMPIRE
Budapest

3 Crusaders use more than one route to the Holy Land.

5 Fourth Crusaders loot this Christian city.

Toulouse

Venice

Danube R.

Black Sea

Marseille

Rome

PAPAL STATES

BYZANTINE EMPIRE

Constantinople

CORDOBA CALIPHATE

1096
1099 First Crusade

1202–1204 Fourth Crusade

1098 Antioch

GREAT SELJUK EMPIRE

ALMORAVIDS   HAMMADITES

Area shown in map A

1248–1254 Seventh Crusade

Cyprus

4 First Crusaders capture Jerusalem.

Mediterranean Sea

1250 Damietta

1099

1187 Jerusalem

NORTH AMERICA   EUROPE   ASIA

AFRICA

SOUTH AMERICA   AUSTRALIA

ANTARCTICA

6 Seventh Crusade fails to end Muslim rule of Egypt.

1249

FATIMID CALIPHATE

See maps D and E for more detail on this area.

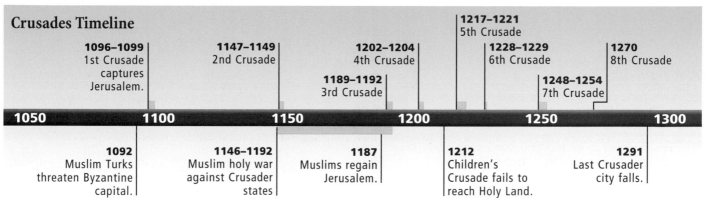

Crusades Timeline

1050	1100	1150	1200	1250	1300

1096–1099 1st Crusade captures Jerusalem.

1147–1149 2nd Crusade

1202–1204 4th Crusade

1189–1192 3rd Crusade

1217–1221 5th Crusade

1228–1229 6th Crusade

1248–1254 7th Crusade

1270 8th Crusade

1092 Muslim Turks threaten Byzantine capital.

1146–1192 Muslim holy war against Crusader states

1187 Muslims regain Jerusalem.

1212 Children's Crusade fails to reach Holy Land.

1291 Last Crusader city falls.

C Over a span of two centuries, Crusaders left for the Holy Land eight times. Which crusade was the longest?

D The First Crusaders divided the land they captured in the Middle East into four states. They also built castles to protect these states.

Pilgrimage or crusade?

Before the Crusades, journeys to holy sites—**pilgrimages**—were a way for people to show their faith. A **crusade** was seen as an armed pilgrimage, a war for a religious cause. For Christians, the word "crusade" came to mean a struggle for an important cause.

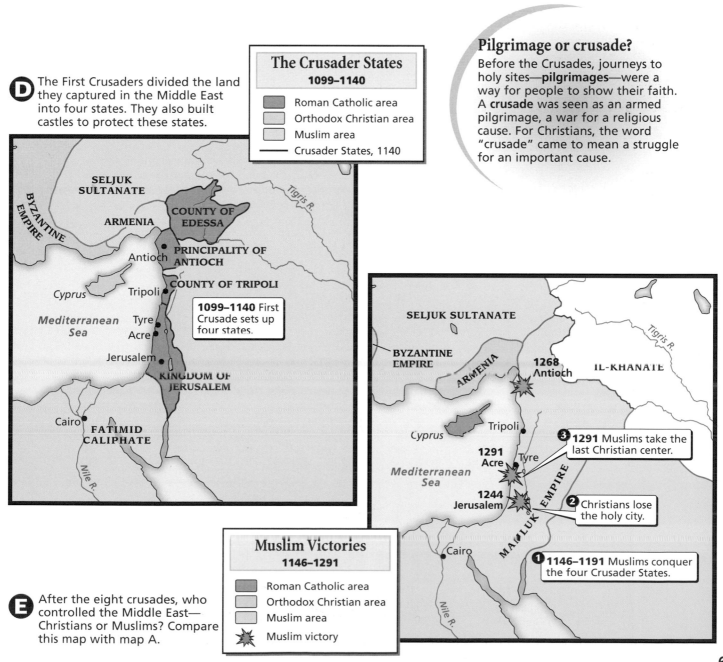

The Crusader States
1099–1140

- Roman Catholic area
- Orthodox Christian area
- Muslim area
- — Crusader States, 1140

1099–1140 First Crusade sets up four states.

Muslim Victories
1146–1291

- Roman Catholic area
- Orthodox Christian area
- Muslim area
- ✹ Muslim victory

1268 Antioch

3 1291 Muslims take the last Christian center.

1291 Acre

2 Christians lose the holy city.

1244 Jerusalem

1 1146–1191 Muslims conquer the four Crusader States.

E After the eight crusades, who controlled the Middle East—Christians or Muslims? Compare this map with map A.

Trade Routes and Plague

Increased trade spread new goods across Europe. However, it also spread the worst disease in European history—the bubonic plague.

- Northern Europeans traded wool cloth, grain, wine, and silver for silk, perfume, and spices from Asia.

- Goods from Asia passed through the Mediterranean, and so did the bubonic plague. Rats, fleas, and people spread the plague along trade routes.

- In five years the bubonic plague killed a quarter of the people in Europe.

Top 10 Cities, 1200

Rank	City (Modern Country)	Population
1	Hangzhou (China)	255,000
2	Fez (Morocco)	200,000
3	Cairo (Egypt)	200,000
4	Pagan (Myanmar [Burma])	180,000
5	Kamakura (Japan)	175,000
6	Angkor (Cambodia)	150,000
7	Constantinople (Turkey)	150,000
8	Palermo (Italy)	150,000
9	Marrakech (Morocco)	150,000
10	Seville (Spain)	150,000

A In 1200 most of the largest cities were in Asia and Africa. In what region were the largest European cities?

B As trade increased, European cities grew. To protect their trade routes, a number of northern cities formed an alliance called the Hanseatic League.

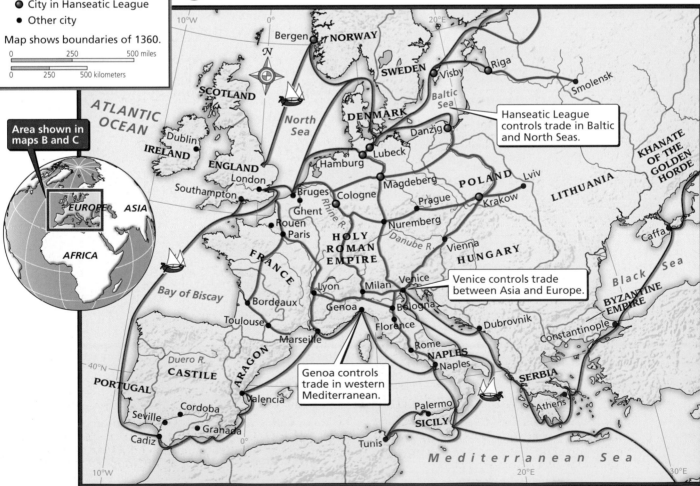

European Trade
1200–1360

Main Trade Routes

——— By land and river

——— By sea

⬤ City in Hanseatic League

• Other city

Map shows boundaries of 1360.

0   250   500 miles

0   250   500 kilometers

Area shown in maps B and C

Hanseatic League controls trade in Baltic and North Seas.

Venice controls trade between Asia and Europe.

Genoa controls trade in western Mediterranean.

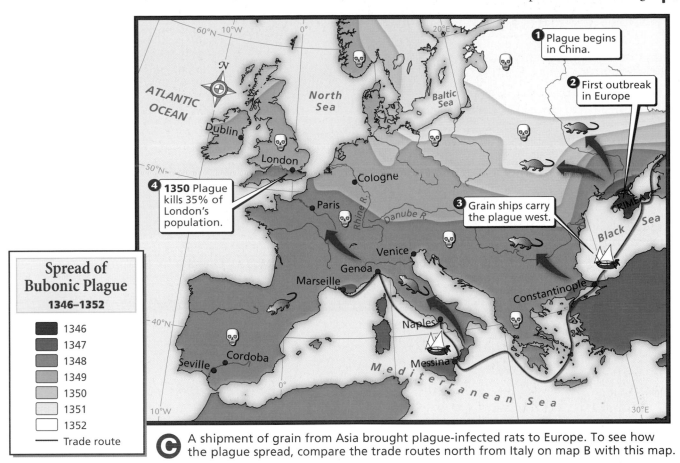

Spread of Bubonic Plague

1346–1352

- 1346
- 1347
- 1348
- 1349
- 1350
- 1351
- 1352
- —— Trade route

1 Plague begins in China.

2 First outbreak in Europe

3 Grain ships carry the plague west.

4 **1350** Plague kills 35% of London's population.

C A shipment of grain from Asia brought plague-infected rats to Europe. To see how the plague spread, compare the trade routes north from Italy on map B with this map.

How did the plague change Europe?

A disease as deadly as the bubonic plague can alter a society. After the plague years, surviving European peasants demanded higher wages and lower taxes. Nobles had to accept their demands because so few workers were left.

D Trade from the eastern Mediterranean made Venice rich. But trade also added plague to its overcrowding and poor sanitation, devastating the city.

Population of Europe 800–1500

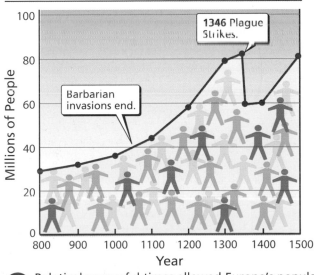

1346 Plague Strikes.

Barbarian invasions end.

E Relatively peaceful times allowed Europe's population to rise—until the plague struck. How many years did it take for the population of Europe to recover?

65

Moorish Spain

For almost 800 years, Muslims and Christians fought for Spain and Portugal.

- In 711 the Moors, Muslims from northwest Africa, invaded Spain. Moorish armies pushed north to what is now France.

- Over the centuries, Christians from northern Spain, France, and England struggled to "reconquer" Moorish Spain.

- In 1492 the Christian kingdoms of Castile and Aragon drove the Moors from their last stronghold.

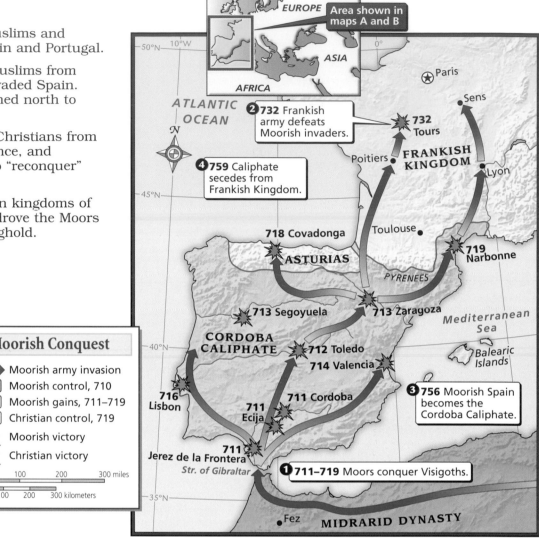

Area shown in maps A and B

EUROPE
ASIA
AFRICA

2 732 Frankish army defeats Moorish invaders.

732 Tours

4 759 Caliphate secedes from Frankish Kingdom.

Paris
Sens
Poitiers
FRANKISH KINGDOM
Lyon
Narbonne
719
Toulouse
718 Covadonga
ASTURIAS
PYRENEES
713 Segoyuela
713 Zaragoza
Mediterranean Sea
CORDOBA CALIPHATE
712 Toledo
714 Valencia
Balearic Islands
716 Lisbon
711 Ecija
711 Cordoba
3 756 Moorish Spain becomes the Cordoba Caliphate.
711 Jerez de la Frontera
Str. of Gibraltar
1 711–719 Moors conquer Visigoths.
Fez
MIDRARID DYNASTY
ATLANTIC OCEAN

A

The Moors quickly fought their way across Spain and Portugal. Christian forces retreated and held out in Asturias.

Moorish Conquest

➤ Moorish army invasion
▢ Moorish control, 710
▢ Moorish gains, 711–719
▢ Christian control, 719
✸ Moorish victory
✸ Christian victory

0   100   200   300 miles
0 100 200 300 kilometers

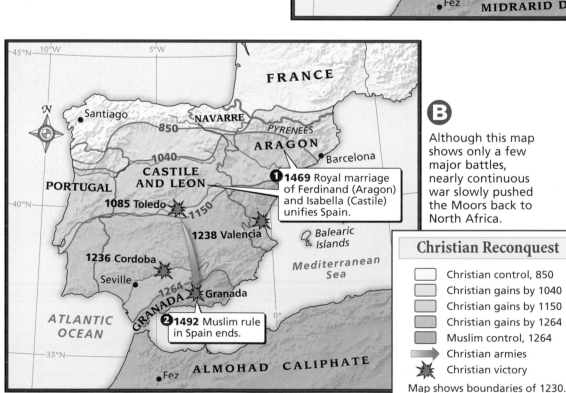

FRANCE
Santiago
NAVARRE
850
PYRENEES
ARAGON
Barcelona
1040
CASTILE AND LEON
1 1469 Royal marriage of Ferdinand (Aragon) and Isabella (Castile) unifies Spain.
PORTUGAL
1085 Toledo
1150
1238 Valencia
Balearic Islands
1236 Cordoba
Mediterranean Sea
Seville
1264
GRANADA
Granada
2 1492 Muslim rule in Spain ends.
ATLANTIC OCEAN
ALMOHAD CALIPHATE
Fez

B

Although this map shows only a few major battles, nearly continuous war slowly pushed the Moors back to North Africa.

Christian Reconquest

▢ Christian control, 850
▢ Christian gains by 1040
▢ Christian gains by 1150
▢ Christian gains by 1264
▢ Muslim control, 1264
➤ Christian armies
✸ Christian victory
Map shows boundaries of 1230.

The Hundred Years' War

After the Norman Conquest, England controlled much of France and claimed the rest. English and French kings fought for control of France in what is known as the Hundred Years' War.

- The war began in 1337 when the king of England, son of a French princess, claimed to be the ruler of France too.

- Some French nobles supported the English. At one point, an English king was chosen to be the next king of France.

- In 1453 the war finally ended with the defeat of the English.

C England and its ally Burgundy won major battles in the first part of the war. By 1420 they seemed to be the victors.

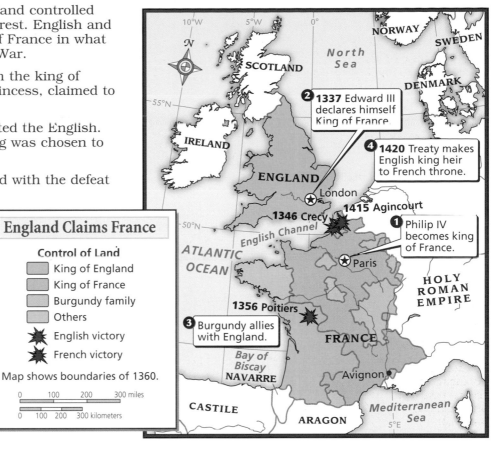

England Claims France

Control of Land
- King of England
- King of France
- Burgundy family
- Others
- ✸ English victory
- ✸ French victory

Map shows boundaries of 1360.

0   100   200   300 miles
0   100   200   300 kilometers

2 1337 Edward III declares himself King of France

4 1420 Treaty makes English king heir to French throne.

1415 Agincourt

1 Philip IV becomes king of France.

1346 Crecy

1356 Poitiers

3 Burgundy allies with England.

D Joan of Arc was a French peasant girl. She became the leader of a French army that repeatedly defeated the English until she was captured and killed.

Area shown in maps C and E

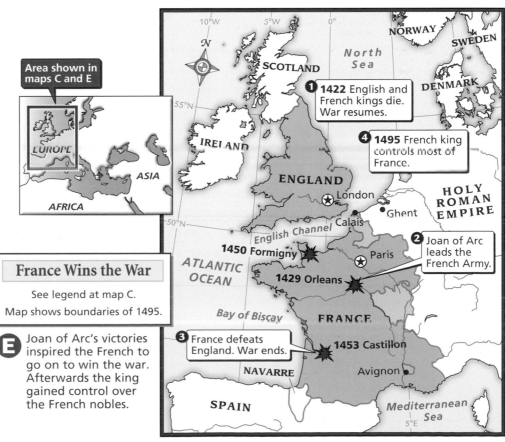

France Wins the War

See legend at map C.
Map shows boundaries of 1495.

1 1422 English and French kings die. War resumes.

4 1495 French king controls most of France.

Calais

Ghent

1450 Formigny

2 Joan of Arc leads the French Army.

1429 Orleans

3 France defeats England. War ends.

1453 Castillon

Avignon

E Joan of Arc's victories inspired the French to go on to win the war. Afterwards the king gained control over the French nobles.

Age of European Exploration

Exotic trade goods from Southeast Asia—the **Indies**—and from East Asia were highly desired by Western Europeans. These goods were extremely expensive.

▬ Competing European powers developed new technologies in shipbuilding and navigation that allowed them to explore new routes to the Indies.

▬ Europeans encountered American, African, and Asian cultures they had never known before.

▬ Often the European power that first explored an area later returned to conquer it.

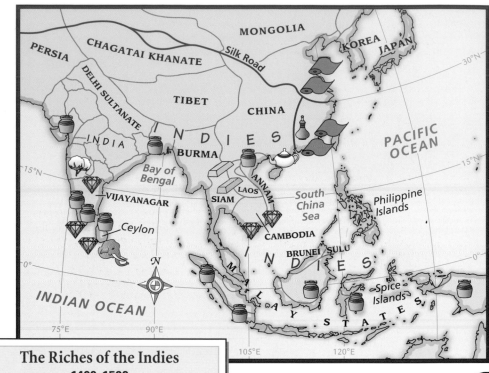

A Merchants in Central Asia and the Middle East controlled trade from the Indies to Europe (see page 43). Europeans wanted to bypass them to increase their own profits.

The Riches of the Indies
1400–1500

▭	Gold	🫙	Perfume
▱	Silver	🫙	Spices
◈	Precious stones		Cotton
🐘	Ivory		Silk
🫖	Porcelain	—	Trade route

Whose land is it?

When European explorers arrived in an area, they claimed it for their country. For years most **claims** were just lines on European maps. The people already living in those areas didn't realize they had new rulers until European soldiers arrived to enforce their paper claims.

B The map shows the key voyages of discovery that gave Europeans more complete knowledge of geography than ever before. Which countries explored which areas?

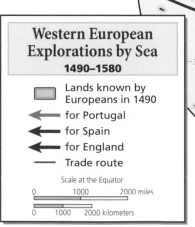

❼ Drake explores American and Pacific lands for England.

NORTH AMERICA

1577–1580 Drake

❽ See page 76 for more about the Americas.

PACIFIC OCEAN

EQUATOR

1519–1522 Magellan

❺ **1519** Rejected by Portugal, Magellan seeks Spice Islands for Spain.

Western European Explorations by Sea
1490–1580

▭ Lands known by Europeans in 1490
→ for Portugal
→ for Spain
→ for England
— Trade route

Scale at the Equator

0   1000   2000 miles

0   1000   2000 kilometers

C Spices from the Indies, such as cloves, cinnamon, and pepper, were worth as much as gold to Western Europeans. Kings sponsored explorations to win control of the spice trade.

D Francis Drake of England meets with a sultan in the Indies to discuss trade. His voyage provided new knowledge about the western coast of North America and the Pacific.

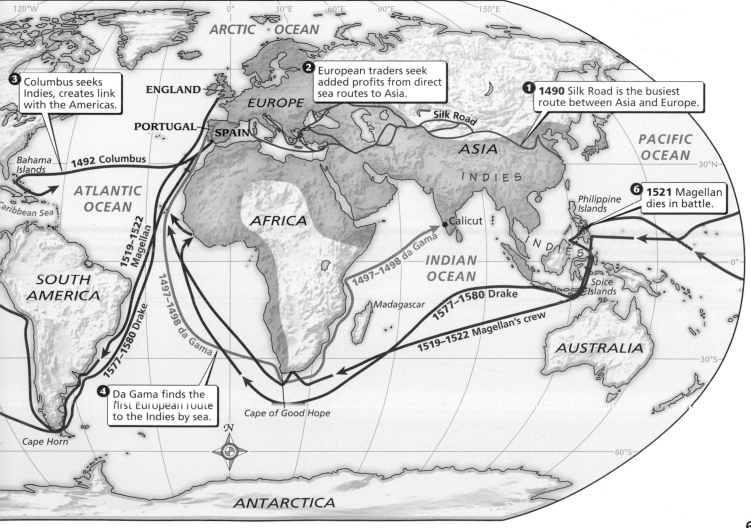

120°W · 0° · 30°E · 60°E · 90°E · 150°E

ARCTIC OCEAN

3 Columbus seeks Indies, creates link with the Americas.

2 European traders seek added profits from direct sea routes to Asia.

1 1490 Silk Road is the busiest route between Asia and Europe.

ENGLAND

EUROPE

Silk Road

ASIA

PACIFIC OCEAN

PORTUGAL

SPAIN

Bahama Islands

1492 Columbus

INDIES

30°N

ATLANTIC OCEAN

Caribbean Sea

AFRICA

Calicut

6 1521 Magellan dies in battle.

Philippine Islands

INDIES

1519–1522 Magellan

1497–1498 da Gama

INDIAN OCEAN

Spice Islands

0°

SOUTH AMERICA

1577–1580 Drake

1497–1498 da Gama

Madagascar

1577–1580 Drake

1519–1522 Magellan's crew

AUSTRALIA

30°S

4 Da Gama finds the first European route to the Indies by sea.

Cape of Good Hope

Cape Horn

N

60°S

ANTARCTICA

69

400 B.C.–250 A.D.
Maya build their first large pyramids.

1500 B.C.	1000 B.C.	500 B.C.	B.C. ◀ ▶ A.D.

1200 B.C.
Olmec city of San Lorenzo dominates Olmec culture.

700 B.C.
Ceremonial mounds are built by Adena civilization.

Olmec and Maya Civilizations

The Olmec and the Maya were the earliest major Native American civilizations. Both developed in Middle America.

- The Olmec civilization developed along the coast of the Gulf of Mexico.

- The Olmec built large sculptures and were the first people in the Americas to build pyramids. Their art and religion influenced later cultures of Middle America, including the Maya.

- The Maya civilization developed east of the Olmec. It was one of the longest lasting civilizations in the Americas.

- The Maya used pictographs to record major events in their history on large stone sculptures. Many of these sculptures still stand today.

A

Giant carvings like this one were used in ceremonies at Olmec religious centers. The largest heads were up to 10 feet tall and weighed several tons.

Area shown in maps B and E

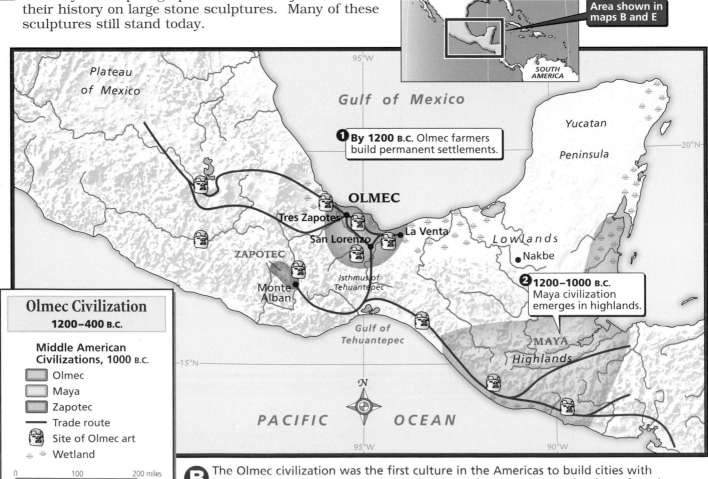

By 1200 B.C. Olmec farmers build permanent settlements.

1200–1000 B.C. Maya civilization emerges in highlands.

Plateau of Mexico

Gulf of Mexico

Yucatan Peninsula

OLMEC

Tres Zapotes

La Venta

Lowlands

Nakbe

San Lorenzo

ZAPOTEC

Monte Alban

Isthmus of Tehuantepec

Gulf of Tehuantepec

MAYA

Highlands

PACIFIC OCEAN

Olmec Civilization
1200–400 B.C.

Middle American Civilizations, 1000 B.C.
- Olmec
- Maya
- Zapotec
- Trade route
- Site of Olmec art
- Wetland

0   100   200 miles
0   100   200 kilometers

B The Olmec civilization was the first culture in the Americas to build cities with large religious centers. It traded with other cultures and its art has been found throughout Middle America.

		1505 **First slaves** arrive at Hispaniola.	1521 **Cortés** conquers Aztecs.		1888 **Slavery** ends in the Americas.
700 **Anasazi** people build the first pueblos.		1492 **Columbus** reaches the Americas.	1535 **New Spain** extends from Mexico to Chile.		

500 A.D.	1000 A.D.	1500 A.D.	2000 A.D.

900 **Hohokam** civilization begins using irrigation.	1325 **Aztec** people settle at Tenochtitlan.	1438–1471 **Inca Empire** rises to power in South America.	1750 **European powers** claim most lands in the Americas.

Built **elaborate limestone pyramids** for religious ceremonies.

Developed accurate **365-day solar calendar**.

Created an **advanced pictographic writing system** to record history.

Made many **advances in astronomy,** including predicting eclipses.

Maya Contributions, 250–950 A.D.

C The Maya produced many achievements in art, astronomy, and mathematics. Use this chart and the one on page 13 to compare Babylonian contributions with those of the Maya.

D Large limestone pyramids with temples at the top were built by the Maya for religious ceremonies. This pyramid is located in the Maya city of Tikal. Find Tikal on map E.

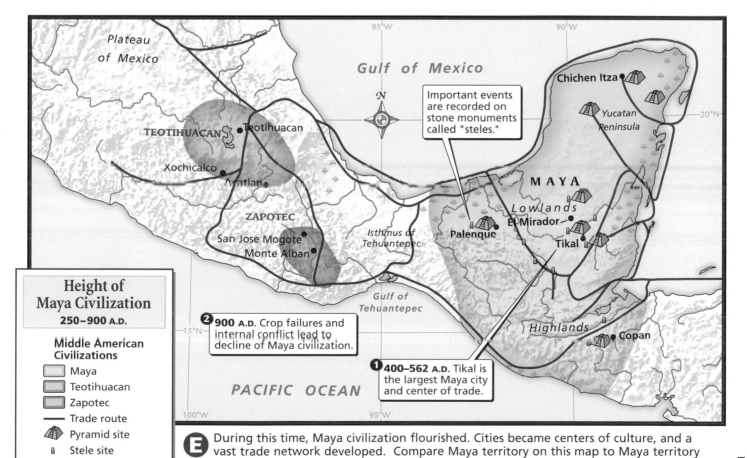

Important events are recorded on stone monuments called "steles."

2 900 A.D. Crop failures and internal conflict lead to decline of Maya civilization.

1 400–562 A.D. Tikal is the largest Maya city and center of trade.

Height of Maya Civilization

250–900 A.D.

Middle American Civilizations

- Maya
- Teotihuacan
- Zapotec
- — Trade route
- Pyramid site
- Stele site

E During this time, Maya civilization flourished. Cities became centers of culture, and a vast trade network developed. Compare Maya territory on this map to Maya territory on map B.

Native American Farming Cultures

During the height of the Olmec and Maya civilizations of Middle America, farming cultures began to develop in two regions of what are today the United States and northern Mexico.

- Early farming groups along the Mississippi and Ohio Rivers had similar cultures and built large structures called **mounds**.

- In the 700s A.D. these cultures were replaced by other mound-building farmers who became known as "Mississippian" people, named for the river.

- Native Americans developed two early farming cultures in the western deserts. They were influenced by the civilizations of Middle America.

- Around 700 A.D. a new culture developed southeast of the Colorado River. They built **pueblos**, unique dwellings many stories high.

A Mounds were built of dirt and stone. Like these at Cahokia, mounds were built for religious ceremonies, for burying the dead, or to house local officials.

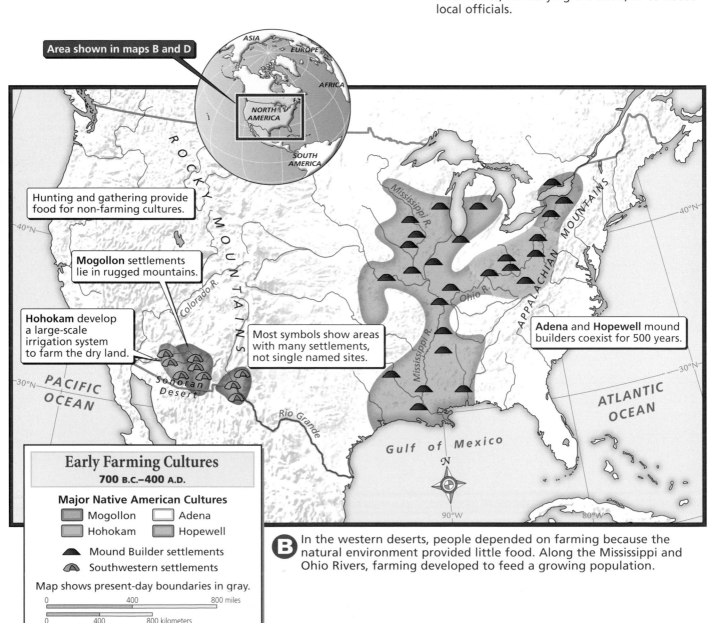

Area shown in maps B and D

Hunting and gathering provide food for non-farming cultures.

Mogollon settlements lie in rugged mountains.

Hohokam develop a large-scale irrigation system to farm the dry land.

Most symbols show areas with many settlements, not single named sites.

Adena and **Hopewell** mound builders coexist for 500 years.

Early Farming Cultures
700 B.C.–400 A.D.

Major Native American Cultures

- Mogollon
- Hohokam
- Adena
- Hopewell
- ⛰ Mound Builder settlements
- ⛰ Southwestern settlements

Map shows present-day boundaries in gray.

```
0          400          800 miles
0          400          800 kilometers
```

B In the western deserts, people depended on farming because the natural environment provided little food. Along the Mississippi and Ohio Rivers, farming developed to feed a growing population.

C Multi-level pueblos were built into the walls of canyons. This cliff dwelling in Mesa Verde, Colorado, was built around 1200. It housed about 400 people and is now called Cliff Palace.

Need roommates for your pueblo?

Pueblos were like modern-day apartment buildings. Dwellings were made of stone or adobe and could be up to four stories high. Ladders linked one floor to the next.

Pueblo and Mound Builders
900–1450 A.D.

Major Native American Civilizations

- Anasazi (Pueblo)
- Hohokam
- Mogollon
- Mississippian

- 🔺 Mound Builder settlement
- 🏠 Pueblo settlement
- — Trade route, 1450

Map shows present-day boundaries in gray.

0   400   800 miles
0   400   800 kilometers

Corn, beans, and squash become the main foods of these farming cultures.

Mississippian mounds are often built in the shapes of animals.

Anasazi people, like their dwellings, become known as "Pueblos."

Vast trade network follows rivers spreading out from Cahokia.

ROCKY MOUNTAINS

APPALACHIAN MOUNTAINS

Aztalan

Great Serpent

Cahokia

Mesa Verde

Chaco Canyon

Wapatki

Taos

Towosaghy

Town Creek

Pueblo Grande

Acoma

Etowah

Moundville

Sonoran Desert

Kolomok

Casas Grandes

Grand Village

Colorado R.

Rio Grande

Mississippi R.

Ohio R.

PACIFIC OCEAN

Gulf of Mexico

ATLANTIC OCEAN

120°W   110°W   90°W   80°W

40°N   30°N

D The Pueblo and the Mound Builders both developed large, structured communities. The mound-building community of Cahokia had a population of more than 100,000 people at its height in 1300. Find Cahokia on the map.

Aztec Empire

The Aztec migrated from the north to a small island in the Valley of Mexico. They built one of the largest empires of Middle America.

- Religion dominated every part of Aztec life. The Aztec worshipped hundreds of gods and performed many kinds of religious ceremonies.

- The Aztec were fierce warriors. They waged war to expand their empire.

- The Spanish came to Mexico in 1519. They conquered the Aztec Empire in 1521 and destroyed its capital.

A The Aztec capital city, shown here, had many temples and public buildings for religious ceremonies. Look at map B. What is the name of the Aztec capital?

Area shown in map B

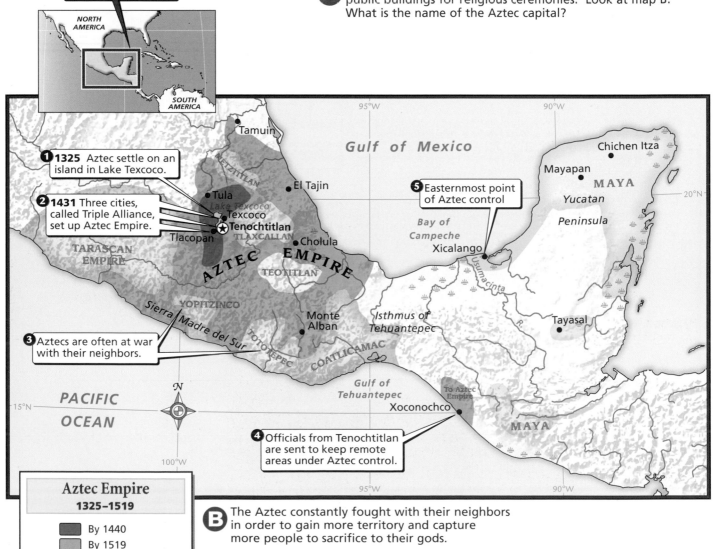

1325 Aztec settle on an island in Lake Texcoco.

1431 Three cities, called Triple Alliance, set up Aztec Empire.

Aztecs are often at war with their neighbors.

Officials from Tenochtitlan are sent to keep remote areas under Aztec control.

Easternmost point of Aztec control

B The Aztec constantly fought with their neighbors in order to gain more territory and capture more people to sacrifice to their gods.

Aztec Empire
1325–1519

- By 1440
- By 1519
- ☆ Aztec capital

0   100   200 miles
0   100   200 kilometers

74

Inca Empire

Around the same time the Aztec were building their empire, the Inca developed a large empire in South America.

▬ The Inca built an empire that extended through the Andes Mountains and along the west coast.

▬ They were excellent architects and engineers and built a vast network of roads and bridges. These helped their strong central government control even the most remote parts of the empire.

▬ The Spanish came to South America in 1532. They killed the Inca Emperor and took over the Empire.

C Powerful emperors greatly expanded Inca territory in less than 100 years. By 1525 the empire stretched 2,600 miles.

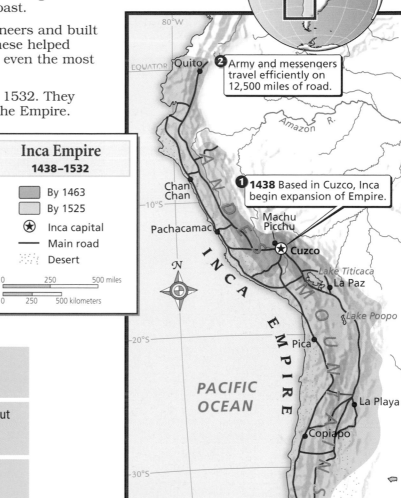

Area shown in map C

2 Army and messengers travel efficiently on 12,500 miles of road.

1 **1438** Based in Cuzco, Inca begin expansion of Empire.

3 **1525–1532** Civil war weakens Empire.

Inca Empire
1438–1532

- By 1463
- By 1525
- ★ Inca capital
- — Main road
- Desert

0   250   500 miles
0   250   500 kilometers

AZTEC

AZTEC	INCA
Built large limestone pyramids for religious ceremonies.	Built enormous stone buildings with great precision.
Used pictographs to record history and myths.	Spread news throughout the Empire using a messenger system.
Created floating gardens to grow food without using additional land areas.	Connected the Empire using an extensive network of roads.

Aztec and Inca Contributions

D Use this chart and the one on page 71 to compare and contrast Aztec, Inca, and Maya contributions.

E The Inca city of Machu Picchu, whose ruins are shown here, was a fortress built on a mountaintop. It could be reached only by crossing a bridge. If enemies were near, the bridge could be removed.

75

Europeans Explore and Settle in the Americas

Early European explorers searching for the Indies found unexpected opportunities in the Americas. By 1750 Europeans controlled most of the Americas.

- Europeans established colonies in the Americas and looked for ways to make a profit from the land and its resources.

- European colonization led to the conquest of Native American peoples, including the Aztec and Inca Empires.

- As European land claims expanded, Native Americans lost control of their traditional lands.

What is colonization?

Colonization is the act of a country claiming, ruling, and settling its people in a territory outside its boundary. The territory is called a "colony."

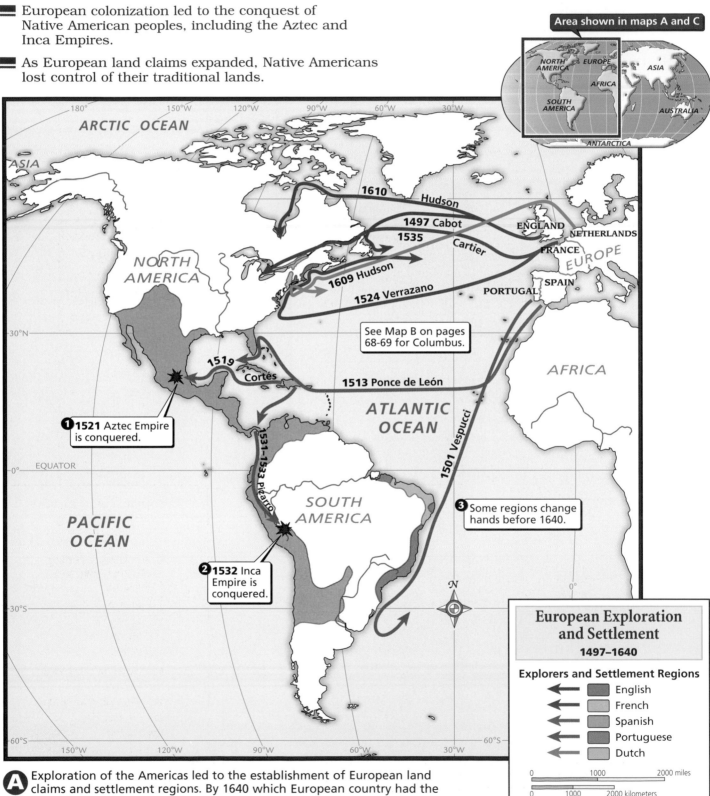

Area shown in maps A and C

NORTH AMERICA · EUROPE · ASIA · AFRICA · SOUTH AMERICA · AUSTRALIA · ANTARCTICA

ARCTIC OCEAN

ASIA

NORTH AMERICA

1610 Hudson
1497 Cabot
1535 Cartier
1609 Hudson
1524 Verrazano

ENGLAND · NETHERLANDS · FRANCE · EUROPE · SPAIN · PORTUGAL

See Map B on pages 68-69 for Columbus.

1519 Cortés

1513 Ponce de León

AFRICA

ATLANTIC OCEAN

❶ **1521** Aztec Empire is conquered.

1531-1533 Pizarro

1501 Vespucci

EQUATOR

PACIFIC OCEAN

SOUTH AMERICA

❸ Some regions change hands before 1640.

❷ **1532** Inca Empire is conquered.

European Exploration and Settlement
1497–1640

Explorers and Settlement Regions

- English
- French
- Spanish
- Portuguese
- Dutch

0 — 1000 — 2000 miles
0 — 1000 — 2000 kilometers

A Exploration of the Americas led to the establishment of European land claims and settlement regions. By 1640 which European country had the largest settlement regions?

B Spanish explorers killed thousands of Native Americans during their conquests. They claimed large areas of land for Spain and in the name of the Roman Catholic Church.

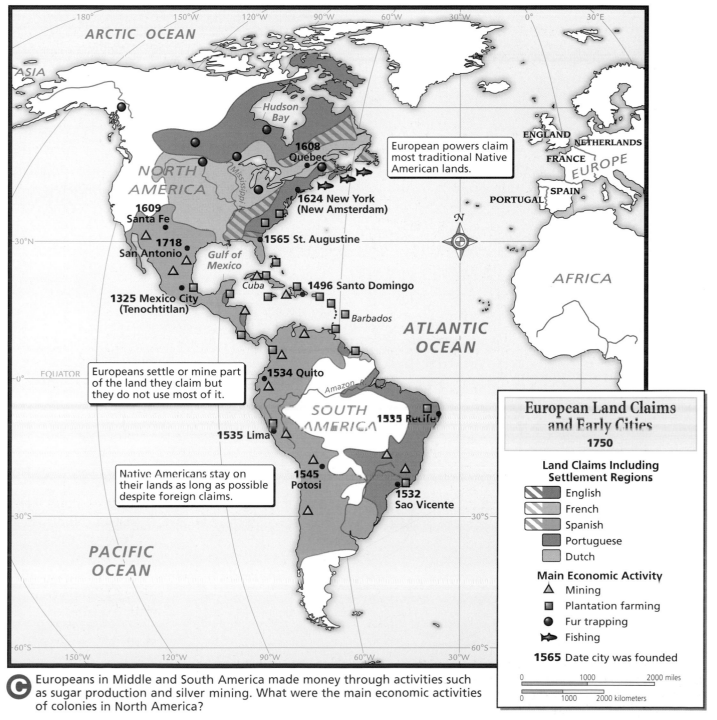

ARCTIC OCEAN

ASIA

Hudson Bay

NORTH AMERICA

1608 Quebec

European powers claim most traditional Native American lands.

1624 New York (New Amsterdam)

ENGLAND NETHERLANDS
FRANCE EUROPE
PORTUGAL SPAIN

1609 Santa Fe

1718 San Antonio

Gulf of Mexico

1565 St. Augustine

AFRICA

Cuba

1325 Mexico City (Tenochtitlan)

1496 Santo Domingo

Barbados

ATLANTIC OCEAN

Europeans settle or mine part of the land they claim but they do not use most of it.

EQUATOR

1534 Quito

Amazon R.

SOUTH AMERICA

1535 Recife

1535 Lima

Native Americans stay on their lands as long as possible despite foreign claims.

1545 Potosi

1532 Sao Vicente

PACIFIC OCEAN

European Land Claims and Early Cities
1750

Land Claims Including Settlement Regions
- English
- French
- Spanish
- Portuguese
- Dutch

Main Economic Activity
- △ Mining
- ◻ Plantation farming
- ● Fur trapping
- ➤ Fishing

1565 Date city was founded

0   1000   2000 miles
0   1000   2000 kilometers

C Europeans in Middle and South America made money through activities such as sugar production and silver mining. What were the main economic activities of colonies in North America?

Three Worlds Meet

European colonization of the Americas changed the lives of millions of people throughout the world. When Europeans and Africans came to the Americas, three separate "worlds," or cultures, were brought together.

- ▬ European ships carried plants and animals across the Atlantic Ocean in both directions. People on both sides of the Atlantic encountered goods that they had never seen before.

- ▬ As Europeans settled in the Americas, they often forced Native Americans to work for them. Millions of Native Americans died from overwork or disease.

- ▬ As the Native American population declined, Europeans began capturing, enslaving, and bringing Africans to the Americas to work as slaves.

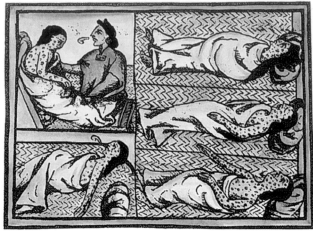

A Diseases brought from Europe, such as smallpox and measles, killed millions of Native Americans who had no resistance to them. This drawing shows Native Americans dying of smallpox.

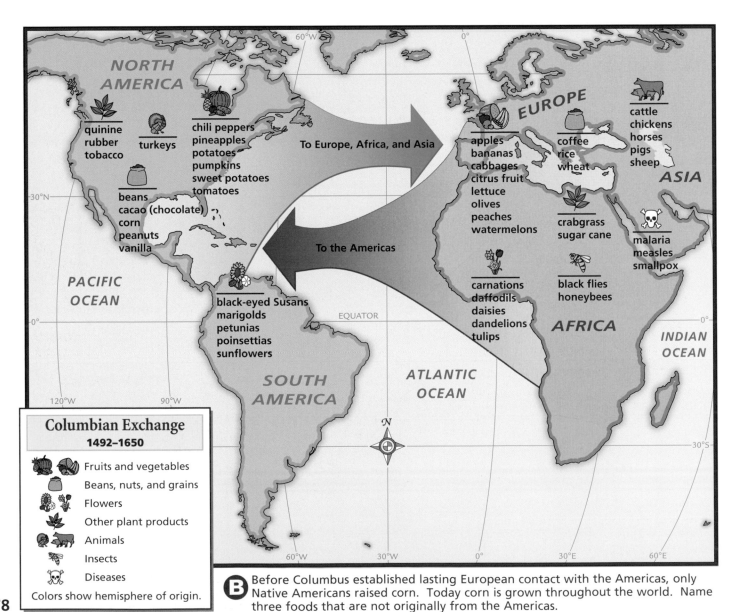

Columbian Exchange
1492–1650

- Fruits and vegetables
- Beans, nuts, and grains
- Flowers
- Other plant products
- Animals
- Insects
- Diseases

Colors show hemisphere of origin.

B Before Columbus established lasting European contact with the Americas, only Native Americans raised corn. Today corn is grown throughout the world. Name three foods that are not originally from the Americas.

Top 10 Cities, 1500

Rank	City (Modern Country)	Population
1	Beijing (China)	672,000
2	Vijayanagar (India)	500,000
3	Cairo (Egypt)	400,000
4	Hangzhou (China)	250,000
5	Tabriz (Iran)	250,000
6	Constantinople (Turkey)	200,000
7	Gaur (India)	200,000
8	Paris (France)	185,000
9	Canton (China)	150,000
10	Nanjing (China)	147,000

C In 1500 none of the world's largest cities was in the Americas. However, cities grew as more people from other regions came to the Americas. Turn to page 121 and compare the cities in this table with the top ten cities of 2000.

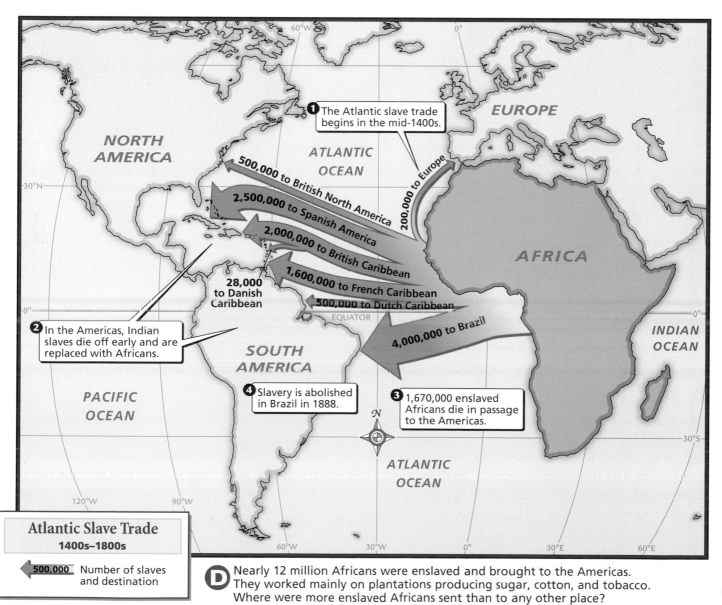

1 The Atlantic slave trade begins in the mid-1400s.

200,000 to Europe

500,000 to British North America

2,500,000 to Spanish America

2,000,000 to British Caribbean

1,600,000 to French Caribbean

28,000 to Danish Caribbean

500,000 to Dutch Caribbean

4,000,000 to Brazil

2 In the Americas, Indian slaves die off early and are replaced with Africans.

4 Slavery is abolished in Brazil in 1888.

3 1,670,000 enslaved Africans die in passage to the Americas.

Atlantic Slave Trade
1400s–1800s

500,000 Number of slaves and destination

D Nearly 12 million Africans were enslaved and brought to the Americas. They worked mainly on plantations producing sugar, cotton, and tobacco. Where were more enslaved Africans sent than to any other place?

1000 B.C.	500 B.C.	B.C. ◀ ▶ A.D.
590 B.C. Meroe is the cultural center of Kush.	**500 B.C.** Bantu migration begins.	**350** Christianity is adopted by king of Axum.

Early Civilizations of Africa

Many different cultures developed in Africa. Two early black African cultures developed around 3000 B.C. A civilization known as Kush developed in northeastern Africa. Bantu cultures developed in West Africa.

- The kingdom of Kush was located along the Nile River in the region of Nubia. Kush is often called Nubia.

- The Kushite civilization became a center for African learning, culture, and trade.

- Bantu people gradually spread farming and ironworking into central and southern Africa.

A Kush was a major trading center linking Central Africa, the Mediterranean region, Arabia, and India. Goods and ideas were exchanged between cultures through Kush.

B These tiles, which show a Kushite in the center, were found in Egypt. Kush and Egypt influenced each other for 2,500 years.

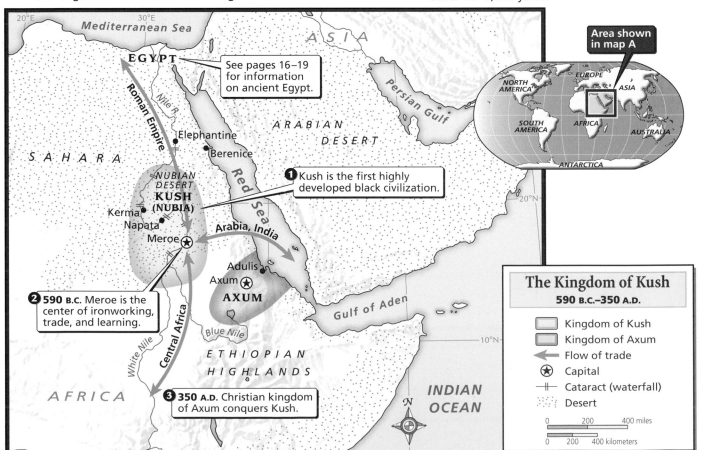

Early Civilizations of Africa map

See pages 16–19 for information on ancient Egypt.

1 Kush is the first highly developed black civilization.

2 590 B.C. Meroe is the center of ironworking, trade, and learning.

3 350 A.D. Christian kingdom of Axum conquers Kush.

Area shown in map A

The Kingdom of Kush
590 B.C.–350 A.D.

- ▢ Kingdom of Kush
- ▢ Kingdom of Axum
- ← Flow of trade
- ⊛ Capital
- ⊣⊢ Cataract (waterfall)
- ⠿ Desert

0   200   400 miles
0   200   400 kilometers

80

639 **Muslim Arabs** invade North Africa.		**1240** **Mali Empire** is established.	**1444** **Atlantic slave trade** begins.	**1500** **Swahili** city-states thrive on trade.	**1780** **Slave trade** reaches its height.

1000   **1500**   **2000**

700 **Ghana** becomes the first empire in West Africa.	**1335** **Songhai Empire** is established.	**1400** **Timbuktu** is the center of Mali culture.	**1914** **Europeans** control most of Africa.

Who is descended from the Bantu?

Descendants of the Bantu live in central and southern Africa. They speak related languages but belong to more than 300 distinct culture groups, including the Swahili, Zulu, and Kikuyu people.

C This farmer in southern Africa is a descendant of Bantu farmers who migrated to the region at least a thousand years ago.

D For about 1,500 years, the Bantu migrated south, mixing with original culture groups across the region. The Bantu brought a new way of life to southern Africa.

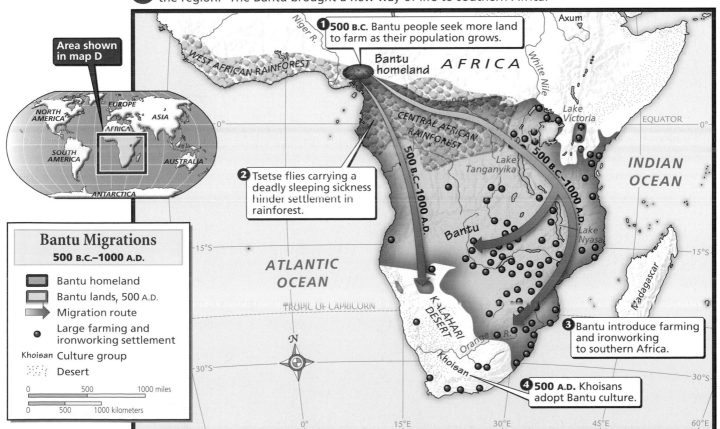

Area shown in map D

1 500 B.C. Bantu people seek more land to farm as their population grows.

2 Tsetse flies carrying a deadly sleeping sickness hinder settlement in rainforest.

3 Bantu introduce farming and ironworking to southern Africa.

4 500 A.D. Khoisans adopt Bantu culture.

Bantu Migrations
500 B.C.–1000 A.D.

- Bantu homeland
- Bantu lands, 500 A.D.
- → Migration route
- • Large farming and ironworking settlement
- Khoisan Culture group
- Desert

0   500   1000 miles
0   500   1000 kilometers

81

Spread of Islam in Africa

In the 600s A.D., invaders from Arabia brought Islam to North Africa. Gradually, Islam spread south and east.

- Hundreds of African religions already existed throughout the continent before the arrival of Arab invaders.

- In addition, Jews and Christians had lived in North Africa since the Roman Empire controlled the region.

- Islamic, or Muslim, empires developed along the Mediterranean Sea in North Africa. Islam came to dominate the culture of North Africa.

A This ancient illustration shows Muslim warriors from the Fatimid Caliphate. The Fatimids conquered Egypt and later founded Cairo.

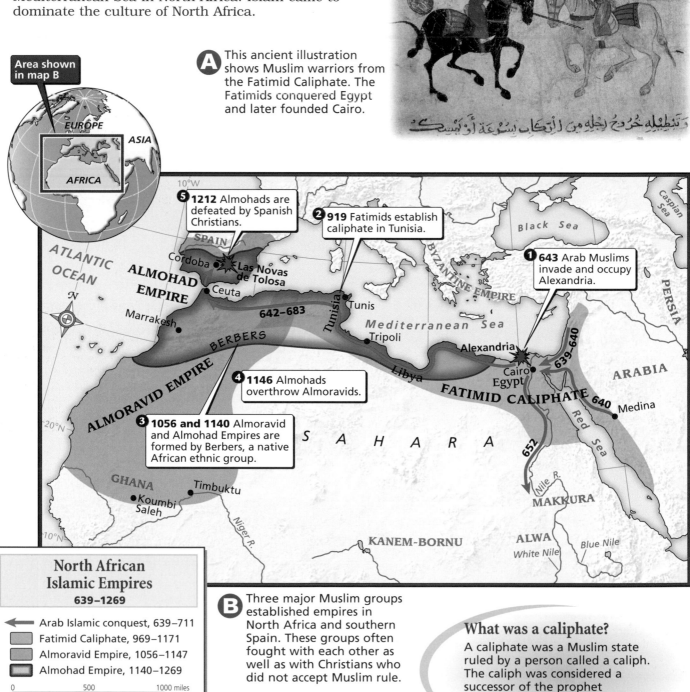

Area shown in map B

5 **1212** Almohads are defeated by Spanish Christians.

2 **919** Fatimids establish caliphate in Tunisia.

1 **643** Arab Muslims invade and occupy Alexandria.

ALMOHAD EMPIRE

ALMORAVID EMPIRE

BERBERS

642–683

4 **1146** Almohads overthrow Almoravids.

3 **1056 and 1140** Almoravid and Almohad Empires are formed by Berbers, a native African ethnic group.

639–640

640

652

FATIMID CALIPHATE

SAHARA

GHANA

Timbuktu

Koumbi Saleh

Niger R.

KANEM-BORNU

MAKKURA

ALWA

White Nile

Blue Nile

Nile R.

Red Sea

ARABIA

Medina

PERSIA

Caspian Sea

Black Sea

BYZANTINE EMPIRE

Mediterranean Sea

SPAIN

Cordoba

Las Navas de Tolosa

Ceuta

Marrakesh

Tunisia

Tunis

Tripoli

Libya

Alexandria

Cairo

Egypt

ATLANTIC OCEAN

10°W

20°N

10°N

North African Islamic Empires
639–1269

← Arab Islamic conquest, 639–711
- Fatimid Caliphate, 969–1171
- Almoravid Empire, 1056–1147
- Almohad Empire, 1140–1269

0   500   1000 miles
0   500   1000 kilometers

B Three major Muslim groups established empires in North Africa and southern Spain. These groups often fought with each other as well as with Christians who did not accept Muslim rule.

What was a caliphate?

A caliphate was a Muslim state ruled by a person called a caliph. The caliph was considered a successor of the prophet Mohammed, the founder of Islam.

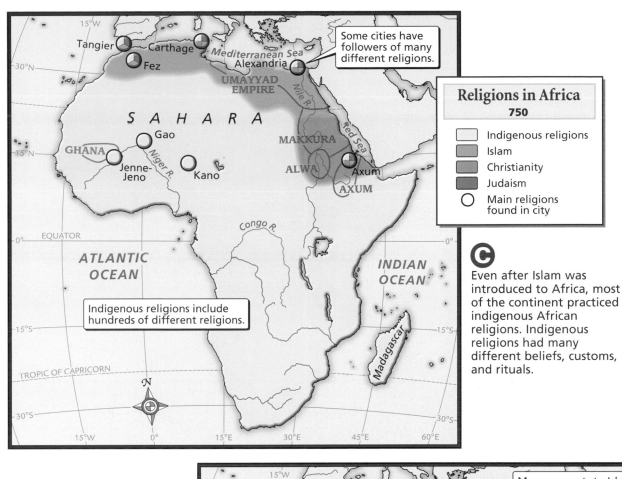

Religions in Africa
750

- ☐ Indigenous religions
- ☐ Islam
- ☐ Christianity
- ☐ Judaism
- ◯ Main religions found in city

Some cities have followers of many different religions.

Indigenous religions include hundreds of different religions.

C Even after Islam was introduced to Africa, most of the continent practiced indigenous African religions. Indigenous religions had many different beliefs, customs, and rituals.

Who was first?

Indigenous describes a region's original people or cultures. The Bantu people are indigenous to Africa, but Arab Muslims are not.

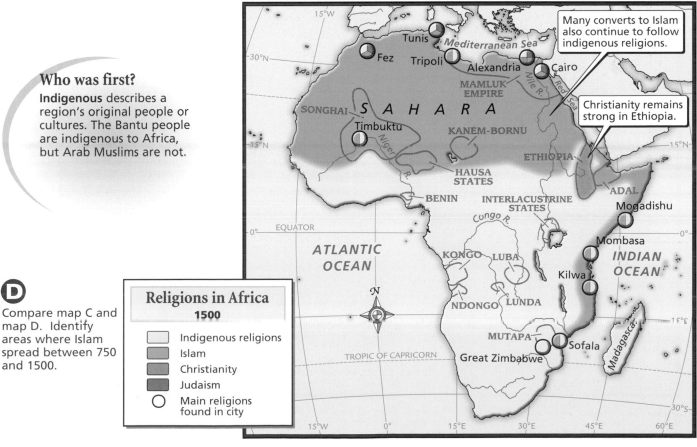

Many converts to Islam also continue to follow indigenous religions.

Christianity remains strong in Ethiopia.

D Compare map C and map D. Identify areas where Islam spread between 750 and 1500.

Religions in Africa
1500

- ☐ Indigenous religions
- ☐ Islam
- ☐ Christianity
- ☐ Judaism
- ◯ Main religions found in city

Empires and States of Africa

Beginning in the 700s, new empires and states developed in Africa.

- West African empires developed south of the Sahara. These empires became wealthy through trade within and outside of Africa.

- In East Africa, Islamic and indigenous African cultures mixed to form a new culture known as Swahili. Swahili city-states developed along the coast.

- Cultures in central and southern Africa developed organized governments. Many different states emerged in the region.

A Cities emerged as centers of trade in North, West, and East Africa. The city of Jenne, in the modern country of Mali, remains a trading center.

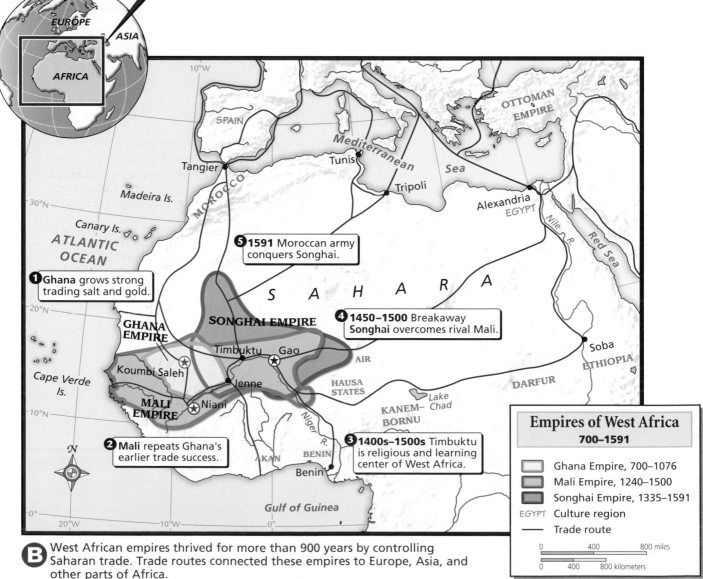

Area shown in map B

EUROPE
ASIA
AFRICA

❺ 1591 Moroccan army conquers Songhai.

❶ Ghana grows strong trading salt and gold.

GHANA EMPIRE

SONGHAI EMPIRE

❹ 1450–1500 Breakaway **Songhai** overcomes rival Mali.

Timbuktu   Gao

Koumbi Saleh

Jenne

MALI EMPIRE   Niani

❷ Mali repeats Ghana's earlier trade success.

❸ 1400s–1500s Timbuktu is religious and learning center of West Africa.

SPAIN
Tangier   Tunis
Mediterranean   Sea
Tripoli
Alexandria
EGYPT   Nile R.   Red Sea
OTTOMAN EMPIRE
Madeira Is.
Canary Is.
ATLANTIC OCEAN
Cape Verde Is.
SAHARA
MOROCCO
AIR
HAUSA STATES
KANEM– BORNU
Lake Chad
Soba
ETHIOPIA
DARFUR
Niger R.
AKAN   BENIN
Benin
Gulf of Guinea

Empires of West Africa
700–1591
Ghana Empire, 700–1076
Mali Empire, 1240–1500
Songhai Empire, 1335–1591
EGYPT   Culture region
—   Trade route

0   400   800 miles
0   400   800 kilometers

B West African empires thrived for more than 900 years by controlling Saharan trade. Trade routes connected these empires to Europe, Asia, and other parts of Africa.

C The Shona people of southeastern Africa built a city called Great Zimbabwe. It became a center of trade. These ruins of the city show a huge stone wall up to 32 feet high. Locate the city of Great Zimbabwe on Map D.

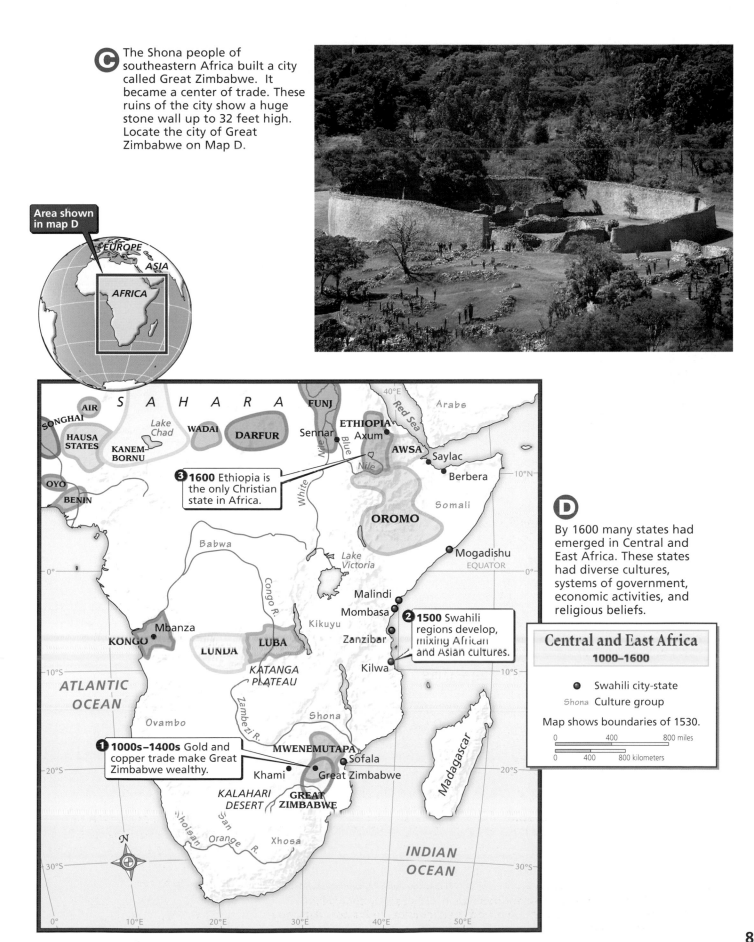

Area shown in map D

EUROPE
ASIA
AFRICA

S A H A R A

AIR
SONGHAI
HAUSA STATES
KANEM-BORNU
Lake Chad
WADAI
DARFUR
FUNJ
Sennar
Nile
Blue Nile
White
ETHIOPIA
Axum
Red Sea
Arabs
AWSA
Saylac
Berbera
10°N

OYO
BENIN

❸ **1600** Ethiopia is the only Christian state in Africa.

OROMO
Somali

Babwa
Lake Victoria
EQUATOR
0°
Mogadishu

D By 1600 many states had emerged in Central and East Africa. These states had diverse cultures, systems of government, economic activities, and religious beliefs.

Congo R.
Kikuyu
Mbanza
KONGO
LUNDA
LUBA
KATANGA PLATEAU
Malindi
Mombasa
Zanzibar
Kilwa

❷ **1500** Swahili regions develop, mixing African and Asian cultures.

10°S
ATLANTIC OCEAN
Ovambo
Zambezi R.
Shona

Khoisan
San
Orange R.
Xhosa

❶ **1000s–1400s** Gold and copper trade make Great Zimbabwe wealthy.

MWENEMUTAPA
Sofala
Khami
Great Zimbabwe
KALAHARI DESERT
GREAT ZIMBABWE

Madagascar

20°S

N

INDIAN OCEAN
30°S

0°   10°E   20°E   30°E   40°E   50°E

Central and East Africa
1000–1600

● Swahili city-state
Shona Culture group

Map shows boundaries of 1530.

0   400   800 miles
0   400   800 kilometers

85

Africa and Trade

Trade strengthened African states and empires as it linked the economies of Africa, Asia, and Europe.

- Caravan routes through the Sahara linked North and West Africa to Europe and the Middle East. Many African states grew wealthy through Saharan trade.

- Salt and gold dominated trade within Africa. Gold and ivory were valuable for trade with other parts of the world.

- The slave trade was at its height during the late 1700s. Millions of Africans were captured, enslaved, and taken from their homelands.

What was slavery?

Slavery was the practice of capturing people, taking them from their homelands, and forcing them to work against their will without pay. Slaves were considered property and were denied the rights of free people.

Area shown in maps A and B

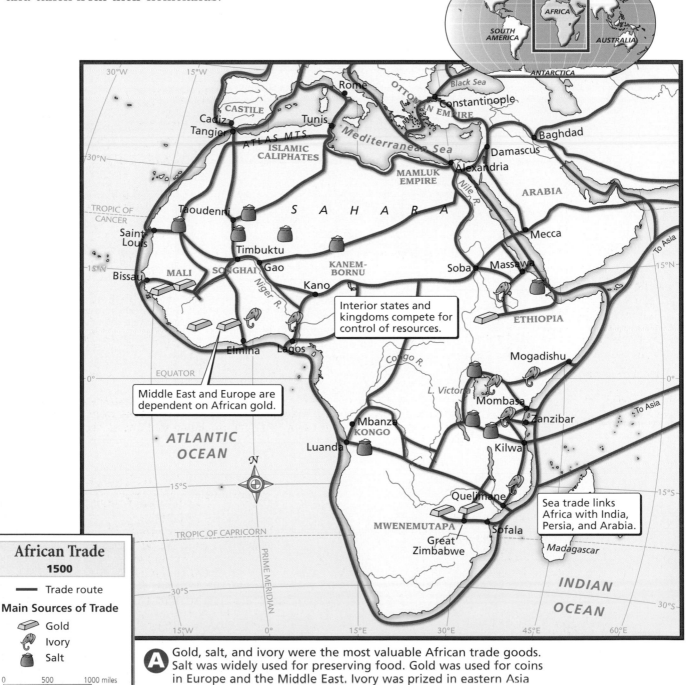

Interior states and kingdoms compete for control of resources.

Middle East and Europe are dependent on African gold.

Sea trade links Africa with India, Persia, and Arabia.

African Trade
1500

— Trade route

Main Sources of Trade

- Gold
- Ivory
- Salt

0   500   1000 miles
0   500   1000 kilometers

A Gold, salt, and ivory were the most valuable African trade goods. Salt was widely used for preserving food. Gold was used for coins in Europe and the Middle East. Ivory was prized in eastern Asia for carved works of art.

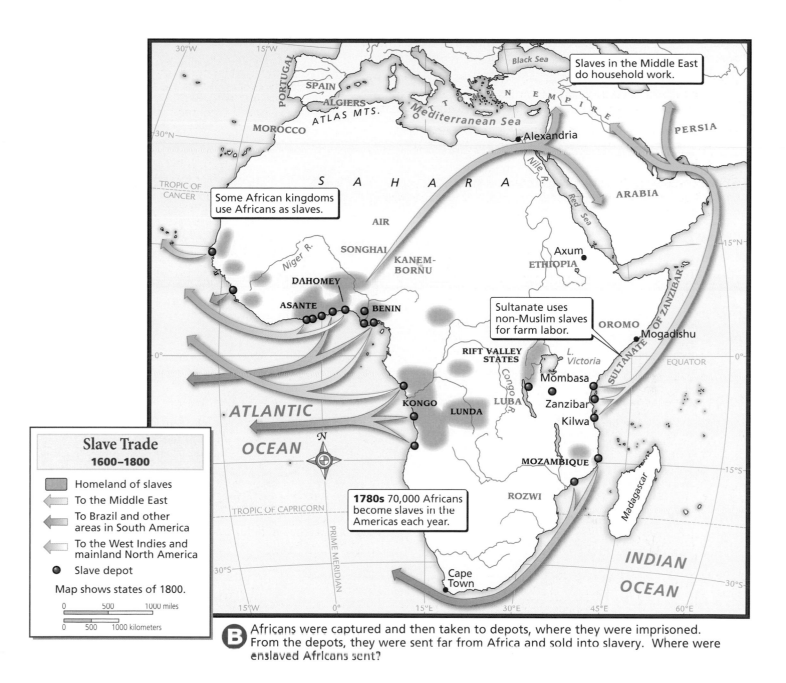

Slaves in the Middle East do household work.

Some African kingdoms use Africans as slaves.

Sultanate uses non-Muslim slaves for farm labor.

1780s 70,000 Africans become slaves in the Americas each year.

Slave Trade
1600–1800

- Homeland of slaves
- ← To the Middle East
- ← To Brazil and other areas in South America
- ← To the West Indies and mainland North America
- ● Slave depot

Map shows states of 1800.

0   500   1000 miles
0   500   1000 kilometers

B Africans were captured and then taken to depots, where they were imprisoned. From the depots, they were sent far from Africa and sold into slavery. Where were enslaved Africans sent?

Top 10 Cities, 1600

Rank	City (Modern Country)	Population
1	**Beijing** (China)	706,000
2	**Constantinople** (Turkey)	700,000
3	**Agra** (India)	500,000
4	**Osaka** (Japan)	360,000
5	**Kyoto** (Japan)	300,000
6	**Hangzhou** (China)	270,000
7	**Paris** (France)	245,000
8	**Naples** (Italy)	224,000
9	**Cairo** (Egypt)	200,000
10	**Bijapur** (India)	200,000

C Many African cities grew and became centers of trade. Even so, cities in Africa had lower populations than the largest cities of Europe and Asia.

European Imperialism in Africa

After the slave trade was abolished, Europeans looked for new sources of wealth in Africa. In less than 50 years, Europeans took over almost all of Africa.

- ▬ European countries claimed land in Africa to make a profit from resources, expand territory, and gain power.

- ▬ The European competition to claim African land became known as "The Scramble for Africa."

- ▬ Africans often tried resisting European imperialism, but only two African states remained independent.

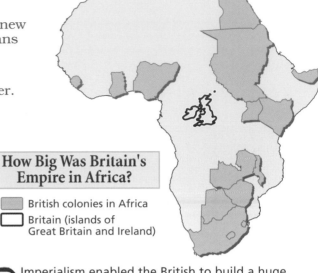

How Big Was Britain's Empire in Africa?

☐ British colonies in Africa
☐ Britain (islands of Great Britain and Ireland)

A Until the late 1800s, there were many independent African states and most European colonies in Africa were along the coast. Compare this map with map D.

B Imperialism enabled the British to build a huge empire. They had colonies in Africa as well as in Asia and the Americas.

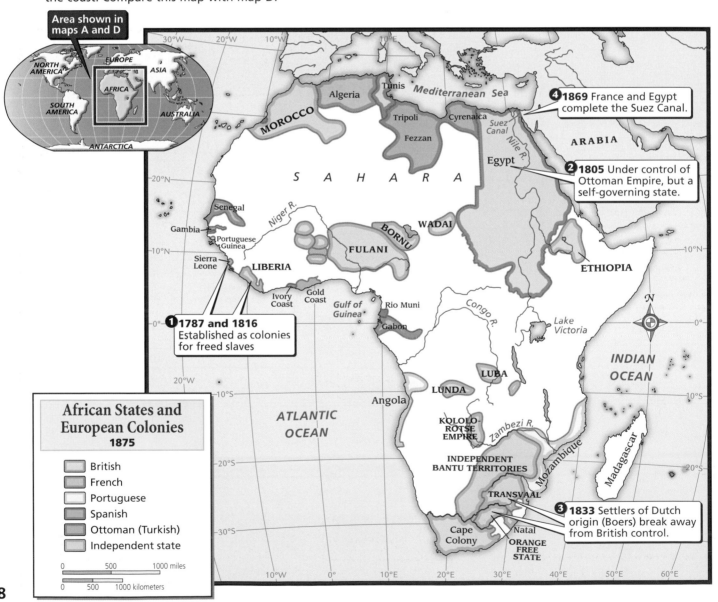

Area shown in maps A and D

4 1869 France and Egypt complete the Suez Canal.

2 1805 Under control of Ottoman Empire, but a self-governing state.

1 1787 and 1816 Established as colonies for freed slaves

3 1833 Settlers of Dutch origin (Boers) break away from British control.

African States and European Colonies
1875

- ☐ British
- ☐ French
- ☐ Portuguese
- ☐ Spanish
- ☐ Ottoman (Turkish)
- ☐ Independent state

0   500   1000 miles
0   500   1000 kilometers

Why are they here?

Imperialism is the national policy of taking control of another country or territory to gain land, power, or wealth. Imperialists can take over by military force, by controlling trade, or by reorganizing the government of another country.

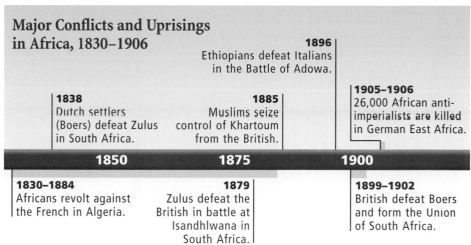

Major Conflicts and Uprisings in Africa, 1830–1906

1896 Ethiopians defeat Italians in the Battle of Adowa.

1838 Dutch settlers (Boers) defeat Zulus in South Africa.

1885 Muslims seize control of Khartoum from the British.

1905–1906 26,000 African anti-imperialists are killed in German East Africa.

1850   **1875**   **1900**

1830–1884 Africans revolt against the French in Algeria.

1879 Zulus defeat the British in battle at Isandhlwana in South Africa.

1899–1902 British defeat Boers and form the Union of South Africa.

C An Ethiopian uprising was the only successful African revolt. Though Africans in many regions tried to retain control of their homelands, Europeans used their military strength to overpower any resistance.

D European leaders met in 1914 to peacefully divide claims on African lands. Africans had no say in this agreement. By 1914 European colonies had been set up in nearly every part of Africa.

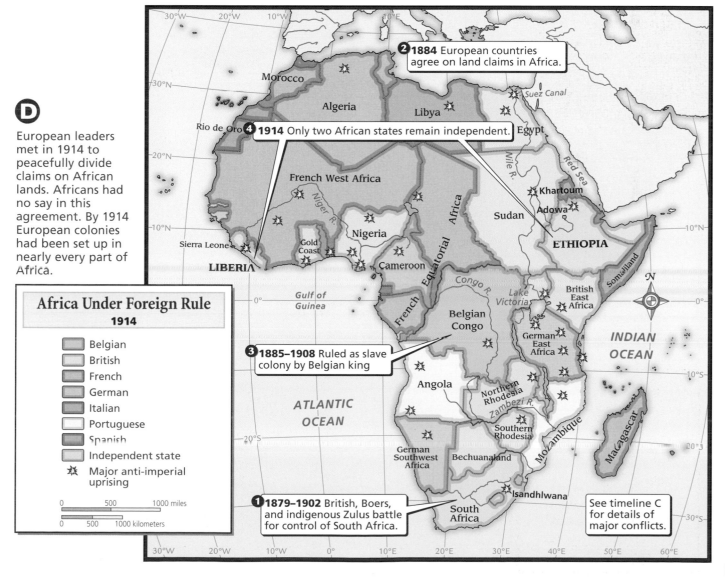

2 1884 European countries agree on land claims in Africa.

4 1914 Only two African states remain independent.

3 1885–1908 Ruled as slave colony by Belgian king

1 1879–1902 British, Boers, and indigenous Zulus battle for control of South Africa.

See timeline C for details of major conflicts.

Africa Under Foreign Rule
1914

- Belgian
- British
- French
- German
- Italian
- Portuguese
- Spanish
- Independent state
- �֎ Major anti-imperial uprising

| 1450 Gutenberg perfects the printing press. | 1517 Reformation is begun by Martin Luther. |

| 1300 | 1400 | 1500 |

1350–1600
Renaissance flourishes in Western Europe.

1453
Constantinople falls to Ottomans.

1503
Leonardo da Vinci paints the *Mona Lisa*.

Europe During the Renaissance

Near the end of the Middle Ages, the **Renaissance**, a "rebirth" of European learning and art, transformed Western Europe.

- The Renaissance began in Italy. Scholars there rediscovered Greek and Roman art, science, and philosophy.

- The great works of the past inspired scientific discoveries, inventions, and new artistic styles.

- Wealthy Italian city-states gave money to support new works of art based on Renaissance ideas.

- The Renaissance spread from Italy to other parts of Western Europe.

A
Leonardo da Vinci and other Renaissance artists developed new styles of painting. His **Mona Lisa** is the most famous portrait of the era.

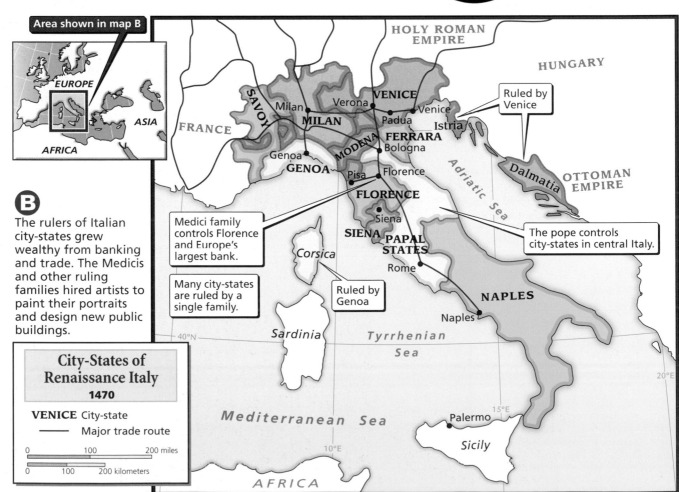

B
The rulers of Italian city-states grew wealthy from banking and trade. The Medicis and other ruling families hired artists to paint their portraits and design new public buildings.

Area shown in map B

EUROPE

ASIA

AFRICA

HOLY ROMAN EMPIRE

HUNGARY

Ruled by Venice

FRANCE

SAVOY

Milan
MILAN

Verona

VENICE
Venice

Padua

Istria

MODENA
FERRARA
Bologna

Genoa
GENOA

Pisa

Florence

Adriatic Sea

Dalmatia

OTTOMAN EMPIRE

Medici family controls Florence and Europe's largest bank.

FLORENCE

Siena

SIENA
PAPAL STATES

Corsica

The pope controls city-states in central Italy.

Rome

Many city-states are ruled by a single family.

Ruled by Genoa

NAPLES

Naples

40°N

Sardinia

Tyrrhenian Sea

20°E

City-States of Renaissance Italy
1470

VENICE City-state

—— Major trade route

| 0 | 100 | 200 miles |
| 0 | 100 | 200 kilometers |

Mediterranean Sea

Palermo

15°E

10°E

Sicily

AFRICA

| 1618–1648 **Thirty Years' War** is fought by religious rivals. | 1683 **Ottomans defeated** at Vienna. | | 1750 **Industrial Revolution** begins in Britain. | | 1850 **Cities** house half the people in Britain. |

1600 — **1700** — **1800** — **1900**

1650 **Dutch** control most European trade in Asia.

1770 **Colonial powers** control most of the Americas.

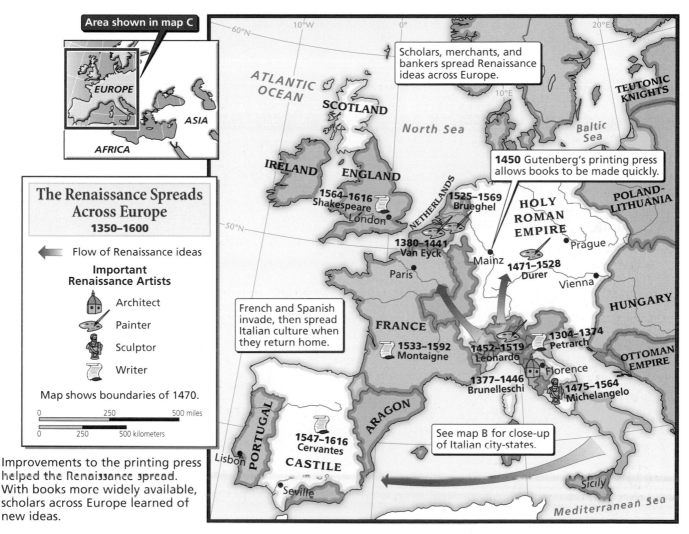

Area shown in map C

ATLANTIC OCEAN

EUROPE

ASIA

AFRICA

Scholars, merchants, and bankers spread Renaissance ideas across Europe.

The Renaissance Spreads Across Europe
1350–1600

⬅ Flow of Renaissance ideas

Important Renaissance Artists

🏛 Architect

🎨 Painter

🗿 Sculptor

📜 Writer

Map shows boundaries of 1470.

0 — 250 — 500 miles
0 — 250 — 500 kilometers

SCOTLAND

North Sea

Baltic Sea

TEUTONIC KNIGHTS

IRELAND   ENGLAND

1564–1616 Shakespeare
London

NETHERLANDS

1525–1569 Brueghel

1450 Gutenberg's printing press allows books to be made quickly.

POLAND-LITHUANIA

HOLY ROMAN EMPIRE

Prague

1380–1441 Van Eyck

Paris

Mainz

1471–1528 Dürer

Vienna

HUNGARY

French and Spanish invade, then spread Italian culture when they return home.

FRANCE

1533–1592 Montaigne

1452–1519 Leonardo

1304–1374 Petrarch

Florence

OTTOMAN EMPIRE

1377–1446 Brunelleschi

1475–1564 Michelangelo

PORTUGAL

ARAGON

1547–1616 Cervantes

Lisbon   CASTILE

Seville

See map B for close-up of Italian city-states.

Sicily

Mediterranean Sea

C Improvements to the printing press helped the Renaissance spread. With books more widely available, scholars across Europe learned of new ideas.

D In the 1400s Italy was made up of several city-states. The powerful city-state of Florence was the cultural and economic center of the Renaissance.

Reformation and Counter Reformation

During the Reformation, Western Christianity split into two separate religious groups: Roman Catholics and Protestants.

- In 1517 Martin Luther, a Catholic monk, began the **Reformation**, a movement to reform the Roman Catholic Church.

- Like Luther, most reformers wanted to change the Catholic Church. Instead their efforts led to the creation of separate **Protestant** churches.

- Conflicts between Catholics and Protestants caused wars throughout Europe.

What were they protesting?

Protestants got their name from protesting, or speaking out against, the authority of the Catholic Church. Protestantism is the name for most non-Catholic and non-Orthodox Christian churches.

A Martin Luther's criticisms changed Christian practices. The swan in this portrait of Luther is a symbol of religious reform.

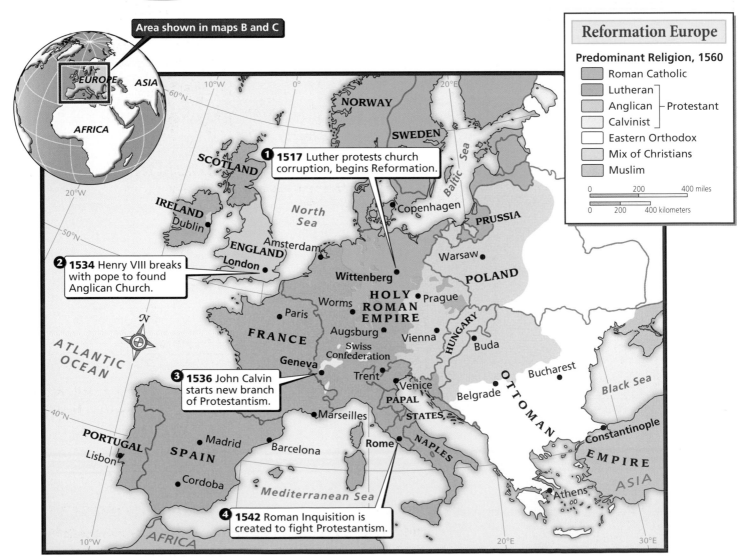

Area shown in maps B and C

1 1517 Luther protests church corruption, begins Reformation.

2 1534 Henry VIII breaks with pope to found Anglican Church.

3 1536 John Calvin starts new branch of Protestantism.

4 1542 Roman Inquisition is created to fight Protestantism.

Reformation Europe

Predominant Religion, 1560

- Roman Catholic
- Lutheran ⎫
- Anglican ⎬ Protestant
- Calvinist ⎭
- Eastern Orthodox
- Mix of Christians
- Muslim

0   200   400 miles
0   200   400 kilometers

B Lutheran, Calvin, Anglican, and other Protestant churches rapidly gained followers. Which regions had become mostly Protestant by 1560?

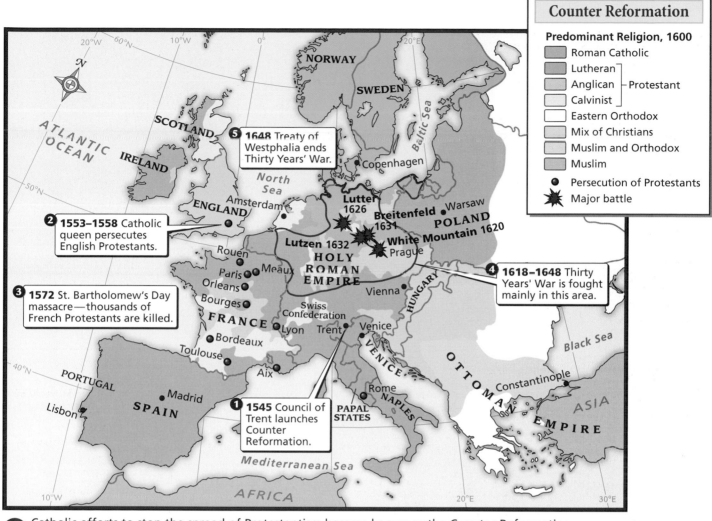

Counter Reformation

Predominant Religion, 1600
- Roman Catholic
- Lutheran ⎤
- Anglican ⎬ Protestant
- Calvinist ⎦
- Eastern Orthodox
- Mix of Christians
- Muslim and Orthodox
- Muslim
- ● Persecution of Protestants
- ✦ Major battle

5 **1648** Treaty of Westphalia ends Thirty Years' War.

2 **1553–1558** Catholic queen persecutes English Protestants.

3 **1572** St. Bartholomew's Day massacre—thousands of French Protestants are killed.

4 **1618–1648** Thirty Years' War is fought mainly in this area.

1 **1545** Council of Trent launches Counter Reformation.

Lutter 1626
Breitenfeld 1631
White Mountain 1620
Lutzen 1632

C Catholic efforts to stop the spread of Protestantism became known as the Counter Reformation. Religious conflicts and land disputes erupted into the Thirty Years' war.

D Catholic leaders made it a crime to print or read Protestant books. Forbidden books were burned in public.

Major Christian Churches, 1600

Church	Began	Key Figure	Leadership
Eastern Orthodox	1st century*	Peter	Patriarchs and Bishops
Roman Catholic	1st century*	Peter	Pope, Cardinals, Bishops
Lutheran	1530	Martin Luther	Pastors
Anglican	1534	Henry VIII	King of England
Calvinist	1536	John Calvin	Elected councils

*1054 Christianity splits into two churches: Eastern Orthodox and Roman Catholic.

E The major Christian churches survived the Reformation and Counter Reformation. They still exist today, either with the same names or as the foundations of more recent churches.

93

Rise of the Ottoman Empire

The Ottoman Empire began as a small kingdom in the region known as Anatolia, near the Black Sea. But during the 1600s it was the world's strongest and wealthiest empire.

▬ The Ottomans were Muslim Turks who warred with neighboring Muslim kingdoms and European Christians.

▬ After conquering the Byzantine Empire, the Ottomans gained power and wealth by controlling important trade routes.

▬ Under their rule, Islam spread into Eastern Europe, although the Ottomans allowed their non-Muslim subjects to practice other religions.

A This illustration from an old text shows a European army battling Ottoman invaders. Europeans feared that the invaders would conquer all of Europe and put an end to Christianity.

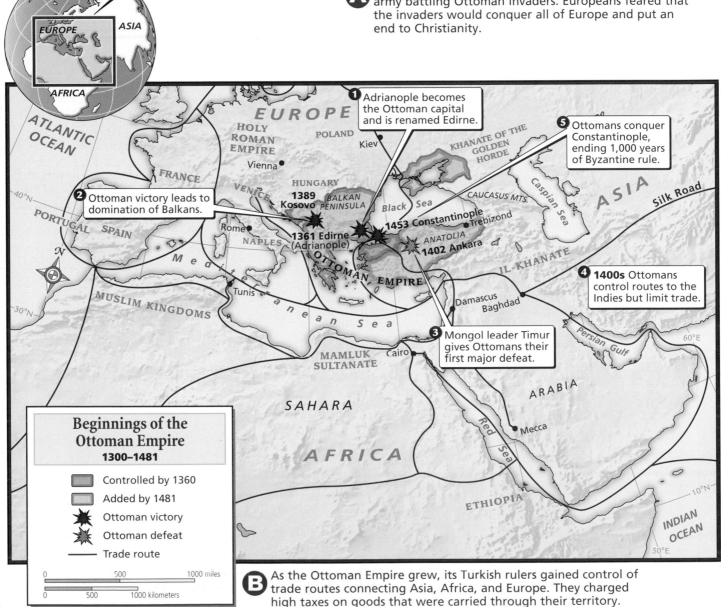

Area shown in maps B and D

1 Adrianople becomes the Ottoman capital and is renamed Edirne.

5 Ottomans conquer Constantinople, ending 1,000 years of Byzantine rule.

2 Ottoman victory leads to domination of Balkans.

4 1400s Ottomans control routes to the Indies but limit trade.

3 Mongol leader Timur gives Ottomans their first major defeat.

1389 Kosovo
1361 Edirne (Adrianople)
1453 Constantinople
1402 Ankara

ATLANTIC OCEAN · EUROPE · HOLY ROMAN EMPIRE · POLAND · Kiev · KHANATE OF THE GOLDEN HORDE · ASIA · Silk Road · Vienna · HUNGARY · BALKAN PENINSULA · Black Sea · CAUCASUS MTS. · Caspian Sea · FRANCE · VENICE · PORTUGAL · SPAIN · Rome · NAPLES · OTTOMAN EMPIRE · ANATOLIA · Trebizond · IL-KHANATE · Mediterranean Sea · Tunis · MUSLIM KINGDOMS · Damascus · Baghdad · Persian Gulf · MAMLUK SULTANATE · Cairo · ARABIA · SAHARA · Red Sea · Mecca · AFRICA · ETHIOPIA · INDIAN OCEAN

Beginnings of the Ottoman Empire
1300–1481

▨ Controlled by 1360
▨ Added by 1481
✸ Ottoman victory
✶ Ottoman defeat
— Trade route

0 ___ 500 ___ 1000 miles
0 ___ 500 ___ 1000 kilometers

B As the Ottoman Empire grew, its Turkish rulers gained control of trade routes connecting Asia, Africa, and Europe. They charged high taxes on goods that were carried through their territory.

Who were the Ottomans?

Groups of Turkish nomads migrated from Central Asia to Anatolia. In 1300 one of these groups began to expand its territory and build an empire. Its leader was named **Osman**, and his followers and successors came to be known as **Ottomans**.

C The Suleimaniye Mosque was built to honor the great Ottoman ruler Suleiman the Magnificent. Today it is one of the largest mosques in Istanbul, the modern name for Constantinople.

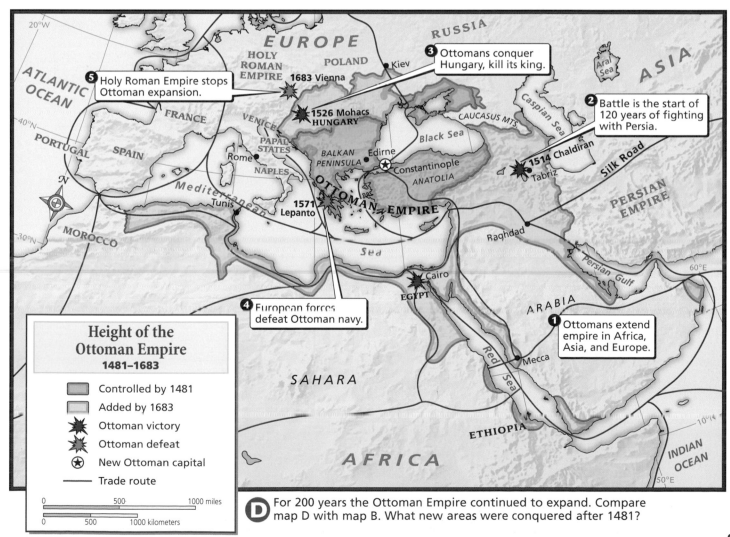

3 Ottomans conquer Hungary, kill its king.

5 Holy Roman Empire stops Ottoman expansion.

2 Battle is the start of 120 years of fighting with Persia.

4 European forces defeat Ottoman navy.

1 Ottomans extend empire in Africa, Asia, and Europe.

Height of the Ottoman Empire
1481–1683

- Controlled by 1481
- Added by 1683
- Ottoman victory
- Ottoman defeat
- New Ottoman capital
- Trade route

D For 200 years the Ottoman Empire continued to expand. Compare map D with map B. What new areas were conquered after 1481?

The Dawn of Worldwide Trade

As Europeans formed colonies overseas, most of the world became linked through trade. Europe became the center of this trade network.

- Based on the voyages of early explorers, Europeans claimed land in Asia, Africa, and the Americas.

- These regions were sources of valuable trade goods. European countries competed for access to these goods.

- As European trade expanded, more and more goods were exchanged among different regions of the world. A world economy began to form.

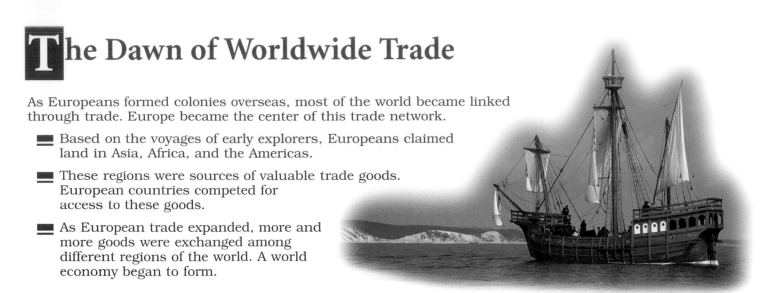

A New ships like the caravel shown here were faster and safer. By the 1500s more goods were being moved by sea than by land.

B Europeans traded in such goods as coffee and silk, and also in slaves. Ports near the sources of trade often were controlled by the major European trading powers.

❶ 1770 Four European powers have trade empires throughout the world.

❷ Spain and Britain claim most of North America.

❸ Spain and Portugal claim most of South America.

Hudson Bay
British North America
Quebec
Boston
Thirteen Colonies
NORTH AMERICA
New Spain
Havana
WEST INDIES
ATLANTIC OCEAN
Acapulco
PACIFIC OCEAN
New Granada
SOUTH AMERICA
Peru
Callao
Brazil
Bahia
Rio de La Plata
Buenos Aires
PACIFIC OCEAN
EQUATOR
30°N
30°S
0°
180°
120°W
90°W
60°W
30°W
60°W

European Trade Empires
1770

Major Colonial Powers and Possessions

- Spanish
- British
- Portuguese
- Dutch
- Other empires

Major Sources of Trade

- Cotton
- Slaves
- Coffee
- Spices
- Furs
- Sugar
- Gold
- Tea
- Silk
- Tobacco
- Silver

— Trade route
⚓ Major port

European Expansion Overseas 1505–1763

1510
Goa becomes capital of Portuguese colonies in Asia.

1575
Brazil becomes world's largest sugar producer.

1695
Gold is discovered in Brazil.

1763
Britain gains French territory in North America after the French and Indian War.

| 1500 | 1600 | 1700 | 1800 |

1505
First European trade settlements are established in Africa.

1545
World's largest silver deposit is discovered in Peru.

1641
Dutch take control of East Indies trade.

1713
British control rapidly growing slave trade.

C During the 1500s Portuguese traders controlled the Atlantic slave trade as well as European trade with Asia. By the 1700s the British and the Dutch were the leaders in worldwide trade.

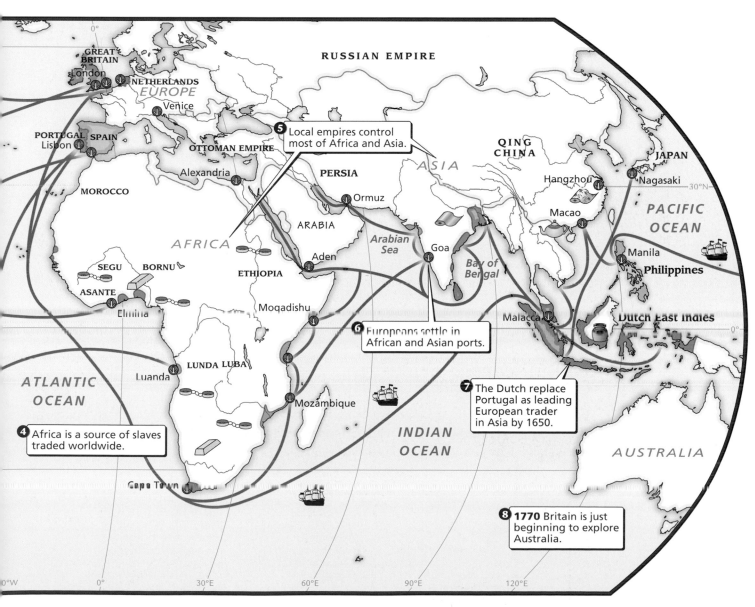

5 Local empires control most of Africa and Asia.

6 Europeans settle in African and Asian ports.

7 The Dutch replace Portugal as leading European trader in Asia by 1650.

4 Africa is a source of slaves traded worldwide.

8 1770 Britain is just beginning to explore Australia.

Industrial Revolution Changes Europe

The Industrial Revolution changed the way goods were produced, and thus changed the way people lived and worked. These changes are known as **industrialization**.

- Machines were developed to produce goods faster and in greater quantities. The fuel that powered the machines was coal.

- Factories were built near coal deposits. Cities near the new industrial areas grew larger and larger.

- The Industrial Revolution began in Great Britain. But industrialization quickly spread to other parts of Europe and to North America.

How did industrialization affect people's lives?

The use of machines to manufacture goods changed where people worked: in factories rather than at home. It also changed where they lived: in cities rather than on farms.

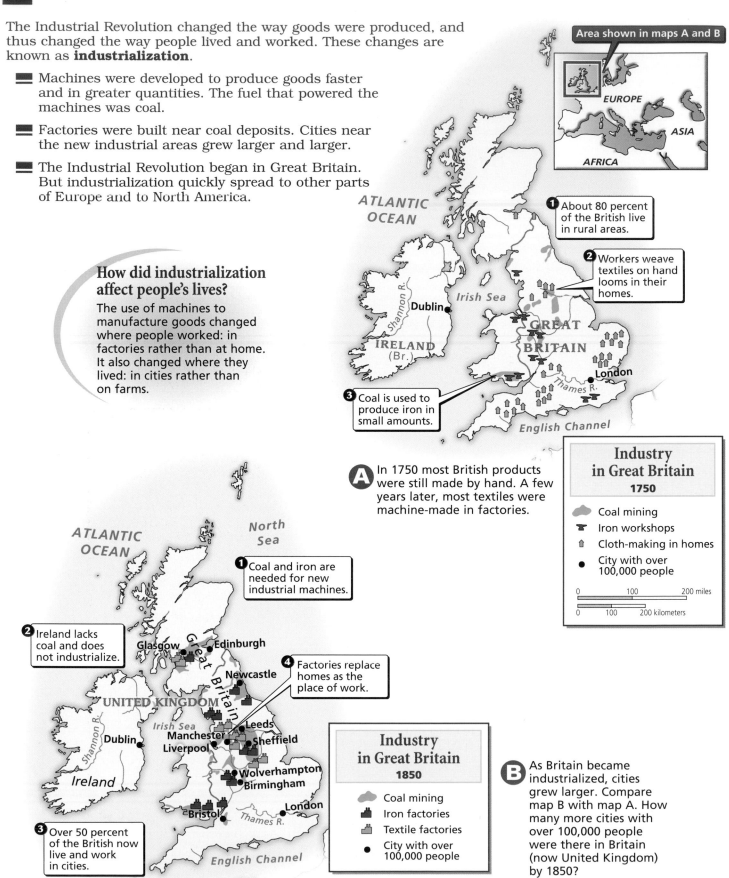

Area shown in maps A and B

EUROPE

ASIA

AFRICA

1 About 80 percent of the British live in rural areas.

2 Workers weave textiles on hand looms in their homes.

3 Coal is used to produce iron in small amounts.

ATLANTIC OCEAN

Irish Sea

Dublin

IRELAND (Br.)

Shannon R.

GREAT BRITAIN

London

Thames R.

English Channel

A In 1750 most British products were still made by hand. A few years later, most textiles were machine-made in factories.

Industry in Great Britain 1750

- Coal mining
- Iron workshops
- Cloth-making in homes
- City with over 100,000 people

0   100   200 miles
0   100   200 kilometers

North Sea

1 Coal and iron are needed for new industrial machines.

2 Ireland lacks coal and does not industrialize.

ATLANTIC OCEAN

Glasgow   Edinburgh

4 Factories replace homes as the place of work.

Great Britain

Newcastle

UNITED KINGDOM

Shannon R.

Irish Sea

Dublin

Manchester   Leeds
Liverpool   Sheffield

Ireland

Wolverhampton
Birmingham

Bristol

London

Thames R.

English Channel

3 Over 50 percent of the British now live and work in cities.

Industry in Great Britain 1850

- Coal mining
- Iron factories
- Textile factories
- City with over 100,000 people

B As Britain became industrialized, cities grew larger. Compare map B with map A. How many more cities with over 100,000 people were there in Britain (now United Kingdom) by 1850?

98

Top 10 Cities, 1800

Rank	City (Modern Country)	Population
1	**Beijing** (China)	1,100,000
2	**London** (United Kingdom)	861,000
3	**Canton** (China)	800,000
4	**Edo** (Japan)	685,000
5	**Constantinople** (Turkey)	570,000
6	**Paris** (France)	547,000
7	**Naples** (Italy)	430,000
8	**Hangzhou** (China)	387,000
9	**Osaka** (Japan)	383,000
10	**Kyoto** (Japan)	377,000

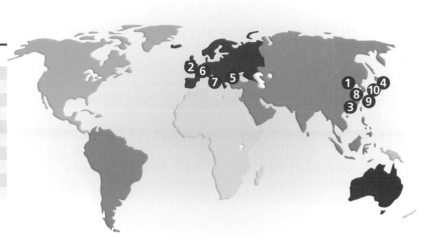

C Between 1700 and 1800, the population of London increased by nearly 60 percent (see page 87). Many parts of the city became overcrowded and had poor living conditions.

Area shown in map D

EUROPE

ASIA

AFRICA

D The Industrial Revolution spread more quickly in some countries than in others. Industrial development depended on having enough natural resources, government support, and money for new factories and technologies.

Industrial Revolution Spreads in Europe
1870

- Coal mining
- Iron factories
- Textile factories
- City with over 100,000 people

0   200   400 miles
0   200   400 kilometers

1800 Belgium is second only to Britain as a coal and iron producer.

Industrialization spreads from the northwest to the north, south, and east.

Mediterranean countries industrialize more slowly.

ATLANTIC OCEAN

NORWAY

SWEDEN

DENMARK

North Sea

Baltic Sea

Glasgow   Edinburgh

UNITED KINGDOM   Leeds

Dublin

Birmingham   Amsterdam   NETH.   Hamburg   Warsaw

London   Berlin   RUSSIA

BELG.   Brussels

Paris   GERMANY   Prague

Rhine R.   Danube R.   Vienna

SWITZ.   AUSTRIA-HUNGARY

FRANCE   Lyon   Milan   Venice

Po R.   OTTOMAN EMPIRE

Marseille   ITALY   Adriatic Sea

PORTUGAL   Madrid   Barcelona   Rome

SPAIN   Naples

Lisbon

Palermo

Mediterranean Sea

60°N   10°W   0°   20°E

50°N

1789
French Revolution begins.

1821
Mexico wins independence from Spain.

1775	1800	1825

1775–1781
American Revolution frees United States from Britain.

1815
Napoleon is defeated at Waterloo.

1819
Bolívar becomes first president of Grand Colombia.

Independence in the Americas

Most colonies in the Americas—British, French, Spanish, and Portuguese—won their independence over a period of just 50 years.

- Colonists throughout the Americas resented European rule. They could not govern themselves. Their businesses were hurt by taxes and trade limits. Their protests were ignored by European governments.

- In 1776 colonists in 13 British colonies rebelled. Their struggle encouraged colonists in other parts of the Americas to fight for independence.

Are we going in circles?

When the king took away some of their rights, Americans declared a **revolution** ("movement in a circle") to restore their rights. They ended up creating a new country. Now "revolution" means a dramatic change.

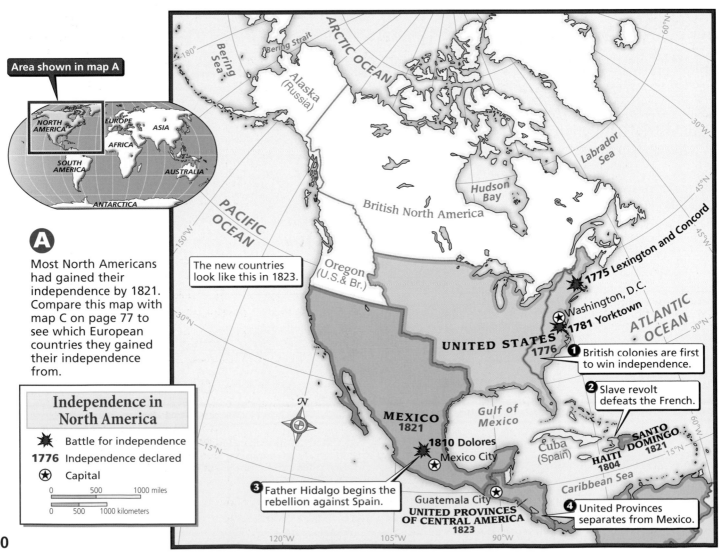

A Most North Americans had gained their independence by 1821. Compare this map with map C on page 77 to see which European countries they gained their independence from.

Area shown in map A

NORTH AMERICA — EUROPE — ASIA — AFRICA — SOUTH AMERICA — AUSTRALIA — ANTARCTICA

The new countries look like this in 1823.

❶ British colonies are first to win independence.

❷ Slave revolt defeats the French.

❸ Father Hidalgo begins the rebellion against Spain.

❹ United Provinces separates from Mexico.

1775 Lexington and Concord
Washington, D.C.
1781 Yorktown
UNITED STATES 1776
1810 Dolores
Mexico City
MEXICO 1821
Guatemala City
UNITED PROVINCES OF CENTRAL AMERICA 1823
Cuba (Spain)
HAITI 1804
SANTO DOMINGO 1821
Caribbean Sea
Gulf of Mexico
Oregon (U.S.& Br.)
British North America
Alaska (Russia)
Hudson Bay
Labrador Sea
ARCTIC OCEAN
PACIFIC OCEAN
ATLANTIC OCEAN
Bering Sea
Bering Strait

Independence in North America

- ✸ Battle for independence
- **1776** Independence declared
- ✪ Capital

0   500   1000 miles

0   500   1000 kilometers

1848 Revolutions erupt throughout Europe.	1857 Indian troops mutiny against British commanders.	1867 Japanese emperor regains power from shoguns.		1898 Spanish-American War
		1869 Suez Canal links Red and Mediterranean Seas.	1895 Sino-Japanese War ends.	1900 Boxer Rebellion pits Chinese against foreigners.

1850   **1875**   **1900**   **1925**

1853
Perry's fleet opens the way to U.S.-Japanese trade.

1884–1914
Control of Africa is seized by European powers.

1910
Japan annexes Korea.

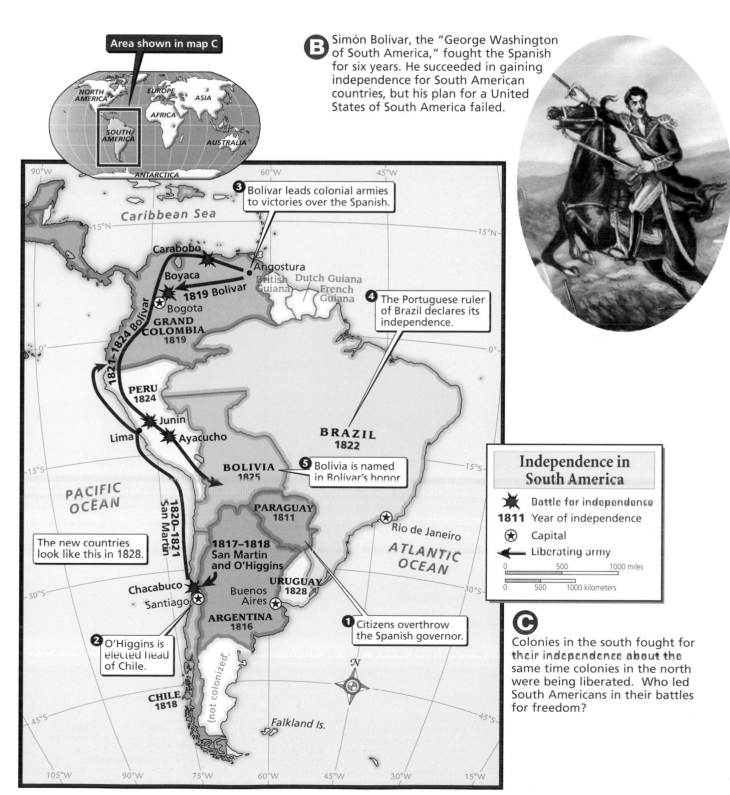

B Simón Bolívar, the "George Washington of South America," fought the Spanish for six years. He succeeded in gaining independence for South American countries, but his plan for a United States of South America failed.

Area shown in map C

3 Bolívar leads colonial armies to victories over the Spanish.

4 The Portuguese ruler of Brazil declares its independence.

5 Bolivia is named in Bolívar's honor

The new countries look like this in 1828.

2 O'Higgins is elected head of Chile.

1 Citizens overthrow the Spanish governor.

Independence in South America

✸	Battle for independence
1811	Year of independence
★	Capital
←	Liberating army

0   500   1000 miles
0   500   1000 kilometers

C

Colonies in the south fought for their independence about the same time colonies in the north were being liberated. Who led South Americans in their battles for freedom?

101

French Revolution

French kings had complete power. By 1789, however, France was bankrupt and the French people wanted a new government.

- The people of Paris revolted and formed a new revolutionary government that took power away from the king.
- The new government promised freedom and equality to all people in France. By 1791 France was a republic.
- King Louis XVI plotted to overthrow the government. Instead, the government overthrew the king, tried him for treason, and had him beheaded.

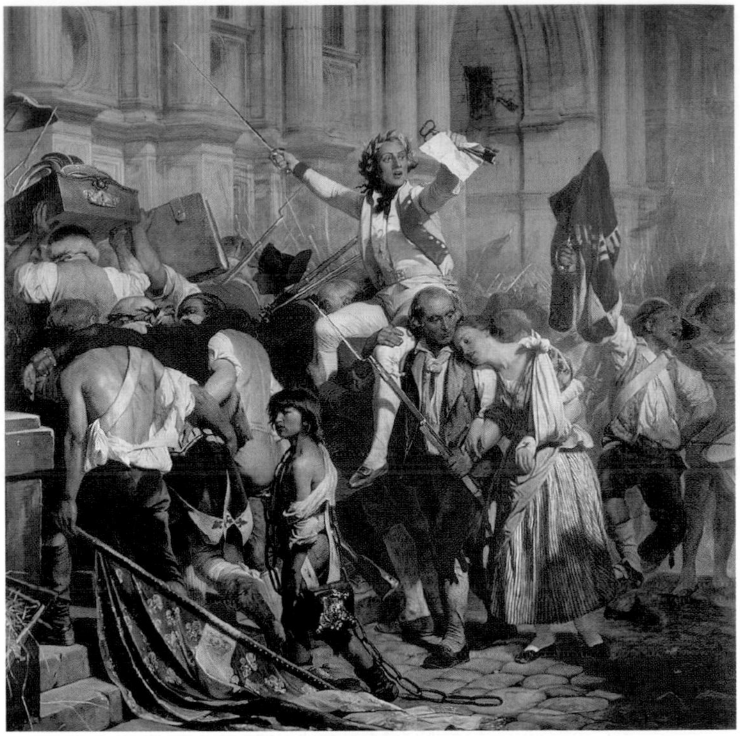

A The people of Paris were determined to protect their new government. Mobs seized weapons to prevent royal troops from arresting the revolutionaries.

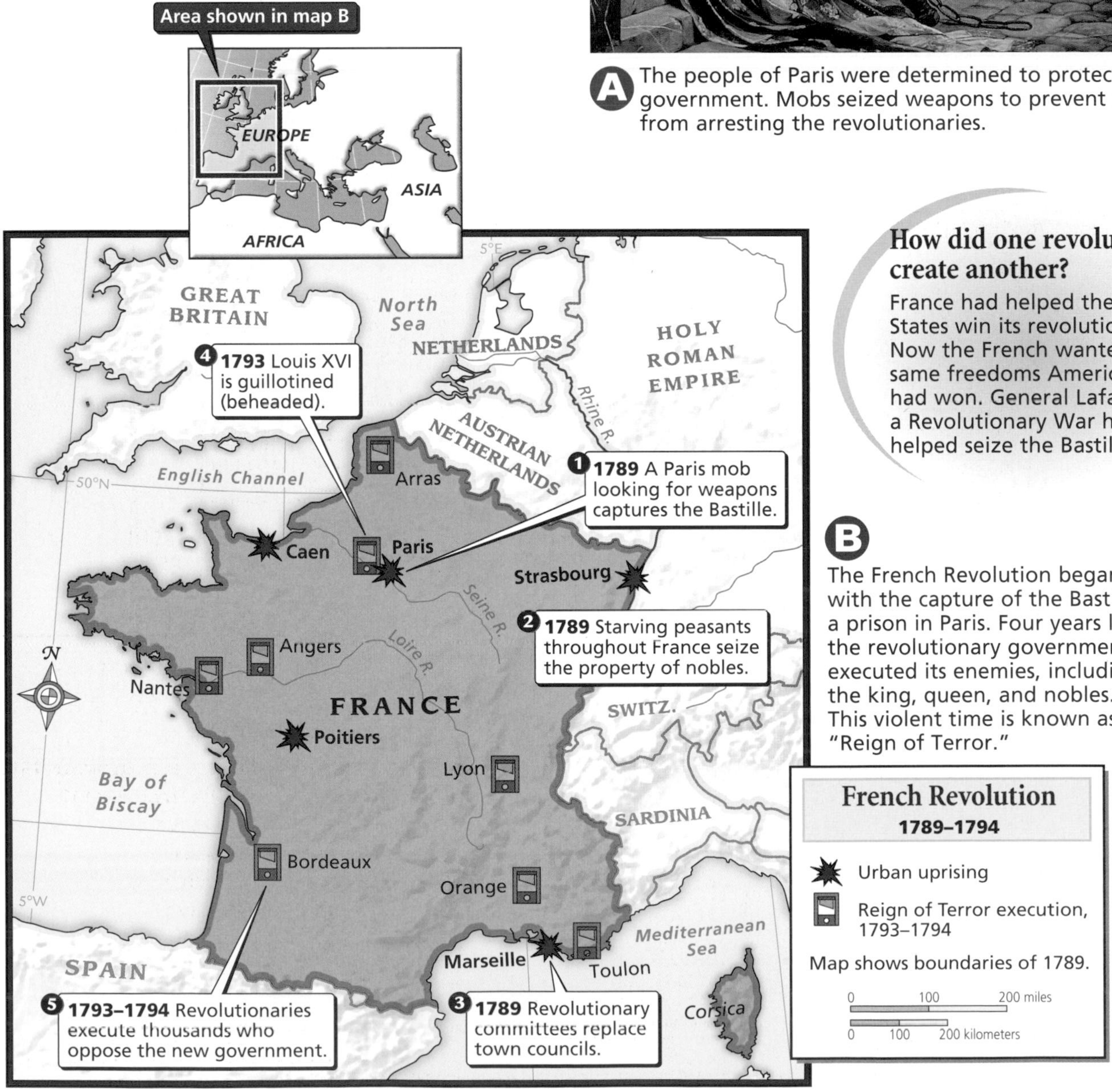

Area shown in map B
EUROPE
ASIA
AFRICA
GREAT BRITAIN
North Sea
NETHERLANDS
HOLY ROMAN EMPIRE
Rhine R.
AUSTRIAN NETHERLANDS
English Channel
50°N
5°E
5°W
Arras
Caen
Paris
Strasbourg
Seine R.
Loire R.
Angers
Nantes
FRANCE
SWITZ.
Poitiers
Lyon
Bay of Biscay
SARDINIA
Bordeaux
Orange
Marseille
Toulon
Mediterranean Sea
Corsica
SPAIN
1 1789 A Paris mob looking for weapons captures the Bastille.
2 1789 Starving peasants throughout France seize the property of nobles.
3 1789 Revolutionary committees replace town councils.
4 1793 Louis XVI is guillotined (beheaded).
5 1793–1794 Revolutionaries execute thousands who oppose the new government.
N
French Revolution 1789–1794
Urban uprising
Reign of Terror execution, 1793–1794
Map shows boundaries of 1789.
0 100 200 miles
0 100 200 kilometers

How did one revolution create another?

France had helped the United States win its revolution. Now the French wanted the same freedoms Americans had won. General Lafayette, a Revolutionary War hero, helped seize the Bastille.

B The French Revolution began with the capture of the Bastille, a prison in Paris. Four years later the revolutionary government executed its enemies, including the king, queen, and nobles. This violent time is known as the "Reign of Terror."

Empire of Napoleon

Napoleon Bonaparte was a young, popular, and very successful general during the French Revolution.

- In 1799 Napoleon seized power from the French government. Five years later, he crowned himself emperor.

- Napoleon expanded the French Empire with conquests across Europe. He placed his relatives and friends on thrones in Italy, Spain, Holland, Germany, and Poland.

- After terrible losses in Russia and again at Waterloo, Napoleon's enemies removed him from power and sent him into exile.

C Napoleon invaded Russia with 600,000 men. They reached Moscow, but winter forced them to retreat. Disease, cold, hunger, and Russian attacks nearly destroyed Napoleon's army.

D Napoleon defeated most of the major nations of Europe, forcing them to become his allies. Only Britain and Russia never surrendered to him. Compare the size of France in 1799 when Napoleon took power with the areas under French control by 1812.

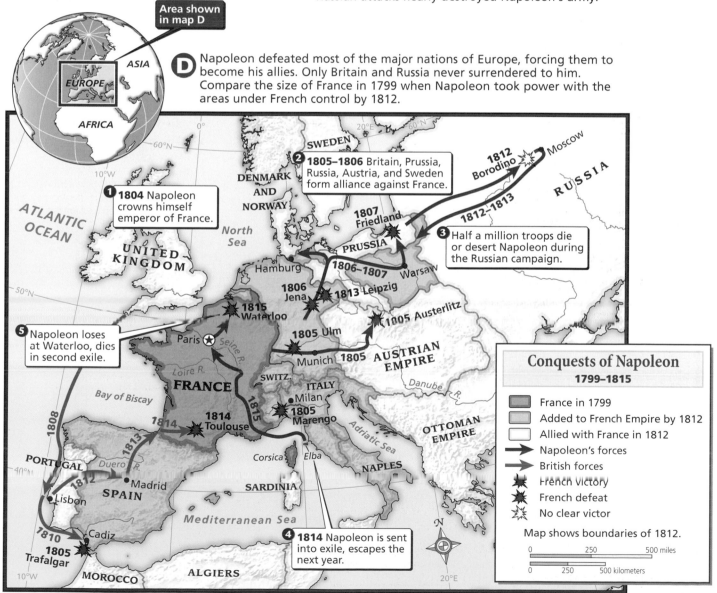

Area shown in map D

1 **1804** Napoleon crowns himself emperor of France.

2 **1805–1806** Britain, Prussia, Russia, Austria, and Sweden form alliance against France.

1812 Borodino — Moscow

1812–1813

3 Half a million troops die or desert Napoleon during the Russian campaign.

1807 Friedland

1806–1807 Warsaw

1806 Jena

1813 Leipzig

1815 Waterloo

1805 Austerlitz

1805 Ulm

Munich **1805**

5 Napoleon loses at Waterloo, dies in second exile.

1814 Toulouse

1805 Marengo

Milan

1814

1813

1812

Madrid

1810

1805 Trafalgar

Lisbon

Cadiz

4 **1814** Napoleon is sent into exile, escapes the next year.

ATLANTIC OCEAN · UNITED KINGDOM · North Sea · SWEDEN · DENMARK AND NORWAY · PRUSSIA · RUSSIA · Hamburg · Paris · Seine R. · Loire R. · FRANCE · SWITZ. · ITALY · AUSTRIAN EMPIRE · Danube R. · Adriatic Sea · OTTOMAN EMPIRE · Bay of Biscay · PORTUGAL · Duero R. · SPAIN · Corsica · Elba · NAPLES · SARDINIA · Mediterranean Sea · MOROCCO · ALGIERS

ASIA · EUROPE · AFRICA

Conquests of Napoleon
1799–1815

- France in 1799
- Added to French Empire by 1812
- Allied with France in 1812
- → Napoleon's forces
- → British forces
- French victory
- French defeat
- No clear victor

Map shows boundaries of 1812.

0 250 500 miles
0 250 500 kilometers

New Boundaries in Europe

After the fall of Napoleon, kings tried to return Europe to its condition before the French Revolution.

- In 1815 many kings and princes of Europe met at the Congress of Vienna. They returned power to kings who had been removed by Napoleon.

- In 1848 uprisings erupted across Europe. Many people were unhappy with their rulers and governments.

- By 1878 the map of Europe had changed again. New countries and boundaries were created.

B The Red Shirts were a revolutionary group that wanted to unite all Italian-speaking people. Here the Red Shirts battle to free the Kingdom of the Two Sicilies from its French ruler and unite it with the rest of Italy.

Whose country is this?

The Austrian Empire ruled Hungarians, Italians, Czechs, and others. Supporters of **nationalism** argued that their own groups should have their own countries.

A At the Congress of Vienna, the boundaries of Europe were redrawn. Compare this map with map D on the previous page. Notice that Prussia and the Austrian Empire grew in size.

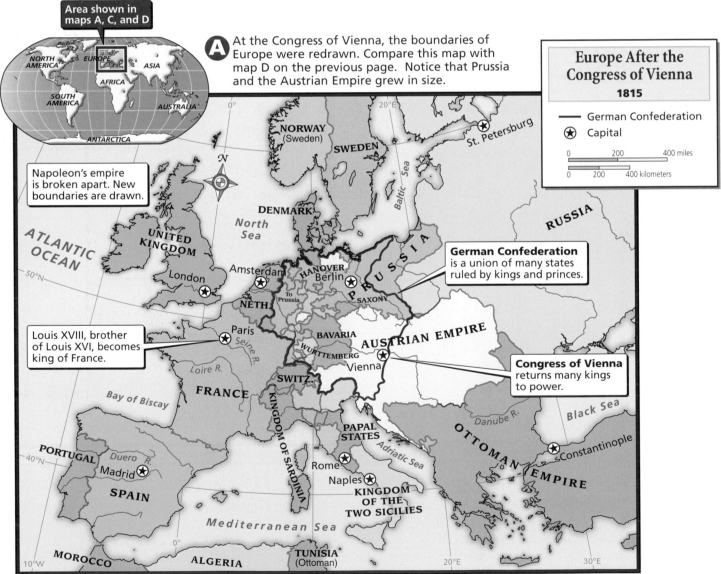

Area shown in maps A, C, and D

Europe After the Congress of Vienna

1815

— German Confederation
⊛ Capital

0   200   400 miles
0   200   400 kilometers

Napoleon's empire is broken apart. New boundaries are drawn.

German Confederation is a union of many states ruled by kings and princes.

Louis XVIII, brother of Louis XVI, becomes king of France.

Congress of Vienna returns many kings to power.

NORWAY (Sweden)
SWEDEN
St. Petersburg
RUSSIA
DENMARK
North Sea
Baltic Sea
ATLANTIC OCEAN
UNITED KINGDOM
London
Amsterdam
HANOVER
Berlin
PRUSSIA
SAXONY
NETH.
To Prussia
Paris
Seine R.
BAVARIA
AUSTRIAN EMPIRE
WÜRTTEMBERG
Vienna
Loire R.
SWITZ.
Bay of Biscay
FRANCE
Danube R.
Black Sea
PORTUGAL
Duero R.
Madrid
SPAIN
KINGDOM OF SARDINIA
PAPAL STATES
Rome
Adriatic Sea
OTTOMAN EMPIRE
Constantinople
Naples
KINGDOM OF THE TWO SICILIES
Mediterranean Sea
MOROCCO
ALGERIA
TUNISIA (Ottoman)

50°N
40°N
10°W
0°
20°E
30°E

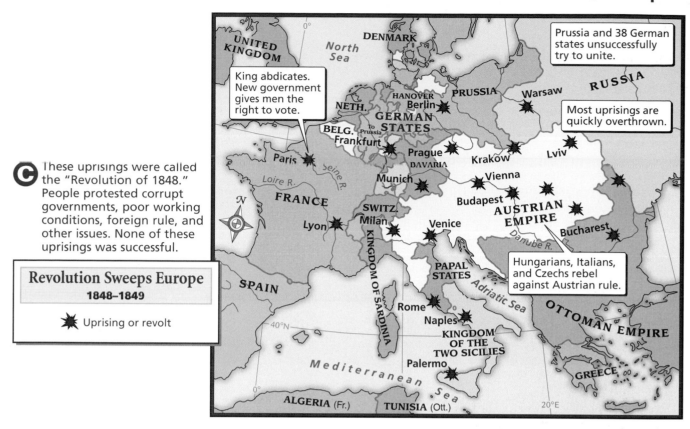

C These uprisings were called the "Revolution of 1848." People protested corrupt governments, poor working conditions, foreign rule, and other issues. None of these uprisings was successful.

Revolution Sweeps Europe
1848–1849

✹ Uprising or revolt

Prussia and 38 German states unsuccessfully try to unite.

King abdicates. New government gives men the right to vote.

Most uprisings are quickly overthrown.

Hungarians, Italians, and Czechs rebel against Austrian rule.

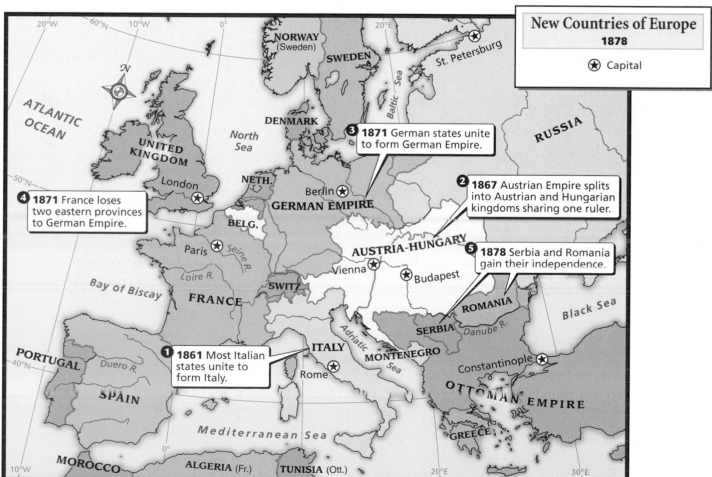

New Countries of Europe
1878

⍟ Capital

4 **1871** France loses two eastern provinces to German Empire.

3 **1871** German states unite to form German Empire.

2 **1867** Austrian Empire splits into Austrian and Hungarian kingdoms sharing one ruler.

5 **1878** Serbia and Romania gain their independence.

1 **1861** Most Italian states unite to form Italy.

D In some places nationalism united countries, while in other places it divided them. Compare this map with map A. Notice that by 1878 Italy was united; so was the German Empire. Also notice that a few countries had gained their independence from the Ottoman Empire.

Imperialism in East Asia and the Pacific

For centuries European imperialists had claimed land in Asia and the Pacific for the purpose of controlling trade.

■ Asian products such as tea, porcelain, and silk were very popular and valuable in Europe and the Americas.

■ Most of Japan's and China's ports, however, were closed to European ships and goods. By 1860 American and British troops had forced them to open.

■ Rebel lords overthrew Japan's ruling shogun for not protecting the country from foreigners.

B Commodore Matthew Perry of the United States (center) threatened to attack Edo, the capital of Japan, unless government officials agreed to meet with him. Perry forced them to sign a treaty opening Japan to trade with the United States.

A European countries controlled vast territories from northern Asia to the South Pacific. Which countries in eastern Asia were not under European control?

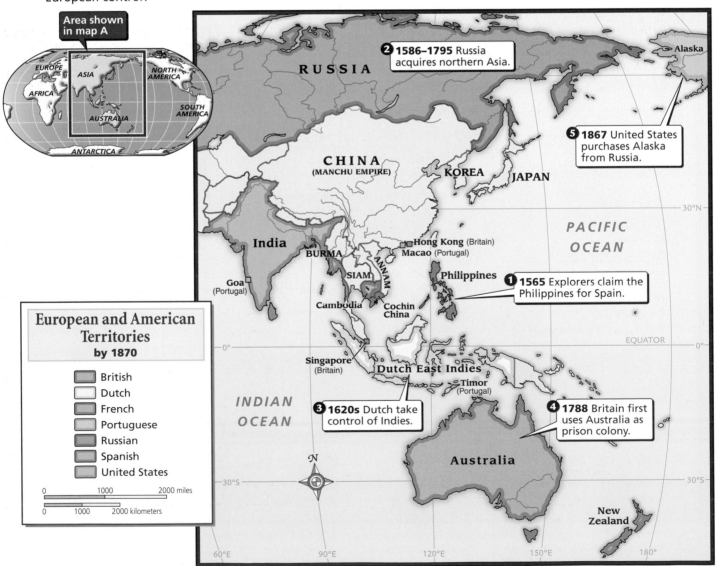

Area shown in map A

2 1586–1795 Russia acquires northern Asia.

5 1867 United States purchases Alaska from Russia.

1 1565 Explorers claim the Philippines for Spain.

3 1620s Dutch take control of Indies.

4 1788 Britain first uses Australia as prison colony.

European and American Territories by 1870

- British
- Dutch
- French
- Portuguese
- Russian
- Spanish
- United States

0   1000   2000 miles
0   1000   2000 kilometers

RUSSIA

Alaska

CHINA
(MANCHU EMPIRE)

KOREA   JAPAN

PACIFIC OCEAN

India

BURMA

Goa (Portugal)

SIAM   ANNAM

Hong Kong (Britain)
Macao (Portugal)

Philippines

Cambodia   Cochin China

Singapore (Britain)

Dutch East Indies

Timor (Portugal)

INDIAN OCEAN

EQUATOR

Australia

New Zealand

30°N

30°S

30°S

60°E   90°E   120°E   150°E   180°

EUROPE   ASIA   NORTH AMERICA
AFRICA   SOUTH AMERICA
AUSTRALIA
ANTARCTICA

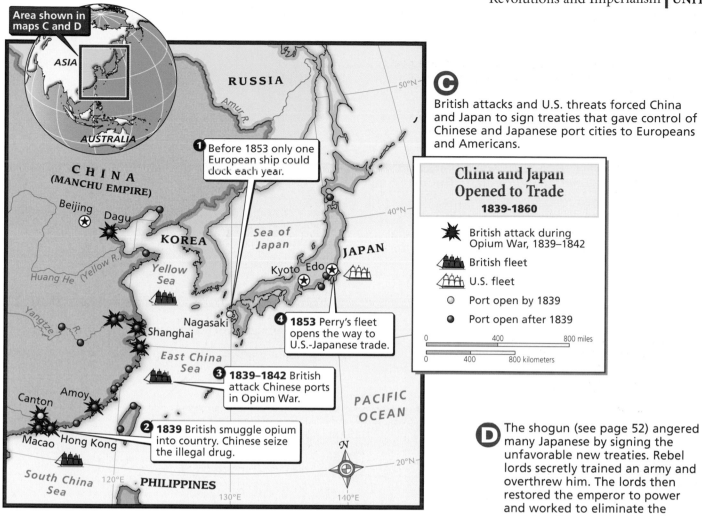

Area shown in maps C and D

ASIA

AUSTRALIA

RUSSIA

CHINA
(MANCHU EMPIRE)

Beijing
Dagu
KOREA
Sea of Japan
JAPAN
Huang He (Yellow R.)
Yellow Sea
Kyoto Edo
Yangtze R.
Nagasaki
Shanghai
East China Sea
Canton
Amoy
Macao Hong Kong
South China Sea
PHILIPPINES
PACIFIC OCEAN

❶ Before 1853 only one European ship could dock each year.

❹ 1853 Perry's fleet opens the way to U.S.-Japanese trade.

❸ 1839–1842 British attack Chinese ports in Opium War.

❷ 1839 British smuggle opium into country. Chinese seize the illegal drug.

120°E 130°E 140°E 20°N 40°N 50°N

China and Japan Opened to Trade
1839-1860

✶ British attack during Opium War, 1839–1842

⛵ British fleet

⛵ U.S. fleet

○ Port open by 1839

● Port open after 1839

0   400   800 miles
0   400   800 kilometers

C British attacks and U.S. threats forced China and Japan to sign treaties that gave control of Chinese and Japanese port cities to Europeans and Americans.

D The shogun (see page 52) angered many Japanese by signing the unfavorable new treaties. Rebel lords secretly trained an army and overthrew him. The lords then restored the emperor to power and worked to eliminate the new treaties.

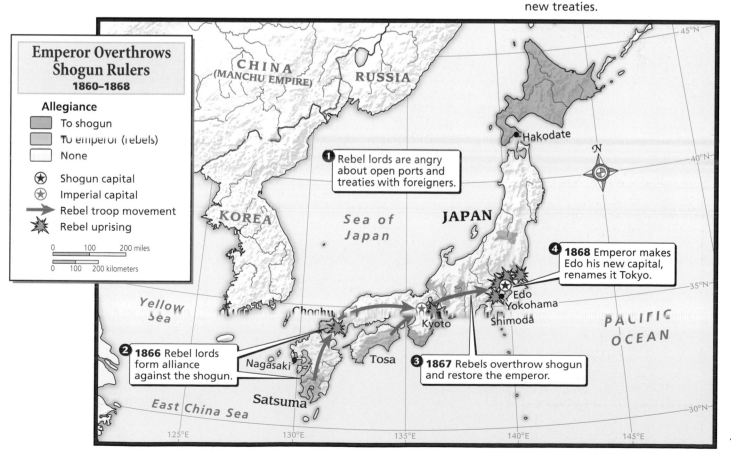

Emperor Overthrows Shogun Rulers
1860-1868

Allegiance

▨ To shogun
▨ To emperor (rebels)
☐ None

✪ Shogun capital
✪ Imperial capital
→ Rebel troop movement
✶ Rebel uprising

0   100   200 miles
0   100   200 kilometers

CHINA
(MANCHU EMPIRE)
RUSSIA
Hakodate
KOREA
Sea of Japan
JAPAN
Choshu
Kyoto
Edo
Yokohama
Shimoda
Nagasaki
Tosa
Satsuma
Yellow Sea
East China Sea
PACIFIC OCEAN

❶ Rebel lords are angry about open ports and treaties with foreigners.

❹ 1868 Emperor makes Edo his new capital, renames it Tokyo.

❷ 1866 Rebel lords form alliance against the shogun.

❸ 1867 Rebels overthrow shogun and restore the emperor.

125°E 130°E 135°E 140°E 145°E 30°N 35°N 40°N 45°N

107

Imperialism Continues

As European countries and the United States expanded their empires in Asia and the Pacific, Asian resistance increased.

- In European and American territories, Asians rebelled against imperialist control.

- The Chinese royal family tried to protect ancient traditions. They supported an uprising, the Boxer Rebellion, to force foreigners out. The revolt failed.

- Japan's emperor decided his country needed to change. Japan developed a western army and an economy. Soon Japan, too, became powerful and imperialistic, and it quickly won two wars.

A Many Chinese resented foreign interference. One group called "Boxers" killed thousands of foreigners, including the German ambassador (shown here).

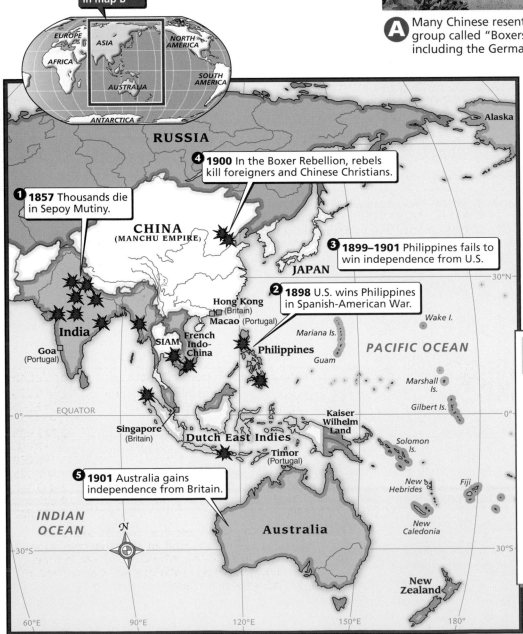

Area shown in map B

① **1857** Thousands die in Sepoy Mutiny.

④ **1900** In the Boxer Rebellion, rebels kill foreigners and Chinese Christians.

③ **1899–1901** Philippines fails to win independence from U.S.

② **1898** U.S. wins Philippines in Spanish-American War.

⑤ **1901** Australia gains independence from Britain.

RUSSIA

Alaska

CHINA (MANCHU EMPIRE)

JAPAN

Hong Kong (Britain)
Macao (Portugal)

India

Goa (Portugal)

SIAM

French Indo-China

Philippines

Guam

Mariana Is.

Wake I.

PACIFIC OCEAN

Marshall Is.

Gilbert Is.

Singapore (Britain)

Dutch East Indies

Timor (Portugal)

Kaiser Wilhelm Land

Solomon Is.

New Hebrides

Fiji

New Caledonia

INDIAN OCEAN

Australia

New Zealand

EQUATOR

B

Asians fought to protect their lands from foreign rule. Indian soldiers hired by the British, called "Sepoys," rebelled against British rule in 1857. Like most other Asians who rebelled, the Sepoys were defeated.

Resisting Imperialism
1857–1901

Territories and Colonies

- British
- Dutch
- French
- German
- Portuguese
- Russian
- United States
- ✳ Rebellion

Map shows boundaries of 1900.

0   1000   2000 miles
0   1000   2000 kilometers

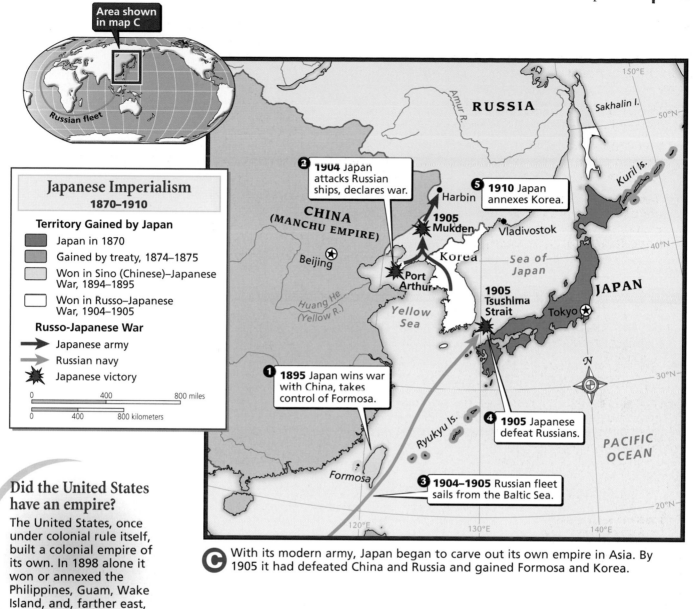

Area shown in map C

Russian fleet

Japanese Imperialism
1870–1910

Territory Gained by Japan

- Japan in 1870
- Gained by treaty, 1874–1875
- Won in Sino (Chinese)–Japanese War, 1894–1895
- Won in Russo–Japanese War, 1904–1905

Russo-Japanese War

- → Japanese army
- → Russian navy
- ✸ Japanese victory

0   400   800 miles
0   400   800 kilometers

RUSSIA

Sakhalin I.

Amur R.

Kuril Is.

② **1904** Japan attacks Russian ships, declares war.

⑤ **1910** Japan annexes Korea.

Harbin

CHINA (MANCHU EMPIRE)

1905 Mukden ✸

Vladivostok

Beijing ✪

Korea

Sea of Japan

JAPAN

Huang He (Yellow R.)

✸ Port Arthur

Yellow Sea

1905 Tsushima Strait ✸

Tokyo ✪

① **1895** Japan wins war with China, takes control of Formosa.

④ **1905** Japanese defeat Russians.

Ryukyu Is.

PACIFIC OCEAN

Formosa

③ **1904–1905** Russian fleet sails from the Baltic Sea.

C With its modern army, Japan began to carve out its own empire in Asia. By 1905 it had defeated China and Russia and gained Formosa and Korea.

Did the United States have an empire?

The United States, once under colonial rule itself, built a colonial empire of its own. In 1898 alone it won or annexed the Philippines, Guam, Wake Island, and, farther east, Hawaii and Puerto Rico.

Top 10 Cities, 1900

Rank	City (Modern Country)	Population
1	London (United Kingdom)	6,480,000
2	New York (United States)	4,242,000
3	Paris (France)	3,330,000
4	Berlin (Germany)	2,707,000
5	Chicago (United States)	1,717,000
6	Vienna (Austria)	1,698,000
7	Tokyo (Japan)	1,497,000
8	St. Petersburg (Russia)	1,439,000
9	Manchester (United Kingdom)	1,435,000
10	Philadelphia (United States)	1,418,000

D In 1900, the largest cities were in countries that had experienced an industrial revolution (see pages 98–99). Where were most of these countries located? Which Asian country had an industrial revolution?

| 1947 |
| India is independent. |

1945
UN is formed.

1939–1945
World War II

1948
Israel is founded.

| **1910** | **1920** | **1930** | **1940** | **1950** |

1914–1918
World War I

1917
Russian Revolution

1930
Gandhi leads first protests against British in India.

1946–1991
Cold War between East and West

World War I Changes Europe

In 1914 an Austrian archduke was assassinated by a Serbian nationalist. Austria-Hungary declared war on Serbia, and military alliances soon brought most of Europe into the conflict.

▬ The war was fought between the Central Powers and the Allies. The main Central Powers were Germany, Austria-Hungary, and the Ottoman Empire. The Allies included the United Kingdom, France, Russia, Serbia, and later the United States.

▬ New technology, especially machine guns and chemical weapons, made World War I deadlier than previous wars.

▬ The war ended in 1918 with the surrender of Germany. New countries were formed out of the defeated empires.

Where was the front?
A **front** is the long battle zone that forms where two armies meet. The bloodiest fighting in World War I took place on the Western Front. There both sides fought from elaborate defensive trenches.

Area shown in maps A and D

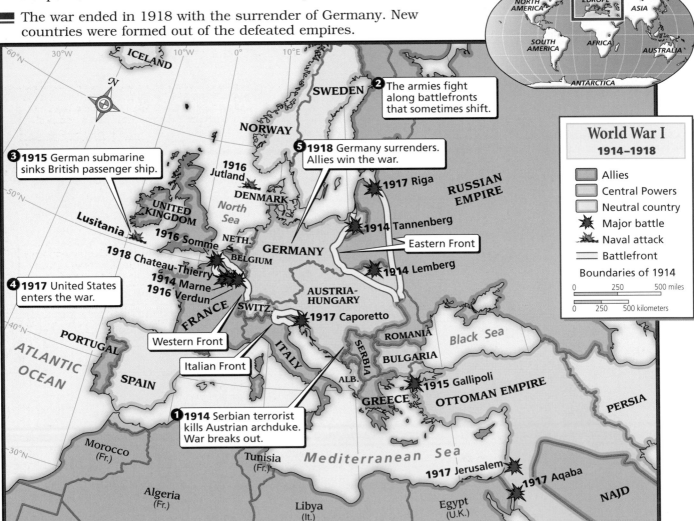

A Fighting along the Western Front, the most important battleground, was deadlocked. For over three years, the defensive strength of the trenches prevented the armies on both sides from gaining ground.

1960–1980
Independence comes to dozens of former colonies.

1980
Solidarity Union begins challenging communist rule in Poland.

1991
Soviet Union collapses, 15 new countries are formed.

2001
Terrorists attack World Trade Center and Pentagon.

1960 **1970** **1980** **1990** **2000**

1961
Berlin Wall is built.

1965–1973
Vietnam War involves U.S. forces

1975
Vietnam War ends.

1979
Iranian Revolution

1991
Persian Gulf War

2003
War in Iraq

B Both sides used poison gases that burned eyes, skin, and lungs, and killed thousands of troops. After the war, most countries agreed to ban chemical warfare.

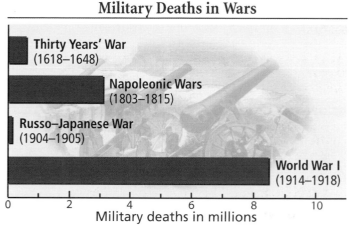

Military Deaths in Wars

Thirty Years' War
(1618–1648)

Napoleonic Wars
(1803–1815)

Russo–Japanese War
(1904–1905)

World War I
(1914–1918)

0   2   4   6   8   10
Military deaths in millions

C Fighting in World War I was so deadly that people hoped it was "the war to end all wars."

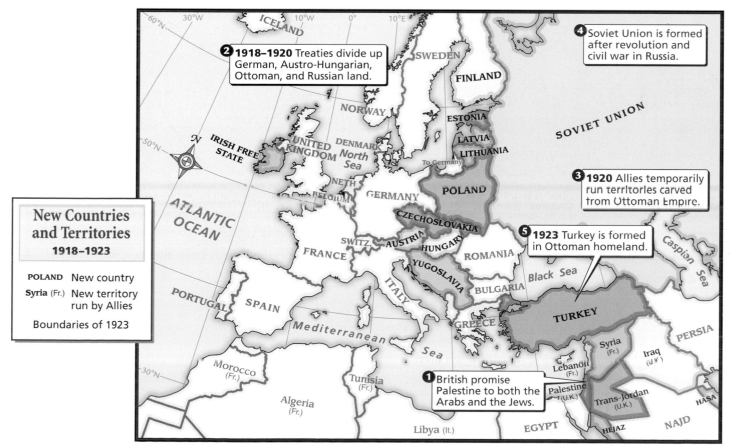

2 **1918–1920** Treaties divide up German, Austro-Hungarian, Ottoman, and Russian land.

4 Soviet Union is formed after revolution and civil war in Russia.

3 **1920** Allies temporarily run territories carved from Ottoman Empire.

5 **1923** Turkey is formed in Ottoman homeland.

1 British promise Palestine to both the Arabs and the Jews.

New Countries and Territories
1918–1923

POLAND New country

Syria (Fr.) New territory run by Allies

Boundaries of 1923

D After the war, boundaries were changed and new countries were carved from the defeated Central Powers—and also from Russia, which had been one of the Allies. Compare the countries on this map with the countries on map A.

111

Rise of Communism

In the early 1900s, the people of Russia and China were unhappy with their rulers and governments. Some were attracted to communism as a way of achieving radical changes in their countries.

- In 1917 angry Russian soldiers, workers, and peasants overthrew the czar. Civil war followed.

- The communists won the war and remade Russia as the Soviet Union.

- After the Chinese emperor lost power in 1912, China collapsed into chaos and civil war. The Chinese communists finally gained control in 1949.

- Afterward the victorious communists in both countries murdered millions of their enemies.

A Lenin was the leader of the Bolshevik (or Communist) Party. His army and secret police crushed all opponents in Russia.

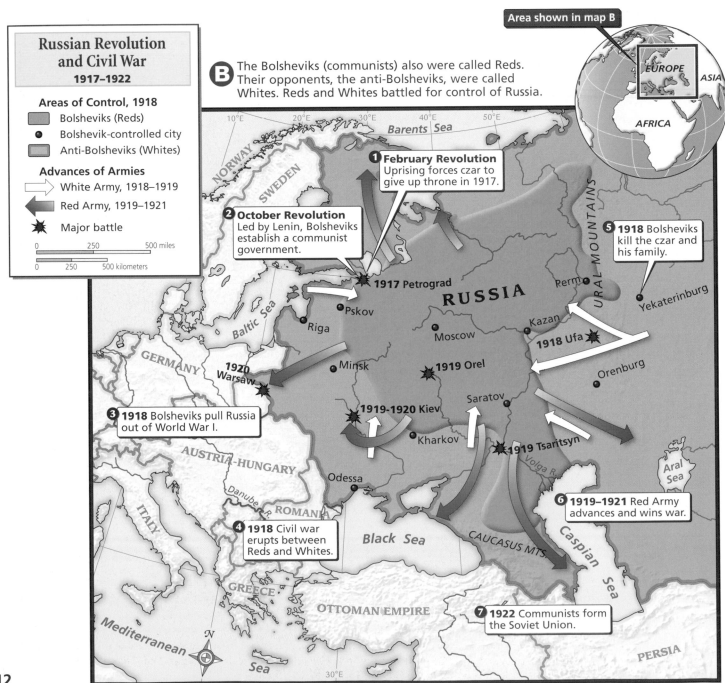

B The Bolsheviks (communists) also were called Reds. Their opponents, the anti-Bolsheviks, were called Whites. Reds and Whites battled for control of Russia.

Area shown in map B

Russian Revolution and Civil War
1917–1922

Areas of Control, 1918
- Bolsheviks (Reds)
- Bolshevik-controlled city
- Anti-Bolsheviks (Whites)

Advances of Armies
- White Army, 1918–1919
- Red Army, 1919–1921
- ✹ Major battle

0   250   500 miles
0   250   500 kilometers

1 **February Revolution** Uprising forces czar to give up throne in 1917.

2 **October Revolution** Led by Lenin, Bolsheviks establish a communist government.

5 **1918** Bolsheviks kill the czar and his family.

3 **1918** Bolsheviks pull Russia out of World War I.

4 **1918** Civil war erupts between Reds and Whites.

6 **1919–1921** Red Army advances and wins war.

7 **1922** Communists form the Soviet Union.

1917 Petrograd
Pskov
Riga
Minsk
Moscow
Kazan
Perm
Yekaterinburg
1918 Ufa
Orenburg
1920 Warsaw
1919 Orel
Saratov
1919-1920 Kiev
Kharkov
1919 Tsaritsyn
Odessa

RUSSIA
URAL MOUNTAINS
NORWAY
SWEDEN
GERMANY
AUSTRIA-HUNGARY
ITALY
ROMANIA
GREECE
OTTOMAN EMPIRE
PERSIA

Barents Sea
Baltic Sea
Black Sea
Mediterranean Sea
Aral Sea
Caspian Sea
CAUCASUS MTS.
Volga R.
Danube R.

EUROPE
ASIA
AFRICA

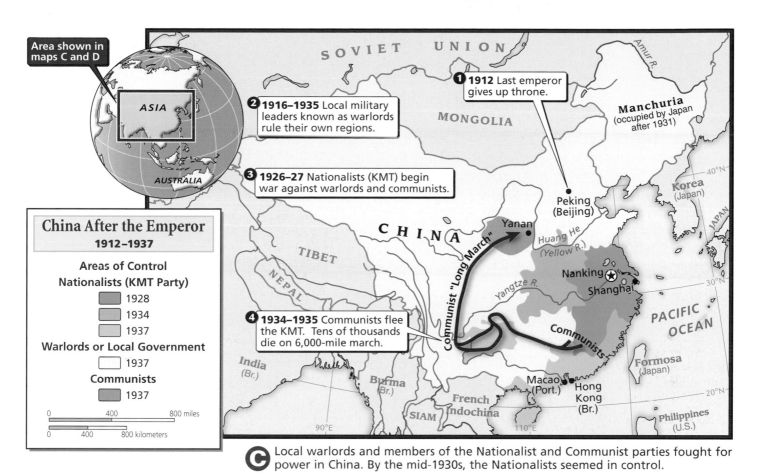

Area shown in maps C and D

ASIA

AUSTRALIA

1 **1912** Last emperor gives up throne.

2 **1916–1935** Local military leaders known as warlords rule their own regions.

3 **1926–27** Nationalists (KMT) begin war against warlords and communists.

4 **1934–1935** Communists flee the KMT. Tens of thousands die on 6,000-mile march.

China After the Emperor
1912–1937

Areas of Control
Nationalists (KMT Party)

    1928
    1934
    1937

Warlords or Local Government

    1937

Communists

    1937

0   400   800 miles
0   400   800 kilometers

SOVIET UNION

MONGOLIA

Manchuria (occupied by Japan after 1931)

Peking (Beijing)

Korea (Japan)

JAPAN

40°N

CHINA

TIBET

NEPAL

Yanan

Huang He (Yellow R.)

Communist "Long March"

Nanking

Shanghai

PACIFIC OCEAN

30°N

Yangtze R.

Communists

Formosa (Japan)

India (Br.)

Burma (Br.)

SIAM

French Indochina

Macao (Port.)

Hong Kong (Br.)

Philippines (U.S.)

20°N

90°E   110°E

C Local warlords and members of the Nationalist and Communist parties fought for power in China. By the mid-1930s, the Nationalists seemed in control.

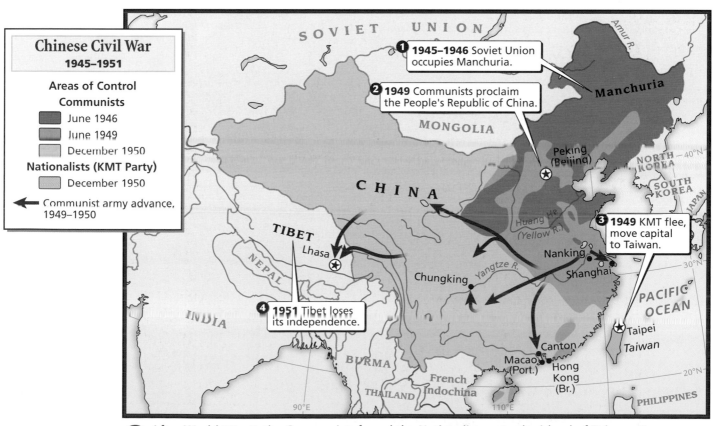

Chinese Civil War
1945–1951

Areas of Control
Communists

    June 1946
    June 1949
    December 1950

Nationalists (KMT Party)

    December 1950

← Communist army advance, 1949–1950

SOVIET UNION

1 **1945–1946** Soviet Union occupies Manchuria.

2 **1949** Communists proclaim the People's Republic of China.

3 **1949** KMT flee, move capital to Taiwan.

4 **1951** Tibet loses its independence.

Amur R.

Manchuria

MONGOLIA

Peking (Beijing)

NORTH KOREA

SOUTH KOREA

JAPAN

40°N

CHINA

TIBET

NEPAL

Lhasa

Huang He (Yellow R.)

Nanking

Shanghai

30°N

INDIA

Chungking

Yangtze R.

PACIFIC OCEAN

Taipei

Taiwan

Canton

Macao (Port.)

Hong Kong (Br.)

BURMA

THAILAND

French Indochina

PHILIPPINES

20°N

90°E   110°E

D After World War II, the Communists forced the Nationalists onto the island of Taiwan. Compare the areas under Communist control by 1937 and by 1950.

113

World War II Engulfs the World

World War II was the most devastating war in history. It was fought between two groups of countries—the Axis and the Allies.

- Before the war, the Axis nations extended their territories by seizing nearby countries. Japan went into China, Italy into Albania, and Germany into Austria. Other nations joined forces as the Allies and tried to stop them.

- Early in the war, the Axis powers defeated every country they attacked. By 1940 only the United Kingdom was left to oppose Germany in Western Europe.

- In 1941 Germany attacked the Soviet Union, and Japan attacked the United States, causing these two powerful nations to join the Allies.

- By the time the Allies had defeated the Axis, Japan and much of Europe were in ruins.

Axis vs. Allies

Axis Powers	Allied Powers
Germany	United Kingdom
Japan	United States
Italy	Soviet Union
	China
	Australia
	Canada
Six other nations were allies of the Axis during the war.	There were 50 Allied nations from around the world.

A The Allies had greater resources than the Axis. The United Kingdom used troops and supplies from its colonies. The United States had vast industrial power.

What was the "final solution"?

The Nazi government of Germany locked up all the Jews and Gypsies they could find. The Nazis considered them inferior and evil: a "problem" to be solved. Their so-called "final solution" was to kill them. Six million Jews and two million Gypsies died in the genocide known as the **Holocaust.**

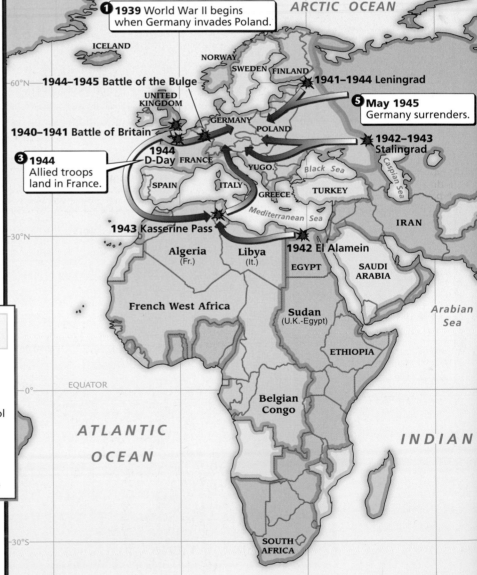

1 1939 World War II begins when Germany invades Poland.

1944–1945 Battle of the Bulge

1940–1941 Battle of Britain

1941–1944 Leningrad

5 May 1945 Germany surrenders.

1942–1943 Stalingrad

3 1944 Allied troops land in France.

1944 D-Day

1943 Kasserine Pass

1942 El Alamein

World War II
1939–1945

- Axis control in 1942
- Allied control in 1942
- Neutral power
- Extent of Japanese control
- ← Allied advance
- Major battle
- Atomic bombing

Map shows boundaries of 1942.

B Unlike the Allies, the Axis was prepared for war and had conquered huge areas by 1942. But the Allies recovered and attacked by land, sea, and air.

Lives Lost in World Wars

Civilian 14%

Military 86%

World War I
10 million dead

Civilian 67%

Military 33%

World War II
51 million dead

C Worldwide, World War II took the lives of more people, mostly civilians, than any other war.

D Winston Churchill, center, inspired the British to continue fighting. During the Battle of Britain, the country withstood nightly German air raids.

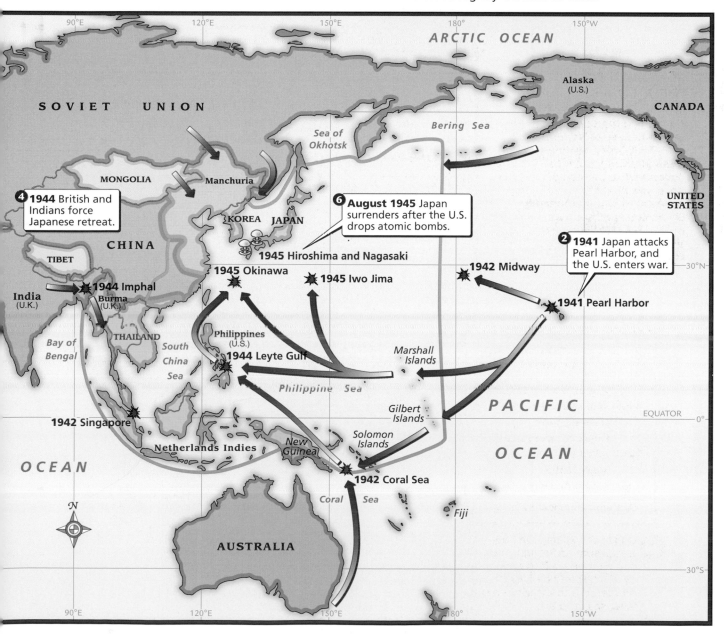

4 **1944** British and Indians force Japanese retreat.

6 **August 1945** Japan surrenders after the U.S. drops atomic bombs.

2 **1941** Japan attacks Pearl Harbor, and the U.S. enters war.

1945 Hiroshima and Nagasaki

1945 Okinawa

1945 Iwo Jima

1942 Midway

1941 Pearl Harbor

1944 Imphal

1944 Leyte Gulf

1942 Singapore

1942 Coral Sea

The Cold War

After World War II, the Communist and anti-Communist nations of the world opposed each other in what came to be called the **Cold War**.

- The two main opponents were the Soviet Union and the United States, the **superpowers** that had been allies in World War II.

- The Cold War was mainly a political and economic struggle, but sometimes it erupted into regional shooting wars.

- The Cold War ended when the Soviet Union broke up in 1991.

A The Berlin Wall was built to prevent people from escaping from communist East Germany to democratic West Germany. The wall became a symbol of the division of Germany, Europe, and the world.

B At first only the United States and the Soviet Union had nuclear weapons. Both countries often tested new bombs above ground until they agreed to ban such tests in 1963.

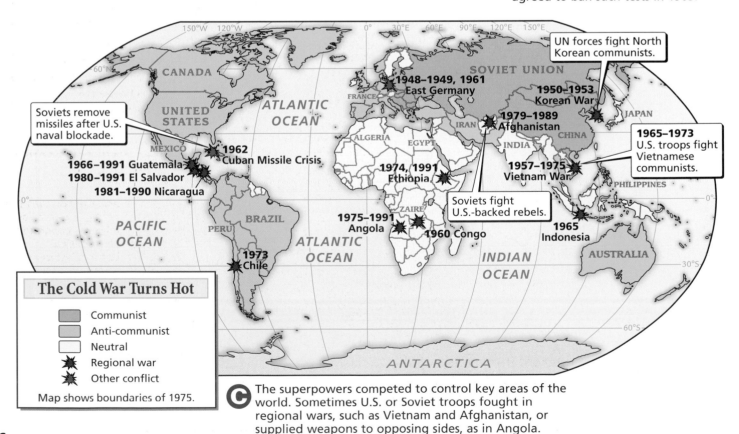

UN forces fight North Korean communists.

1948–1949, 1961 East Germany

1950–1953 Korean War

1979–1989 Afghanistan

Soviets remove missiles after U.S. naval blockade.

1962 Cuban Missile Crisis

1965–1973 U.S. troops fight Vietnamese communists.

1966–1991 Guatemala
1980–1991 El Salvador
1981–1990 Nicaragua

1974, 1991 Ethiopia

1957–1975 Vietnam War

Soviets fight U.S.-backed rebels.

1975–1991 Angola

1960 Congo

1965 Indonesia

1973 Chile

The Cold War Turns Hot

- Communist
- Anti-communist
- Neutral
- ✶ Regional war
- ✶ Other conflict

Map shows boundaries of 1975.

C The superpowers competed to control key areas of the world. Sometimes U.S. or Soviet troops fought in regional wars, such as Vietnam and Afghanistan, or supplied weapons to opposing sides, as in Angola.

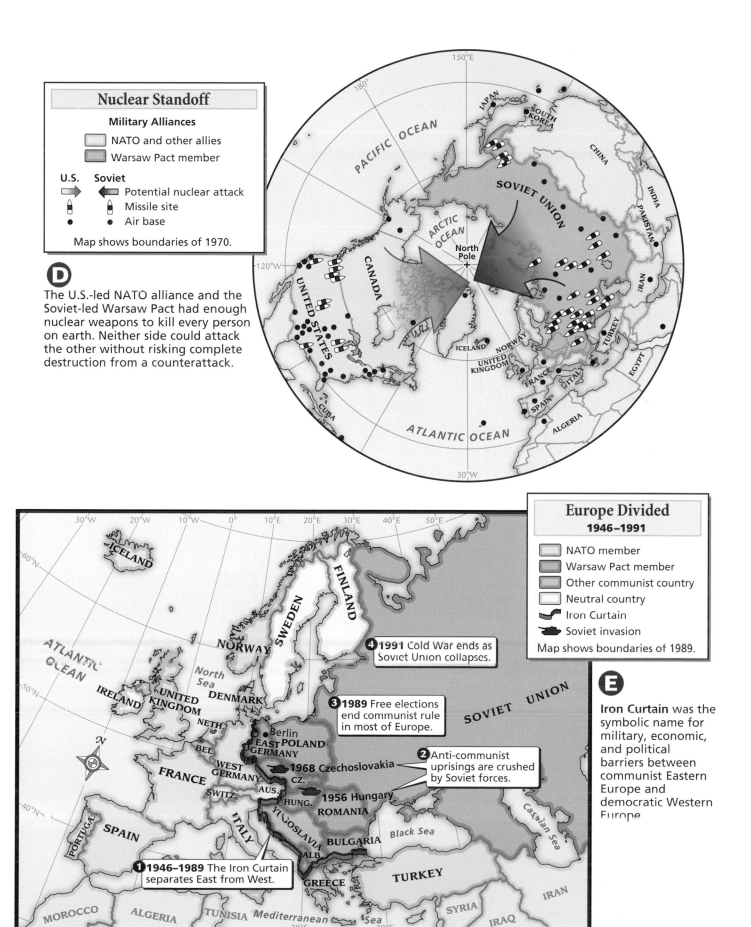

Nuclear Standoff

Military Alliances

NATO and other allies

Warsaw Pact member

U.S.	Soviet	
→	←	Potential nuclear attack
		Missile site
•	•	Air base

Map shows boundaries of 1970.

D The U.S.-led NATO alliance and the Soviet-led Warsaw Pact had enough nuclear weapons to kill every person on earth. Neither side could attack the other without risking complete destruction from a counterattack.

PACIFIC OCEAN
JAPAN
SOUTH KOREA
CHINA
INDIA
PAKISTAN
SOVIET UNION
ARCTIC OCEAN
North Pole
IRAN
TURKEY
CANADA
UNITED STATES
ICELAND
NORWAY
UNITED KINGDOM
FRANCE
ITALY
EGYPT
SPAIN
ALGERIA
CUBA
ATLANTIC OCEAN

Europe Divided
1946–1991

NATO member

Warsaw Pact member

Other communist country

Neutral country

Iron Curtain

Soviet invasion

Map shows boundaries of 1989.

E **Iron Curtain** was the symbolic name for military, economic, and political barriers between communist Eastern Europe and democratic Western Europe.

ICELAND
FINLAND
SWEDEN
NORWAY
ATLANTIC OCEAN
IRELAND
UNITED KINGDOM
North Sea
DENMARK
NETH.
BEL.
Berlin
EAST GERMANY
POLAND
SOVIET UNION
FRANCE
WEST GERMANY
CZ.
AUS.
SWITZ.
HUNG.
YUGOSLAVIA
ROMANIA
PORTUGAL
SPAIN
ITALY
ALB.
BULGARIA
Black Sea
Caspian Sea
GREECE
TURKEY
MOROCCO
ALGERIA
TUNISIA
Mediterranean Sea
SYRIA
IRAQ
IRAN

4 **1991** Cold War ends as Soviet Union collapses.

3 **1989** Free elections end communist rule in most of Europe.

2 Anti-communist uprisings are crushed by Soviet forces.

1968 Czechoslovakia

1956 Hungary

1 **1946–1989** The Iron Curtain separates East from West.

117

Independence Sweeps the World

After World War II, numerous European colonies in Africa and Asia began seeking independence. Most succeeded within the next 35 years. In the 1990s, after the fall of communism, a second wave of independence swept Asia and Europe itself.

- The war weakened the economies of the European colonial powers. They could no longer afford to run their overseas empires.

- The colonies felt they could manage their own resources to improve the lives of their citizens. But independence brought unexpected problems, including poverty and civil war.

A In this picture, Eritreans celebrate their independence from Ethiopia after 30 years of war.

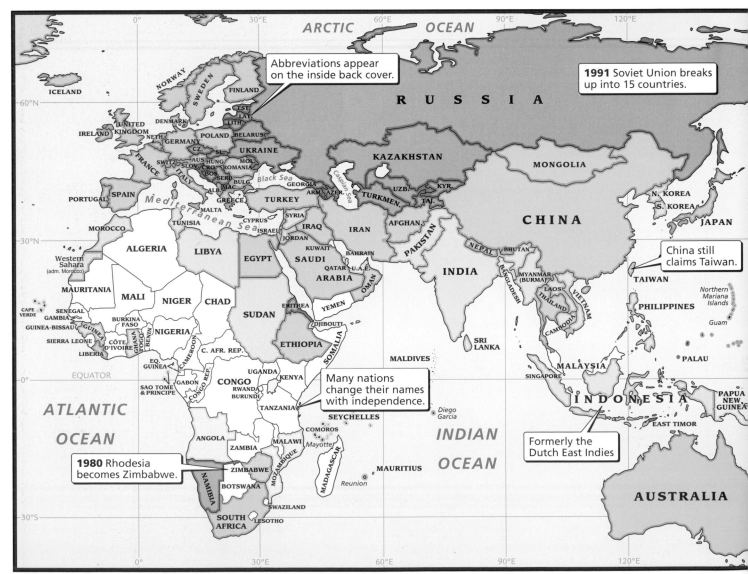

Abbreviations appear on the inside back cover.

1991 Soviet Union breaks up into 15 countries.

China still claims Taiwan.

Many nations change their names with independence.

Formerly the Dutch East Indies

1980 Rhodesia becomes Zimbabwe.

B Different regions gained independence at different times. It was common for many countries in the same region to gain independence within a few years of each other. Which regions gained independence in which decades?

Independence Timeline

1945
United Nations (UN) is founded.

1947
India and Pakistan replace British colony of India.

1960–1962
All French colonies in Africa gain independence.

1980
Zimbabwe is last British Colony in Africa to gain independence.

1992–1999
Yugoslavia breaks apart.

1945	1955	1965	1975	1985	1995	2005

1948
Israel is a new nation.

1949
Indonesia is no longer the Dutch East Indies.

1974–1976
Spain, Portugal withdraw from Africa.

1991
Soviet Union breaks up—15 countries created.

1993
Eritrea breaks away from Ethiopia.

2002
East Timor becomes free.

C The United Nations, which was established late in World War II, encouraged decolonization in Asia and Africa. In 1989–1991 the fall of communism led to the breakup of the Soviet Union and Yugoslavia.

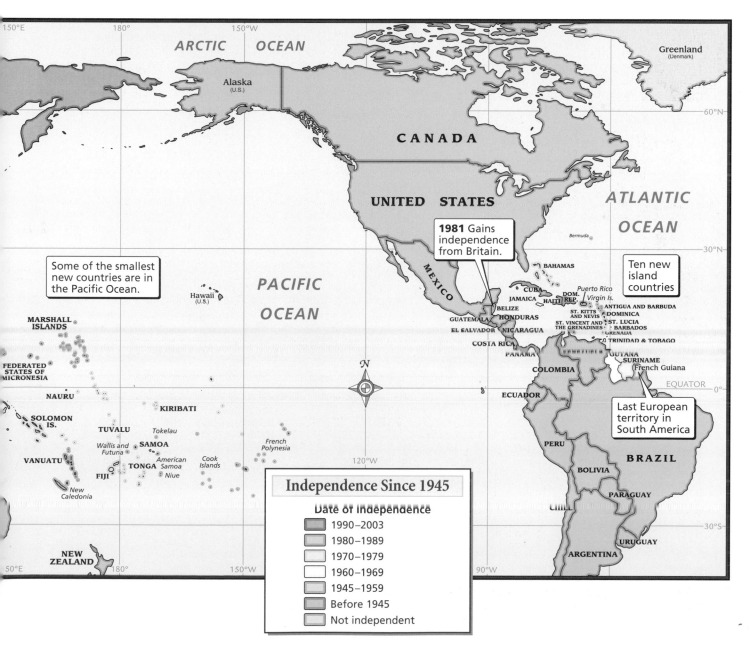

Some of the smallest new countries are in the Pacific Ocean.

1981 Gains independence from Britain.

Ten new island countries

Last European territory in South America

Independence Since 1945

Date of Independence

- 1990–2003
- 1980–1989
- 1970–1979
- 1960–1969
- 1945–1959
- Before 1945
- Not independent

International Challenges Today

Today the world faces serious challenges, many of which can only be solved through global cooperation.

- Even after the Cold War, many regions are trapped in endless violence and war.

- Terrorists use violence against innocent people in hopes of forcing governments to change and eliminating foreign influence in their homelands.

- At the same time, nations are coming together to improve trade, health, nutrition, and international safety.

A Vaccines can now control many diseases that once killed millions. Many private, government, and international groups provide free vaccinations for children in poor nations, such as this boy in Afghanistan.

Where is it from?

Today it's not always easy to say. A car might be designed in Japan, made of U.S. steel, and assembled in Mexico—with parts from all over the world. We now have a **global** economy.

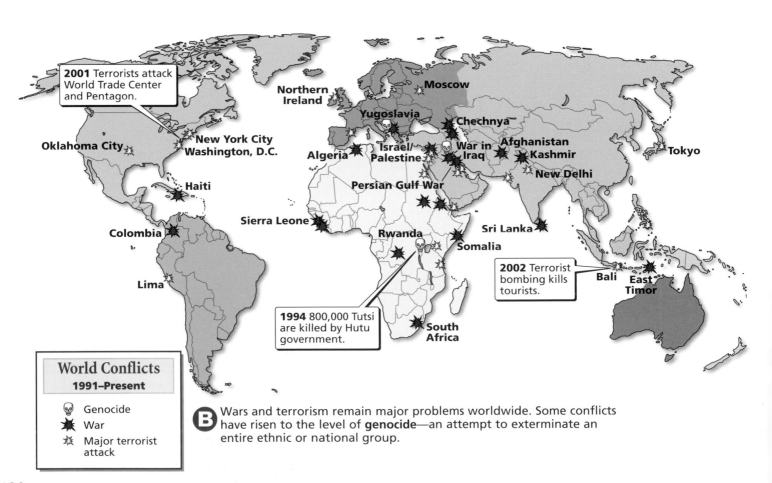

2001 Terrorists attack World Trade Center and Pentagon.

Oklahoma City

New York City
Washington, D.C.

Northern Ireland

Moscow

Yugoslavia

Chechnya

Algeria

Israel/
Palestine

War in
Iraq

Afghanistan

Kashmir

Tokyo

New Delhi

Haiti

Persian Gulf War

Colombia

Sierra Leone

Rwanda

Somalia

Sri Lanka

2002 Terrorist bombing kills tourists.

Bali

East Timor

Lima

1994 800,000 Tutsi are killed by Hutu government.

South Africa

World Conflicts
1991–Present

- ☠ Genocide
- ✹ War
- ✺ Major terrorist attack

B Wars and terrorism remain major problems worldwide. Some conflicts have risen to the level of **genocide**—an attempt to exterminate an entire ethnic or national group.

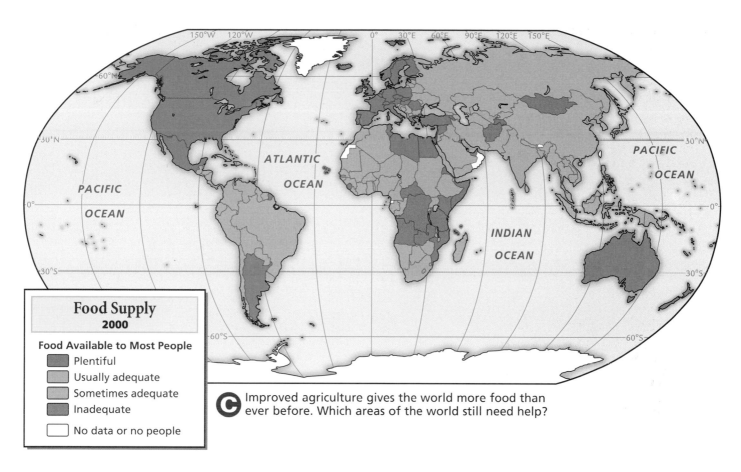

Food Supply
2000

Food Available to Most People
- Plentiful
- Usually adequate
- Sometimes adequate
- Inadequate
- No data or no people

C Improved agriculture gives the world more food than ever before. Which areas of the world still need help?

D Through ports like Vancouver, increased international trade provides opportunities for economic growth.

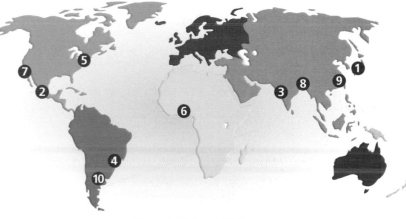

Top 10 Cities, 2000

Rank	City (Modern Country)	Population
1	**Tokyo** (Japan)	26,444,000
2	**Mexico City** (Mexico)	18,131,000
3	**Bombay (Mumbai)** (India)	18,066,000
4	**Sao Paulo** (Brazil)	17,755,000
5	**New York City** (United States)	16,640,000
6	**Lagos** (Nigeria)	13,427,000
7	**Los Angeles** (United States)	13,140,000
8	**Calcutta (Kolkata)** (India)	12,918,000
9	**Shanghai** (China)	12,887,000
10	**Buenos Aires** (Argentina)	12,560,000

E For 50 years the urban populations in many countries have skyrocketed as poor people have left farms to seek better lives. What earlier migration to the cities was similar?

121

ARCTIC OCEAN

Greenland

Baffin
Bay

Norwegian

ARCTIC CIRCLE 66½°N

Iceland

Denmark Strait

Bering
Strait

Yukon R.

60°N

Bering
Sea

Hudson
Bay

Hudson Strait

Aleutian Is.

Great
Lakes

St. Lawrence R.

Missouri

Azores

30°N

Colorado
R.

Río Grande

Mississippi

Gulf of
Mexico

Cuba

Bahama Is.

ATLANTIC

Canary Is.

TROPIC OF CANCER 23½°N

Hawaiian Is.

PACIFIC

TEOTIHUACAN
Teotihuacan

ZAPOTEC

Monte
Alban

MAYAN
CITY-STATES

Caribbean Sea

EQUATOR 0°

Galapagos Is.

N
W   E
S

OCEAN

Amazon River

EQUATOR 0°

OCEAN

Moche

MOCHE

NAZCA

TIWANAKU
Tiwanaku

Samoa

Tahiti

TROPIC OF CAPRICORN 23½°S

Easter I.

30°S

Falkland Is.

South
Georgia I.

In the year 200, only certain
regions have central governments
and can be thought of as countries.

60°S

ANTARCTIC CIRCLE 66½°S

Weddell
Sea

180°

150°W   120°W   90°W   60°W   30°W

Countries of the World in 200

Symbols

∘∘∘∘∘∘∘∘∘∘ Continental boundary

▬▬▬▬▬ Country boundary

■ City-state

⊛ National capital

● Other city

Scale at Equator

0   1000   2000 miles

0   1000   2000 kilometers

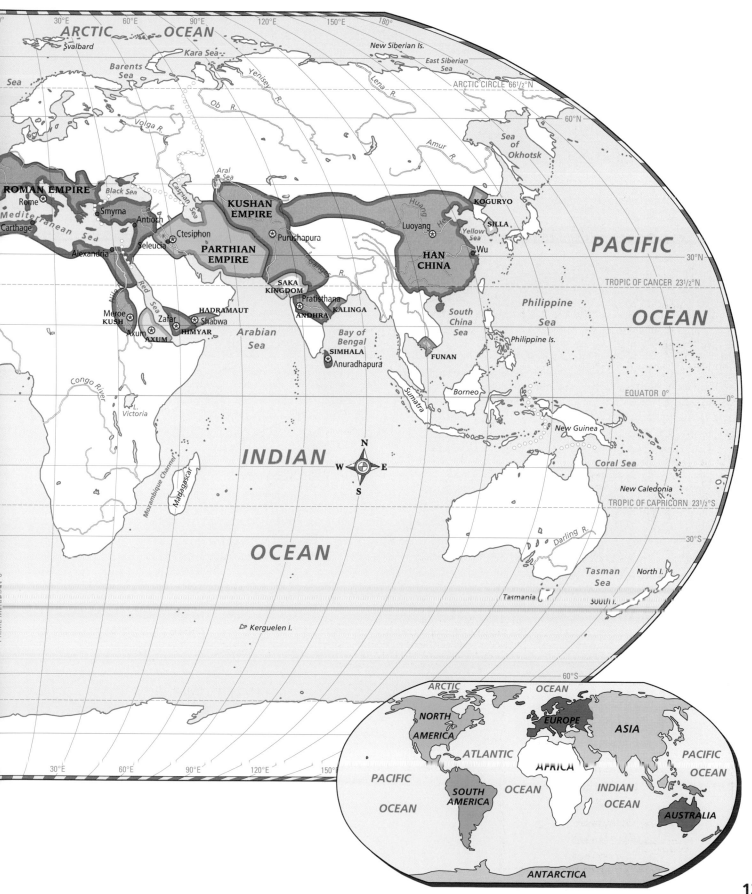

ARCTIC OCEAN

Svalbard

Kara Sea

New Siberian Is.

Barents Sea

East Siberian Sea

Sea

Yenisey R.

Lena R.

ARCTIC CIRCLE 66½°N

Ob R.

Volga R.

60°N

Amur R.

Sea of Okhotsk

Aral Sea

ROMAN EMPIRE

Rome

Black Sea

KUSHAN EMPIRE

Caspian Sea

Huang He

KOGURYO

Mediterranean Sea

Smyrna

Antioch

Ctesiphon

Purushapura

Luoyang

SILLA

Carthage

Alexandria

Seleucia

PARTHIAN EMPIRE

Yellow Sea

Wu

HAN CHINA

PACIFIC

30°N

TROPIC OF CANCER 23½°N

Red Sea

SAKA KINGDOM

Ganges R.

OCEAN

Meroe

KUSH

Zafar

HADRAMAUT

Shabwa

Pratisthana

ANDHRA

KALINGA

South China Sea

Philippine Sea

Axum

AXUM

HIMYAR

Arabian Sea

Bay of Bengal

Philippine Is.

Congo River

SIMHALA

Anuradhapura

FUNAN

L. Victoria

Sumatra

Borneo

EQUATOR 0°

0°

INDIAN

New Guinea

Coral Sea

Mozambique Channel

Madagascar

N

W   E

S

New Caledonia

TROPIC OF CAPRICORN 23½°S

OCEAN

Darling R.

30°S

Tasman Sea

North I.

Tasmania

South I.

Kerguelen I.

60°S

30°E   60°E   90°E   120°E   150°E

ARCTIC   OCEAN

NORTH AMERICA

EUROPE

ASIA

ATLANTIC

PACIFIC

AFRICA

PACIFIC   OCEAN

OCEAN

INDIAN

OCEAN

SOUTH AMERICA

OCEAN

AUSTRALIA

ANTARCTICA

ARCTIC OCEAN

Greenland

Baffin Bay

Denmark Strait

Norwegian

ARCTIC CIRCLE 66½°N

Bering Strait

ICELAND

Yukon R.

Hudson Strait

60°N
Bering Sea

Hudson Bay

SCOTLAND

Aleutian Is.

Great Lakes

St. Lawrence R.

ENGLAND
London
Pari
FRANCE
NAVARRE
LEON

Missouri

Colorado R.

Rio Grande

Mississippi

Azores

Cordoba

30°N

UMAYYID CALIPHATE

TROPIC OF CANCER 23½°N

Canary Is.

Hawaiian Is.

PACIFIC

Gulf of Mexico

Bahama Is.
Cuba

ATLANTIC

Tula
TOLTEC EMPIRE

Koumbi
GHANA Saleh
TAKRUR
MALI

Caribbean Sea

EQUATOR 0°

Galapagos Is.

EQUATOR 0°

OCEAN

0°

Amazon River

OCEAN

CHIMU
HUARI
Huari

Samoa

Tiwanaku

Tahiti

TIWANAKU

TROPIC OF CAPRICORN 23½°S

Easter I.

30°S

Falkland Is.

In the year 1000, only certain regions have central governments and can be thought of as countries.

South Georgia I.

60°S

ANTARCTIC CIRCLE 66½°S

Weddell Sea

Countries of the World in 1000

Symbols

∘∘∘∘∘∘∘∘∘∘∘ Continental boundary

────── Country boundary

▪ City-state

⊛ National capital

• Other city

Scale at Equator

0   1000   2000 miles

0   1000   2000 kilometers

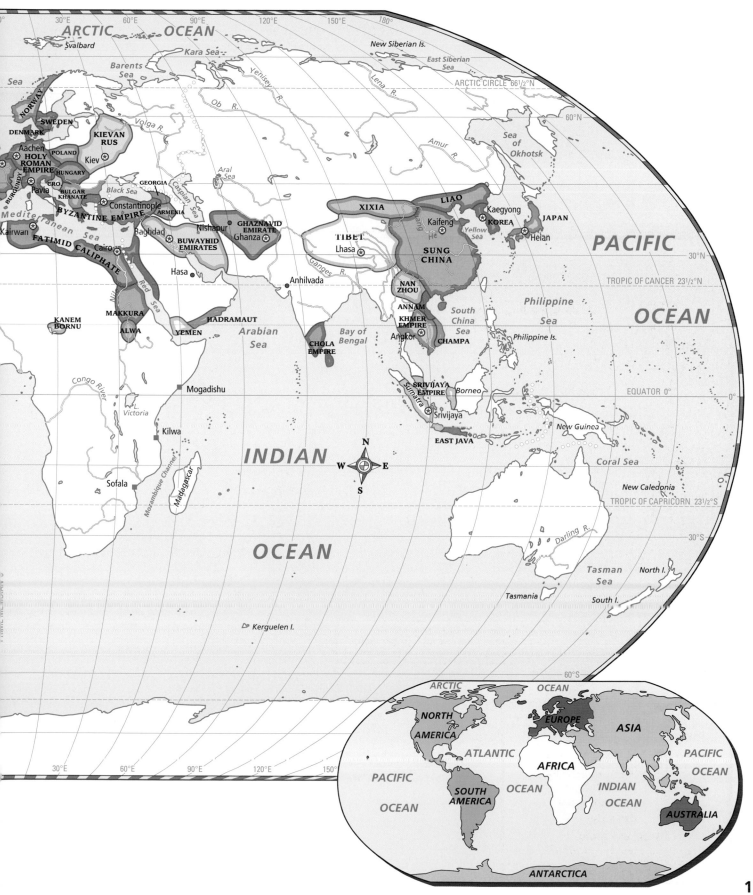

ARCTIC   OCEAN

Svalbard

Kara Sea

New Siberian Is.

East Siberian
Sea

Barents
Sea

Sea

Yenisey R.

ARCTIC CIRCLE 66½°N

60°N

Ob R.

Volga R.

NORWAY

SWEDEN

DENMARK

KIEVAN
RUS

Aachen
HOLY
ROMAN
EMPIRE

POLAND

Kiev

*Aral
Sea*

HUNGARY

Amur R.

Sea of
Okhotsk

BURGUNDY

CRO.

Pavia

BULGAR
KHANATE

GEORGIA

Black Sea

Caspian Sea

BYZANTINE EMPIRE

Constantinople

ARMENIA

XIXIA

LIAO

Kaegyong

KOREA

JAPAN

Mediterranean Sea

Kairwan

Nishapur

Baghdad

GHAZNAVID
EMIRATE
Ghanza

Kaifeng

Huang He

*Yellow
Sea*

PACIFIC

FATIMID CALIPHATE

Cairo

BUWAYHID
EMIRATES

TIBET

Lhasa

Helan

SUNG
CHINA

30°N

Hasa

Anhilvada

Ganges R.

TROPIC OF CANCER 23½°N

NAN
ZHOU

Philippine
Sea

OCEAN

KANEM
BORNU

MAKKURA

HADRAMAUT

Red Sea

ALWA

YEMEN

*Arabian
Sea*

*Bay of
Bengal*

ANNAM
KHMER
EMPIRE

Angkor

South
China
Sea

CHAMPA

Philippine Is.

CHOLA
EMPIRE

Congo River

Mogadishu

SRIVIJAYA
EMPIRE

Sumatra

Borneo

EQUATOR 0°

0°

*L.
Victoria*

Srivijaya

New Guinea

Kilwa

EAST JAVA

INDIAN

N

W   E

S

Coral Sea

Sofala

Mozambique Channel

Madagascar

New Caledonia

TROPIC OF CAPRICORN 23½°S

OCEAN

30°S

Darling R.

Tasman
Sea

North I.

Kerguelen I.

Tasmania

South I.

60°S

30°E   60°E   90°E   120°E   150°E

ARCTIC   OCEAN

NORTH
AMERICA

EUROPE

ASIA

ATLANTIC

AFRICA

PACIFIC
OCEAN

SOUTH
AMERICA

OCEAN

INDIAN
OCEAN

PACIFIC

OCEAN

AUSTRALIA

ANTARCTICA

125

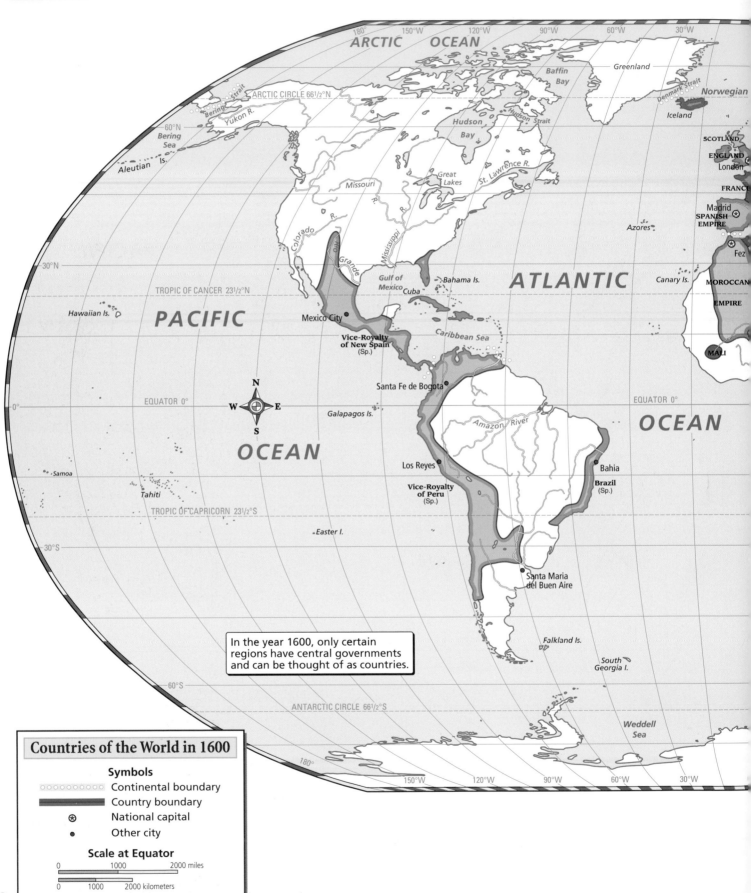

ARCTIC OCEAN

180° 150°W 120°W 90°W 60°W 30°W

Greenland

Baffin Bay

ARCTIC CIRCLE 66½°N

Bering Strait

Yukon R.

60°N

Bering Sea

Hudson Strait

Denmark Strait

Norwegian

Iceland

Aleutian Is.

Hudson Bay

SCOTLAND

ENGLAND

London

Great Lakes

St. Lawrence R.

FRANCE

Missouri

Madrid

SPANISH EMPIRE

30°N

Colorado R.

Rio Grande

Mississippi R.

Fez

TROPIC OF CANCER 23½°N

Gulf of Mexico

Bahama Is.

ATLANTIC

Canary Is.

MOROCCAN

PACIFIC

Hawaiian Is.

Mexico City

Cuba

EMPIRE

Vice-Royalty of New Spain (Sp.)

Caribbean Sea

MALI

N

Santa Fe de Bogota

W   E

Galapagos Is.

EQUATOR 0°

OCEAN

S

0°

Amazon River

Los Reyes

OCEAN

Samoa

Vice-Royalty of Peru (Sp.)

Bahia

Brazil (Sp.)

Tahiti

TROPIC OF CAPRICORN 23½°S

Easter I.

30°S

Santa Maria del Buen Aire

In the year 1600, only certain regions have central governments and can be thought of as countries.

Falkland Is.

South Georgia I.

60°S

ANTARCTIC CIRCLE 66½°S

Weddell Sea

180°

150°W 120°W 90°W 60°W 30°W

Countries of the World in 1600

Symbols

⊙⊙⊙⊙⊙⊙⊙⊙⊙ Continental boundary

▬▬▬▬▬▬ Country boundary

⊗ National capital

● Other city

Scale at Equator

0 ———— 1000 ———— 2000 miles

0 ——— 1000 ——— 2000 kilometers

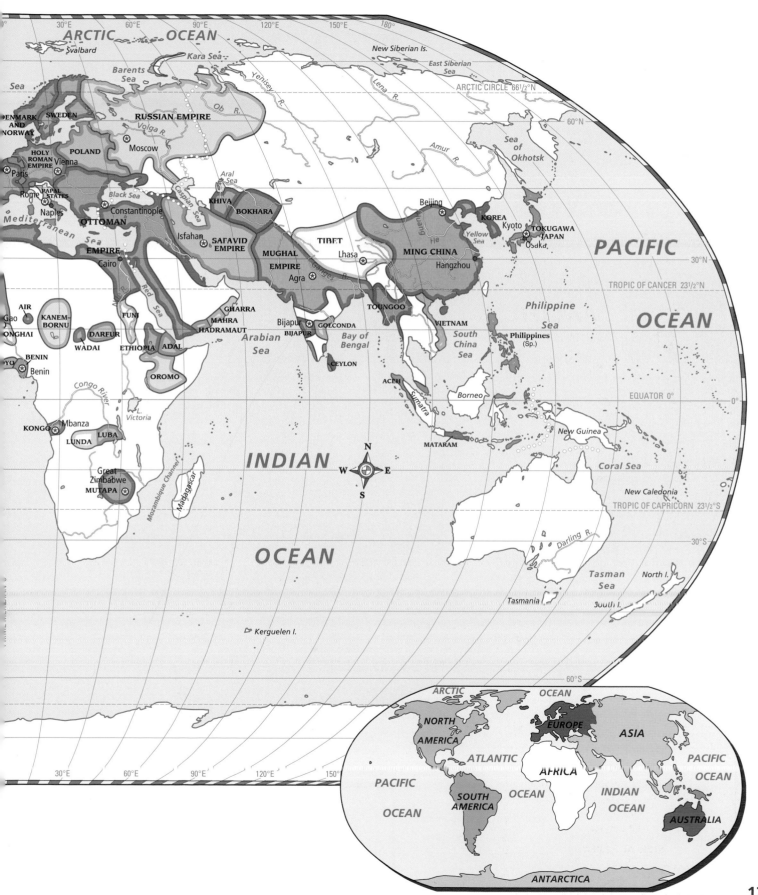

ARCTIC OCEAN

Svalbard

Kara Sea

New Siberian Is.

Barents Sea

East Siberian Sea

ARCTIC CIRCLE 66½°N

DENMARK AND NORWAY

SWEDEN

RUSSIAN EMPIRE

Ob R.

Yenisey R.

Lena R.

Amur R.

60°N

Sea of Okhotsk

Volga R.

Moscow

POLAND

HOLY ROMAN EMPIRE

Vienna

Paris

Aral Sea

KHIVA

BOKHARA

Beijing

KOREA

Kyoto

TOKUGAWA JAPAN

Rome

PAPAL STATES

Black Sea

Caspian Sea

Osaka

Naples

Constantinople

OTTOMAN

Mediterranean Sea

Isfahan

SAFAVID EMPIRE

TIBET

Lhasa

Huang He

Yellow Sea

MING CHINA

PACIFIC

EMPIRE

Cairo

MUGHAL EMPIRE

Agra

Ganges R.

Hangzhou

30°N

OCEAN

TROPIC OF CANCER 23½°N

Red Sea

AIR

KANEM-BORNU

FUNJ

GHARRA

MAHRA

HADRAMAUT

Bijapur

GOLCONDA

TOUNGOO

VIETNAM

Philippine Sea

Gao

ONGHAI

DARFUR

BIJAPUR

Bay of Bengal

South China Sea

Philippines (Sp.)

WADAI

ETHIOPIA

ADAL

Arabian Sea

YO

BENIN

Benin

OROMO

CEYLON

EQUATOR 0°

0°

Congo River

ACEH

Sumatra

Borneo

New Guinea

KONGO

Mbanza

LUBA

L. Victoria

LUNDA

MATARAM

Coral Sea

INDIAN

N

W   E

S

New Caledonia

Great Zimbabwe

MUTAPA

Mozambique Channel

Madagascar

TROPIC OF CAPRICORN 23½°S

OCEAN

Darling R.

30°S

Tasman Sea

North I.

Tasmania

South I.

Kerguelen I.

60°S

30°E

60°E

90°E

120°E

150°E

ARCTIC   OCEAN

NORTH AMERICA

EUROPE

ASIA

ATLANTIC

AFRICA

PACIFIC OCEAN

PACIFIC OCEAN

OCEAN

INDIAN OCEAN

SOUTH AMERICA

AUSTRALIA

ANTARCTICA

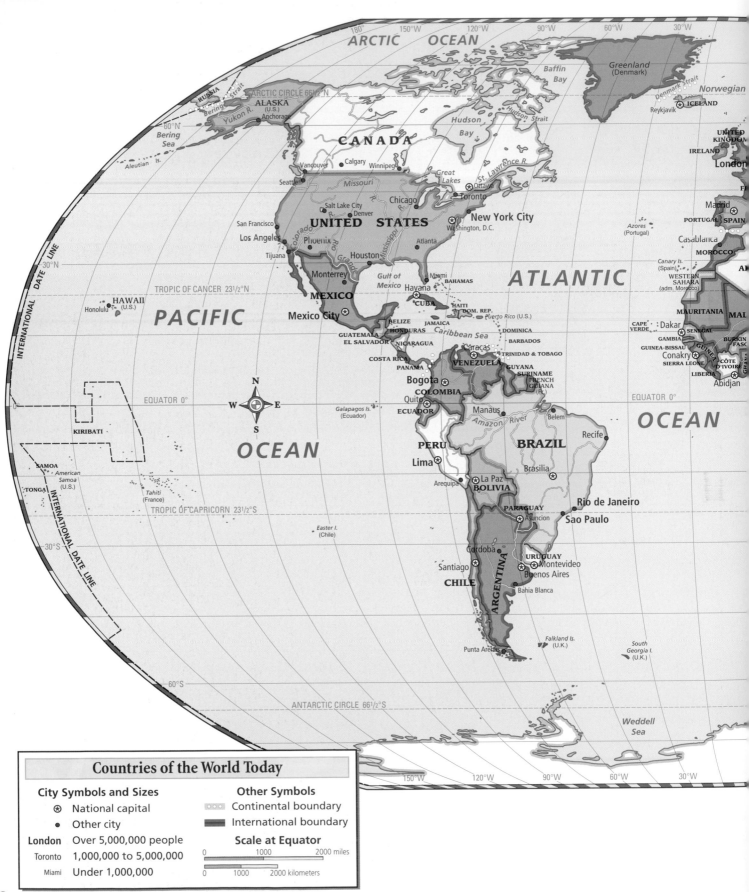

ARCTIC OCEAN

RUSSIA
Bering Strait
Yukon R.
ALASKA (U.S.)
Anchorage
ARCTIC CIRCLE 66½°N
50°N
Bering Sea
Aleutian Is.

CANADA
Hudson Bay
Baffin Bay
Hudson Strait
Denmark Strait
Greenland (Denmark)
Norwegian
Reykjavik ICELAND

Vancouver Calgary Winnipeg
Seattle
Missouri
Great Lakes
St. Lawrence R.
Ottawa Toronto

UNITED KINGDOM
IRELAND
London

Salt Lake City
Denver
Chicago
San Francisco
UNITED STATES
New York City
Washington, D.C.

Madrid
PORTUGAL SPAIN

Los Angeles
Phoenix
Atlanta
Casablanca
MOROCCO

Tijuana
Colorado
Rio Grande
Houston
Mississippi
Miami
Gulf of Mexico
Havana BAHAMAS
ATLANTIC

Azores (Portugal)

Canary Is. (Spain)
WESTERN SAHARA (adm. Morocco)

Monterrey
TROPIC OF CANCER 23½°N
MEXICO
CUBA
HAITI
DOM. REP.
Puerto Rico (U.S.)

MAURITANIA
CAPE VERDE Dakar
MAL

HAWAII (U.S.)
Honolulu
PACIFIC
Mexico City
BELIZE
JAMAICA
GUATEMALA HONDURAS
EL SALVADOR NICARAGUA
Caribbean Sea
DOMINICA
BARBADOS
TRINIDAD & TOBAGO

SENEGAL
GAMBIA
GUINEA-BISSAU
Conakry
SIERRA LEONE
BURKINA FASO
GUINEA
CÔTE D'IVOIRE
LIBERIA

COSTA RICA
PANAMA
Caracas
VENEZUELA
GUYANA
SURINAME
FRENCH GUIANA (Fr.)
Abidjan

Bogota
COLOMBIA
Quito
ECUADOR
EQUATOR 0°
EQUATOR 0°

Galapagos Is. (Ecuador)
Manaus
Amazon River
Belem
OCEAN

N
W E
S

KIRIBATI
PERU
Lima
BRAZIL
Recife
Brasilia

OCEAN

SAMOA
American Samoa (U.S.)
TONGA
Tahiti (France)
Arequipa
La Paz
BOLIVIA

TROPIC OF CAPRICORN 23½°S
Easter I. (Chile)
PARAGUAY
Asuncion
Rio de Janeiro
Sao Paulo

INTERNATIONAL DATE LINE
30°S
Cordoba
Santiago
CHILE
ARGENTINA
URUGUAY
Montevideo
Buenos Aires
Bahia Blanca

60°S
Punta Arenas
Falkland Is. (U.K.)
South Georgia I. (U.K.)

ANTARCTIC CIRCLE 66½°S
Weddell Sea

180° 150°W 120°W 90°W 60°W 30°W
150°W 120°W 90°W 60°W 30°W

INTERNATIONAL DATE LINE

Countries of the World Today

City Symbols and Sizes

⊛ National capital

• Other city

London Over 5,000,000 people

Toronto 1,000,000 to 5,000,000

Miami Under 1,000,000

Other Symbols

ooo Continental boundary

▬▬ International boundary

Scale at Equator

0   1000   2000 miles

0   1000   2000 kilometers

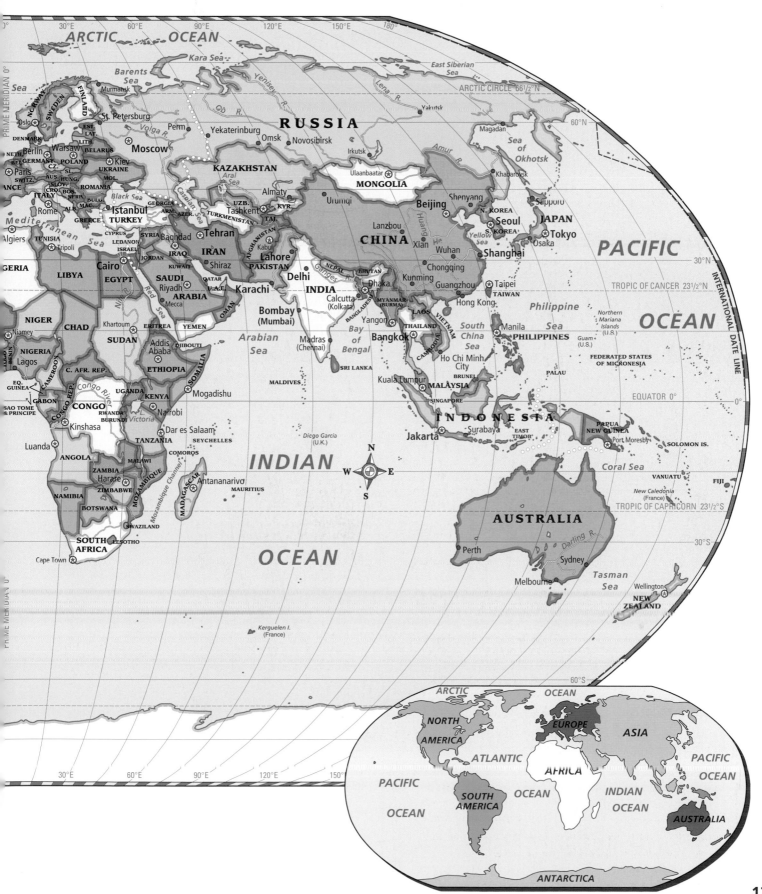

Physical World

Legend / map labels:

ARCTIC OCEAN
Polar ice mass
Banks I.
Victoria I.
Baffin
Baffin Bay
Greenland
ARC
Hudson Strait
Denmark Strait
Norwegian
Iceland
Cape Farewell
British Isles
London
ARCTIC CIRCLE 66½°N
Bering Strait
Yukon R.
Mt. McKinley 20,320 ft.
Mackenzie R.
Canadian Shield
Hudson Bay
60°N
Bering Sea
Kodiak I.
Aleutian Is.
Vancouver I.
Vancouver
Seattle
Rocky Mountains
NORTH AMERICA
Great Lakes
St. Lawrence R.
Toronto
Montreal
Newfoundland
Iberian Peninsula
Madrid
Chicago
Missouri R.
Great Plains
Los Angeles
Appalachian Mts.
New York City
Azores
Strait of Gibraltar
Casablanca
Atlas
S
30°N
Sierra Madre
Rio Grande
Houston
Gulf of Mexico
Cape Hatteras
Canary Is.
Niger
TROPIC OF CANCER 23½°N
Cape San Lucas
Mexico City
Miami
Bahama Is.
ATLANTIC
Hawaiian Islands
PACIFIC
Cuba
West Indies
Puerto Rico
Hispaniola
Caribbean Sea
Cape Verde Is.
Central America
Panama Canal
Caracas
Trinidad
Guiana Highlands
Bogota
Amazon Basin
Amazon River
EQUATOR 0°
Galapagos Is.
Andes Mountains
SOUTH AMERICA
EQUATOR 0°
OCEAN
Lima
Brazilian Highlands
Brasilia
Ascension I.
PACIFIC OCEAN
Samoa Is.
Rio de Janeiro
Sao Paulo
Tuamotu Archipelago
TROPIC OF CAPRICORN 23½°S
Pitcairn I.
Easter I.
30°S
Juan Fernandez Is.
Santiago
Aconcagua 22,831 ft.
Buenos Aires
Pampas
Patagonia
Falkland Is.
Strait of Magellan
Tierra del Fuego
South Georgia I.
Cape Horn
60°S
ANTARCTIC CIRCLE 66½°S
Antarctic Peninsula
Weddell Sea
Ice shelf

Physical World

Natural Regions

Tundra or ice   Forest   Grass   Shrub or desert

Symbols

oooo Continental boundary
— International boundary
• City
▲ Mountain peak

Scale at Equator

0 — 1000 — 2000 miles
0 — 1000 — 2000 kilometers

imetables of World History

	Middle East and Africa	East and South Asia	Europe and Russia	Americas and Oceania
9000 B.C.–4000 B.C.	**9000 B.C.** Farming develops in the Fertile Crescent. **8000 B.C.** First cities are built–Jericho and Catal Huyuk. **6000 B.C.** Farming develops along the Nile River. **5000 B.C.** Irrigation is used in Egypt and Mesopotamia.	**6000 B.C.** Farming develops along the Huang He, Indus, and Yangtze Rivers. **5000 B.C.** Yangshao culture emerges in China.	**5000 B.C.** Farming spreads across Europe. **4500 B.C.** Plow is used in southeastern Europe.	**9000 B.C.** People inhabit the southern tip of South America. **5000 B.C.** Farming develops in Middle America and the Andes Mountains.
4000 B.C.–2000 B.C.	**4000 B.C.** Saharan herders move to West Africa. **3500 B.C.** First bronze tools are made in Sumer. **3100 B.C.** Egypt is unified. **3000 B.C.** Sumerians begin using cuneiform symbols. **2650 B.C.** Egyptians build first pyramid. **2350 B.C.** Akkadians create world's first empire.	**3000 B.C.** Longshan culture emerges in China. **2500 B.C.** First planned cities built in Indus Valley–Harappa and Mohenjo-Daro.	**3000 B.C.** Minoan civilization emerges in Crete. **2900 B.C.** Phoenicians become first sea-going civilization.	**3000 B.C.** Corn (maize) is first cultivated in Middle America.
2000 B.C.–1000 B.C.	**1800 B.C.** Hammurabi of Babylon issues his law code. **1570 B.C.** New Kingdom of Egypt begins. **1504 B.C.** Egypt defeats Kush. **1200 B.C.** Hebrews start kingdom in Canaan. **1070 B.C.** Libyan invasion ends the New Kingdom.	**1766 B.C.** The Shang start China's first dynasty. **1600 B.C.** Chinese begin using pictographs. **1500 B.C.** Aryan invasion ends Indus Valley civilization. Hinduism begins to spread through India. **1122 B.C.** Shang dynasty is overthrown by the Zhou. **1000 B.C.** Hindus write down the world's oldest scriptures.	**1600 B.C.** Mycenaean civilization emerges in Greece. **1450 B.C.** Mycenaens conquer the Minoans. **1200 B.C.** Sea Peoples invade Greece. Mycenaean civilization collapses.	**2000 B.C.** People begin to colonize distant islands in the Pacific. **1200 B.C.** Olmec farmers build permanent settlements. Maya civilization emerges.
1000 B.C.–500 B.C.	**724 B.C.** Kush conquers Egypt. **664 B.C.** Assyrians conquer Egypt. **612 B.C.** Babylonians conquer Assyria. **586 B.C.** Hebrews are exiled to Babylon. **539 B.C.** Persia conquers Babylon.	**551 B.C.** Confucius is born. **528 B.C.** Siddhartha Gautama founds Buddhism.	**900 B.C.** Phoenician ships reach Atlantic Ocean. **750 B.C.** Greek city-states begin colonizing the Mediterranean. Phoenician alphabet is introduced to Greece. **509 B.C.** Rome becomes a republic. **508 B.C.** Greece becomes a democracy.	**700 B.C.** Adena culture builds ceremonial mounds.

Middle East and Africa	East and South Asia	Europe and Russia	Americas and Oceania
500 B.C. Bantu migrations begin in Africa.	**500 B.C.** Hindu kingdoms exist throughout India.	**431 B.C.** Peloponnesian War begins between Athens and Sparta. **399 B.C.** Plato writes down the teachings of Socrates. **336 B.C.** Alexander the Great becomes king of Greece and Macedonia.	**400 B.C.** Maya begin building pyramids.
331 B.C. Alexander the Great conquers the Persian Empire. **264 B.C.** Punic Wars begin between Carthage and Rome.	**326 B.C.** Alexander the Great reaches India. **321 B.C.** Mauryan Empire begins in India. **260 B.C.** Mauryan emperor Asoka becomes Buddhist. **221 B.C.** China's first emperor takes control. **220 B.C.** Construction begins on Great Wall of China. **206 B.C.** Han dynasty expands Chinese empire. **150 B.C.** Silk Road links China and Europe through trade.	**264 B.C.** Rome controls all of Italy.	
146 B.C. Rome destroys Carthage. **30 B.C.** Rome conquers Egypt. **4 B.C.** Jesus Christ is born.		**146 B.C** Rome conquers Greece. **27 B.C.** Rome becomes an empire.	
29 Jesus Christ is crucified. **45** Paul begins to spread Christianity. **70** Jews flee Roman rule in Judea.		**100** Rome is the world's largest city. **117** Roman Empire reaches its greatest extent.	
	220 Han dynasty ends, Chinese empire declines.	**250** Plague spreads through Roman Empire. **303** Rome begins harsh persecution of Christians.	
350 Kush falls to Axum. Axum adopts Christianity.	**320** Gupta dynasty begins in northern India.	**392** Christianity becomes official religion of Roman Empire. **395** Roman Empire divides into eastern and western regions. **476** Western Roman Empire falls to barbarians.	**300** Maya begin to record events on stone slabs.
	500 Gupta Empire collapses after Hun invasion. **552** Buddhism reaches Japan.	**500** Constantinople is the world's largest city.	
622 Muhammad's journey to Medina begins spread of Islam. **639** Muslim armies invade North Africa. **700** Ghana is first empire in West Africa.	**751** Chinese expansion is halted by Muslim armies.	**711** Moors conquer Spain. **789** Vikings raid England for first time. **800** Charlemagne is crowned Emperor of the West. **843** Charlemagne's empire breaks up.	**700** Anasazi begin building pueblos.
900 Baghdad is the world's largest city.	**800** Khmer kingdoms emerge in Southeast Asia.	**936** Otto I of Germany begins the Holy Roman Empire.	**900** Hohokam people begin to use irrigation. Maya Empire declines after crop failures.

Left margin labels: **500 B.C.–1 B.C.** / **1 A.D.–500 A.D.** / **500 A.D.–1000 A.D.**

Middle East and Africa	East and South Asia	Europe and Russia	Americas and Oceania

1000 A.D.–1500 A.D.

Middle East and Africa	East and South Asia	Europe and Russia	Americas and Oceania
1098 First Crusade takes Jerusalem from Muslims. **1240** Mali Empire rises in West Africa. **1270** Last Crusade ends. **1291** Last Crusader state falls to Muslims. **1335** Songhai Empire rises in West Africa. **1444** Atlantic slave trade begins. **1453** Ottomans conquer the Byzantine Empire.	**1001** Chinese perfect gunpowder. **1100** Angkor Wat is built. **1127** Manchurian invasion pushes Chinese south. **1185** Shoguns take power in Japan. **1200** Hangchow is the world's largest city. **1279** Mongols conquer China. **1368** Ming dynasty starts in China. **1398** Timur invades India. **1498** Portuguese reach India.	**1066** Normans conquer England. **1095** Pope calls for crusades to Holy Land. **1215** Magna Carta gives rights to free Englishmen. **1337** France and England begin Hundred Years' War. **1346** Bubonic plague spreads from Asia to Europe. **1350** Plague kills a third of London's population. **1450** Gutenberg perfects the printing press. **1492** Muslim rule in Spain ends.	**1000** Vikings settle in Newfoundland. **1200** Pueblo civilization builds cliff dwellings. **1325** Aztec people settle at Tenochtitlan. **1438** Inca begin to expand their empire in the Andes. **1492** Christopher Columbus reaches America.

1500 A.D.–1700 A.D.

Middle East and Africa	East and South Asia	Europe and Russia	Americas and Oceania
1500 Swahili culture emerges in East Africa. **1505** Portuguese start East African colonies. **1574** Ottomans complete North African expansion. **1591** Songhai is destroyed. **1625** Dutch settle at Capetown, South Africa.	**1500** Beijing is the world's largest city. **1526** Babur begins the Mughal Empire in India. **1565** Spain claims the Philippines. **1602** English and Dutch start trade colonies in India. **1644** Manchus end the Ming dynasty, begin ruling China. **1650** Dutch control most European trade in Asia. **1674** Maratha Kingdom established in India.	**1503** Leonardo paints the *Mona Lisa.* **1517** Luther starts the Protestant Reformation. **1543** Copernicus proposes a sun-centered universe. **1618** Thirty Years' War begins. **1683** Ottoman Empire is defeated at Vienna. **1698** First steam engine invented.	**1500** Portugal claims Brazil. **1521** Spain conquers the Aztec. **1532** Spain conquers the Inca. **1535** New Spain extends from Mexico to Chile. **1606** Europeans first encounter Australia. **1607** Jamestown is settled by the English.

1700 A.D.–1850 A.D.

Middle East and Africa	East and South Asia	Europe and Russia	Americas and Oceania
1798 Napoleon leads French invasion of Egypt. **1815** Zulu kingdom is founded. **1838** Dutch (Boers) defeat the Zulus.	**1707** Mughal Empire reaches its height. **1800** Beijing's population is over 1,000,000. **1803** British take control of Mughal Empire. **1818** British take control of Maratha Kingdom. **1839** Opium War begins between Britain and China.	**1769** Improved steam engine speeds the Industrial Revolution. **1789** French Revolution begins. **1796** World's first vaccine is developed to fight smallpox. **1804** Napoleon crowns himself emperor. **1815** Napoleon is defeated at Waterloo. **1848** Revolutions sweep across Europe.	**1750** Europeans claim most of the Americas. **1775** American Revolution begins. **1787** U.S. Constitution is written. **1788** Britain sends convicts to Australia **1819** Revolutions against Spain begin in Latin America.

	Middle East and Africa	East and South Asia	Europe and Russia	Americas and Oceania
1850 A.D.–1900 A.D.	1869 Suez Canal links Red Sea and Mediterranean Sea. 1884 Seven European nations agree to divide up Africa.	1853 Perry's fleet opens way to U.S.-Japanese trade. 1857 Indian troops mutiny against British commanders. 1867 Japanese emperor regains power from the shogun. 1895 Japan wins Sino-Japanese War.	1850 Over 50 percent of the British live in cities. 1861 Italy is unified. 1870 Industrial Revolution spreads across Europe. 1885 Daimler and Benz build first gasoline-powered car.	1861 American Civil War begins. 1863 Lincoln frees most slaves in the U.S. 1867 Canada gains its independence from Britain. U.S. buys Alaska. 1879 Edison invents the electric light bulb. 1888 Brazil frees the last slaves in the Americas. 1898 U.S. annexes Hawaii.
1900 A.D.–1950 A.D.	1914 European colonies make up most of Africa. 1920 Ottoman Empire is divided into several countries. 1948 State of Israel is created.	1900 Chinese attack foreigners in the Boxer Rebellion. 1904 Japan wins Russo-Japanese War. 1910 Japan annexes Korea. Last Manchu emperor is deposed in China. 1930 Gandhi begins non-violent protests against British in India. 1945 U.S. drops atomic bombs on Japan, ending World War II. 1947 India gains independence. 1949 Communists take control of mainland China.	1900 London is the world's largest city. 1914 World War I begins. 1917 Russian Revolution overthrows the czar. 1919 New nations are created after end of World War I. 1933 Adolf Hitler becomes chancellor of Germany. 1939 World War II begins. 1945 Allies defeat Germany. 1946 Cold War begins.	1901 Australia gains its independence from Britain. 1914 Panama Canal connects Atlantic and Pacific Oceans. 1917 U.S. enters World War I. 1941 Japan attacks Pearl Harbor. U.S. enters World War II. 1945 UN is formed.
1950 A.D.–Present	1960 Eighteen African nations gain independence. 1969 Most of Africa is independent. 1991 UN coalition forces Iraq out of Kuwait. 2003 U.S. leads invasion of Iraq.	1950 U.S. troops enter Korean War. 1965 U.S. troops enter Vietnam War. 1975 Vietnam War ends with communist victory. 1997 China regains control of Hong Kong. 2000 Tokyo is the world's largest city.	1957 Soviet Union launches Sputnik, the first satellite. 1961 Soviet Union sends first man into space. Berlin wall is built. 1980 Solidarity Union challenges Communist rule in Poland. 1991 Soviet Union collapses and Cold War ends. 2001 European Union introduces a single currency.	1959 Alaska and Hawaii become states. Castro leads communist revolution in Cuba. 1964 Civil Rights Bill passes in U.S. 1969 U.S. lands first men on the moon. 2001 Terrorists attack New York City and Washington, D.C.

Glossary

agriculture Practice of raising plants and animals for food and other products. Farming.

aristocracy Small ruling class that inherits its powers; may control the land and military in its country.

Bantu Large family of ethnic and language groups that extends from West Africa to South Africa.

barbarian A word used by one group to describe another group thought to be less advanced. Often refers to the peoples who invaded the Roman Empire.

boundary Shared border separating places such as countries or continents.

bronze Mixture of copper and tin; main metal used for tools and weapons in Europe and Asia until iron replaced it.

Buddhism Religion from India that includes the belief that happiness is found by eliminating all desires. Founded by Siddhartha Gautama, who was known as *Buddha* or the "Enlightened One."

capital City where a country's government is located.

caravan Group of overland traders and the animals carrying their goods.

Christianity Religion that arose in Israel during Roman times and includes belief in Jesus as the Son of God.

church 1. Organization of Christians with shared beliefs, such as the Roman Catholic Church or the Lutheran Church. 2. A group of Christians who worship together. 3. Building where they worship.

city Very large settlement of people. Unlike those in villages, people in cities do not farm.

city-state Independent city and its surrounding farms.

civil war War between different groups or regions within a country, usually for control of the country.

civilization A society that has writing, cities, agriculture, artisans, and public monuments.

Cold War Rivalry from 1946 to 1991 between the United States and its allies and the Soviet Union and its allies.

colony Settlement or region usually governed by a distant parent country. Settling the area is called *colonization.*

Communism System of government ownership and control of the property and equipment used for producing food, goods, and services.

Confucianism Philosophy from China that includes belief in government by an educated, moral elite. Based on the teachings of Confucius.

Counter Reformation Efforts by the Catholic Church to counter or reverse the Protestant Reformation.

country Land with one government.

culture The beliefs, customs, and practices of a group of people.

culture group Ethnic, racial, or religious group.

culture region Where a particular culture is found; usually outlasts the countries established there.

czar One of the emperors who ruled Russia until the revolution of 1917.

democracy Government by voting citizens, developed in Greece and Rome; country with democratic government.

desert Dry natural region with little rain and few if any plants; usually hot.

domestic Term used to describe tame animals or plants cultivated by people.

Dutch People from the Netherlands, a country in Europe.

dynasty Family of rulers, usually powerful for generations.

Eastern Orthodox Church Main branch of Christianity in Eastern Europe and the Middle East, originally the Eastern Christian Church. Often called *Orthodox.*

economy System of making, distributing, and buying goods and services.

emperor A man who rules an empire.

empire Separate nations or regions under a single ruler or government.

export Something that is sold to another country.

feudalism System of government that gives most power to large landowners. Common in Europe from 500 until 1500 and in Japan from 1100 to 1860.

genocide Deliberate murder of every man, woman, and child from an ethnic or racial group.

globalization Modern process of connecting worldwide communications and trade for the benefit of companies or of humanity, but not specific countries.

Hinduism Religion from India based on belief in reincarnation and in spiritual connections between all things.

Holy Roman Empire A weak government that ruled Germany and Italy from about 1000 to 1806.

hunting and gathering Way of life using only wild animals and wild plants for food.

imperialism Policy of expanding a country's power by gaining territory, by controlling other countries, or both.

import Something that is bought from another country.

independence State of being free from rule by another country.

Indies European name for the islands and mainland of Southeast Asia, India, and coastal China.

indigenous Coming from a particular area or environment.

Industrial Revolution Social change in the 1700s and 1800s caused by replacing goods made by hand at home with goods made by machinery in factories.

irrigation Artificially supplying water to land so that crops will grow.

Islam Religion from Arabia that includes belief in one god (*Allah* in Arabic) and the unity of all believers. Based on the life and teachings of Muhammad.

Jew Believer in Judaism. Originally called *Hebrew.*

Jewish Diaspora Migration of Jews away from Israel to the rest of the Middle East, the Mediterranean lands, and Europe.

Judaism Religion from the Hebrews based on belief in one god and obeying the laws of Moses, especially the Ten Commandments.

kingdom Country ruled by an inherited ruler, often a king or queen.

manufacturing Making products in large amounts.

merchant A person who makes a living by selling and transporting goods.

Middle East Region including Southwest Asia and Northeast Africa.

migration Mass movement from one region to another.

monarchy Country ruled by one person whose position passes to his or her children.

Mound Builder North American culture marked by agriculture, extensive trade, and construction of large earthen mounds.

Muslim Believer in Islam.

nationalism Belief that a people with similar language, religion, history, and customs should have their own country.

Nazi Related to the German fascist political party that ruled Germany from 1933 to 1945 and that was responsible for World War II and the Holocaust, genocide aimed at European Jews.

nomad Person who lives by herding animals, moving from place to place in search of food, water, and grazing land.

Ottoman Empire A Muslim, Turkish empire that ruled much of the Middle East and Balkan Peninsula from 1307 to 1920.

peasant Member of a poor farming or laboring family that has little or no personal property.

persecution Violence and discrimination against a particular group of people.

pictograph Simple picture of an object, used as a symbol in early writing.

plague Highly infectious disease, often deadly; bubonic plague, which struck Europe and Asia in the 1300s, is spread by rats and fleas.

plantation Large tract of land where one labor-intensive cash crop is grown. Work on colonial plantations was usually done by slaves.

pope Head of the Roman Catholic Church on earth. Often written as *Pope*.

Protestant churches Non-Catholic groups that grew out of Western Christianity.

Reformation Movement beginning in the 1500s to change Western Christianity; led to the emergence of Protestant Christianity.

region Large area that is different from the areas around it. Defined by a single feature or several features, either natural or cultural.

Renaissance Intellectual and cultural movement in Europe from 1300 to 1600; the rebirth of cultural progress after the Middle Ages.

republic Country governed by officials elected by citizens and their chosen representatives.

revolution 1. Overthrow of a country's government by its citizens. 2. Other enormous change in government or society.

Roman Catholic Church Largest branch of Christianity, originally the Western Christian Church, led by the pope. Often called *Catholic*.

Sea Peoples Peoples of unknown origin who attacked eastern Mediterranean civilizations in the 1200s and 1100s B.C.

Semite Member of a culture group that began as herders in the ancient Middle East and included Assyrians and Babylonians. Modern Semitic groups include Hebrews and Arabs.

settlement 1. Community, usually small, with permanent residents. 2. The act of establishing homes in a new place.

Shinto Traditional religion of Japan based on respect for ancestors and worship of spirits in nature.

shogun Military ruler of Japan, a position that lasted from 1192 to 1867.

Silk Road Ancient overland trade route between China and Europe.

slavery Practice of owning people and forcing them to work without pay. A person treated this way is a slave.

state 1. Area with its own government, not ruled by outsiders. 2. Part of a country, such as the United States of America, with laws and leaders of its own.

superpower Country with widespread political and military power; the United States and the Soviet Union during the Cold War.

Swahili Civilization that developed in East Africa combining Bantu, Arabic, Persian, and Indian cultures; the language of Swahili civilization.

Taoism 1. Philosophy from China that emphasizes personal harmony with nature. 2. Related religion influenced by traditional Chinese beliefs.

terrorism Use of deliberate attacks on civilians, usually by non-military groups, to cause fear in order to advance a cause.

textiles Woven or knitted cloth. Textiles are made from wool, cotton, silk, or other fibers.

trade Exchanging goods and services for other goods and services or for money.

United Nations Organization of nearly all countries set up in 1945 to promote peace and improve the standard of living for the world's people.

village Settlement, usually small, where most people work on nearby farms.

Index

N

O

P